Stephen Manley • Michelle Cha...
Chris Francis • Simon Topliss • M...

edexcel
advancing learning, changing lives

Edexcel Diploma

Construction and the Built Environment

Level 2 Higher Diploma

A PEARSON COMPANY

Published by Pearson Education Limited, a company incorporated in England and Wales, having its registered office at Edinburgh Gate, Harlow, Essex, CM20 2JE. Registered company number: 872828

www.edexceldiplomas.co.uk

Edexcel is a registered trademark of Edexcel Limited

Text © Pearson Education Limited, 2008

First published 2008

12 11 10 09 08

10 9 8 7 6 5 4 3 2

British Library Cataloguing in Publication Data

A catalogue record is available from the British Library for this book.

ISBN 978 0435499 91 4

Edited by Sarah Christopher

Typeset by HL Studios

Original illustrations © Pearson Education Limited, 2008

Illustrated by HL Studios

Cover photo/illustrations – Inspector © iStockphoto/Justin Horrocks; Blueprint © iStockphoto/Branko Miokovic; Building © iStockphoto/Yury Asotov; Tower © iStockphoto/knape; Dumper truck © iStockphoto/Trevor Fisher; Worker © iStockphoto/Hotizov Ivan

Printed in the UK by Scotprint

Websites

The websites used in this book were correct and up-to-date at the time of publication. It is essential for tutors to preview each website before using it in class so as to ensure that the URL is still accurate, relevant and appropriate. We suggest that tutors bookmark useful websites and consider enabling students to access them through the school/college intranet.

Contents

WELCOME TO THE CONSTRUCTION AND THE BUILT ENVIRONMENT DIPLOMA

The Construction and the Built Environment Diploma is a ground-breaking qualification created by employers, the government and the leading education bodies to create a twenty-first century workforce. The Diploma will give you skills and experience that employers value and will provide you with opportunities to progress on to Level 3 studies.

Get stuck in!

The Higher Diploma includes the following components:

Principal learning The seven units covered by this book aims to provide a broad understanding and working knowledge, understanding and skills essential to working in the Construction sector.

Generic learning Functional skills in IT, English and maths, and personal learning and thinking skills have been embedded in this book to give you opportunities to develop and practise your skills.

The project You will have the opportunity to set your own brief and plan, develop, deliver and review a construction related project. The final section of this book will give you guidance on completing this part of the diploma.

Additional/specialist learning You can choose from a number of different qualifications – including GCSEs and BTECs – to complement or contrast your construction and the built environment principal learning.

Getting involved

As part of your Diploma, you will also need to take at least 10 days work experience. Ideally this should be relevant to your subject. In fact, employer engagement and applied learning are such key parts of the Diploma that you should consider which local companies may be willing to offer you work experience as early as possible to find the right placement for you.

Your school or college may already have strong links with local employers, or they may use a work-placement service like Trident. Remember that you should always speak to your teacher or tutor before contacting an employer.

Going further

The Diploma is available at Foundation (Level 1, equivalent to 5 GCSEs at grades D–G), Higher (Level 2, equivalent to 5 GCSEs at grades A–C) and Advanced (Level 3, equivalent to 3.5 A Levels at grades A*–E). The Advanced Diploma is recognised by universities and through the full qualification you could achieve up to 420 UCAS points.

From the Higher Diploma, you can progress to:

* Advanced Diploma

* A Levels

* BTEC National 3 or other Level 3 vocational courses

* Work through Apprenticeship and Advanced Apprenticeship.

We hope you enjoy your studies on this cutting-edge course and that you feel inspired by the real-life scenarios and opportunities to follow your own interests in the project. Good luck!

How to use this book

This book has been divided into seven units to match the Higher Construction and the Built Environment Diploma qualification structure. Each unit follows the Edexcel learning outcomes and each double-page spread covers an individual theme or topic.

Features of the book

The features in this book are described over the next few pages.

Want to achieve more?

The book concludes with advice on getting the best from the assessment. This section tells you how you will be assessed, how your work will be marked and gives you useful reminders for key unit themes. Hints and tips give you guidance on how to aim for the higher mark band so you use your new skills and knowledge to best effect.

Unit 5 also provides supporting information for Additional Specialist learning. This is provided for four areas: carpentry and joinery, brickwork, painting and decorating and building services.

Starter stimulus

A discussion point or short activity that will introduce the key concepts of the double-page spread.

Key words

Key concepts and new words are explained clearly and simply to make sure you don't miss anything important.

Functional Skills

Functional skills have been built into many of the activities in this book. These features highlight opportunities to develop and practise your functional skills in IT, English or maths. Remember, you will need a Pass in all three functional skills to achieve the full Diploma.

Personal Learning and Thinking Skills

Elements of the generic learning are embedded in the principal learning. These features highlight opportunities to develop and demonstrate your personal learning and thinking skills.

Case study

Case studies show the concepts covered in this book applied to the real world through real-life scenarios. Questions and activities will encourage you to push your understanding further.

WHY DO WE USE CONSTRUCTION PLANT?

Think about the vast amounts of materials and equipment involved in constructing domestic and commercial buildings. How would we manage if we only had manual labour to move and process these resources?

... range of equipment available extends ... and tools to large earth-moving vehicles.

The range of construction plant

In the construction industry we use a wide range of plant and equipment; here is a list of some of the common types that are in use on ...

* ...
* ... and compressors
* Small tools and plant
* Concrete batching plant or silos.

Construction plant – mechanical machines used on construction sites

Excavator – a digging machine that can swivel its excavator arm 180° or 360°; the most common is the JCB 3CX

Mechanisation – the use of mechanical plant instead of manual labour

Tower cranes – a crane sitting on a mast, comprising sections bolted together, which can lift materials to great heights; these cranes tower over the project, and can climb up a structure as it is built

Four main reasons for use

Time	Clients require their buildings to be handed over, completed, earlier than originally planned; plant makes the job faster.
Safety	Some situations would be dangerous for manual working, for example, if you need to excavate to 2 m depth in loose ground, working by hand could cause ground to collapse in on the workers.
Efficiency	For many types of work, using plant is more cost effective than using manual labour.
Height	Particular building structures require specialist tower cranes to lift materials to great heights.

* Larger designed structures – Terminal 4 at Heathrow ... open-span passenger terminal that would have been impossi...

... ngs – tower cranes have enabled us to build tall structures. We can now use climbing cranes where the crane climbs up with the structure as it is built. This reduces the restrictions on the height of buildings.

Activity 4.21

1 Taking a well-known excavator manufacturer, visit their website and look for a plant specification sheet. Find out how deep it can excavate, how much the front bucket holds, and how high it can reach vertically.

2 Now find out if there are any attachments that can be fitted to the rear arm of the machine and check what they can be used for.

3 Look closely at the specification of the excavator. What items are going to have to be maintained, and so will slow down the usage of the machine?

Personal Learning and Thinking Skills

During your visit to look at this site, make a short list that illustrates the range of construction plant being used. When you return, expand this list with short explanations of what each piece of plant is being used for.

Elect a team leader and debate the factors that affect plant choice. Choose one particular piece of construction plant to discuss. The team leader should ensure that each member is encouraged and able to contribute.

Just checking

* Why do people use construction plant?
* What sort of tasks is plant used for?
* What effect has the development of plant had on buildings?

Functional Skills

Find a plant manufacturer's website and investigate the costs of different items of plant.

Case Study

Have a look locally for a construction project where some construction plant is being used. Look for one item of plant and, in small groups, list what factors you think would have to be considered before bringing it onto the site (e.g. for an excavator, you might have to think about how much earth you had to move). Groups should then compare lists, checking with the tutor to see if you are correct.

5.27 Building services 4: Jointing methods

For both plumbers and electricians, jointing is an everyday part of the job. In each case, there are a variety of different methods and components to choose from. It takes a lot of skill to be able to carry out these methods of jointing. It is important that care is taken, as the safety of the worker and the customer is of utmost importance.

Plumbing

J...

Co...
th...

Soldere... ...ry joints are normally soft soldered. This is done in one ...ays:

* ...gral solder ring – where the solder is already in the fitting

* end-feed – where the solder is end-fed from some separate solder.

Push-fit joints are available in metal, but are most commonly plastic. They involve simply pushing the fitting onto either plastic or copper pipe, where a grab ring is used to hold the fitting in place and an O-ring is used to make a watertight joint.

Electrical work

Cable joints and connections should be avoided. In domestic installations, joints are not generally used because most installation is behind plasterboard walls and therefore inaccessible. Joints in electrical circuits are also a weakness, which can cause overheating and, in extreme cases, fire. Where a joint or connection is unavoidable, a suitable type must be selected. Joints and connections include:

* plastic connectors
* porcelain connectors
* compression joints
* uninsulated connectors
* junction boxes
* soldered joints.

Terminating cables

When a cable is joined to a socket, consumer unit, switches or any ...ation. There are different ...shers, strip connectors and ...commonly used.

...ole in the side where ...h and held in place by a

... s – the conductor (cable) is ...placed around the shaft of the ...e screw or nut will close the joint and ... hold it in place.

screw or nut. The ro...

Non-manipulative compression joints

Backnut — Compression ring — Fitting body — Tube

Manipulative compression joints

Tube — Swaged end of tube — Adaptor — Fitting body — Tube

HOW MANY JOINTS?

The water and electricity in your house have to travel. Think about where they have to go from and to. Estimate how many joints are involved in (a) the plumbing system and (b) the electrical circuit.

Activity 5.27

1 Find images of the following brass fittings: straight adaptors, straight couplers, tap connectors, stop ends, tees, elbows, wall-plate elbows, bent and straight tank connectors. Make a file of what you find.

2 Find a manufacturer's list of push-fit and capillary fittings. Compare them in terms of cost, what the manufacturer says about them and how they look.

3 Find two different sockets or light switches. Inspect them and describe how you would terminate a cable in each accessory.

Activity

Each double-page spread contains an activity or a short sequence of questions to test your understanding and give you opportunities to apply your knowledge and skills.

For your project

These are useful things to consider when working on your project.

For your project

For Unit 5 of the Diploma, learners are required to carry out two pieces of practical work. These involve mounting and wiring electrical components, and mounting pipes and components. Use what you have learnt in this section about jointing methods to complete your work.

Just checking

The most important points to understand summarised so you can quickly refresh your knowledge.

Just checking

* What is the difference between a type A and a type B compression joint?
* ...hat are the two ways of soldering a capillary joint?
* Why should jointing in electrical circuits be avoided?

Acknowledgements

The authors and publishers would like to thank the following for their kind permission to reproduce photos:

Alamy/Ace Stock Ltd – page 186; Alamy/Alan Oliver – page 76; Alamy/Andrew Holt – pages 77, 200; Alamy/Bildarchiv Monheim GmbH – page 187 [housing]; Alamy/Blickwinkel – page 13 [infrastructure]; Alamy/Caro – page 193 [bottom]; Alamy/David R. Frazier Photography – pages 176, 195; Alamy/David Hoffman Photo Library – pages 40 [London], 96, 97; Alamy/David Lyons – page 69 [house]; Alamy/David Williams – page 112 [joiner/carpenter/bricklayer]; Alamy/David Wotten – page 112 [engineer]; Alamy/Gabe Palmer – page 43; Alamy/Greg Balfour Evans – page 182; Alamy/Helene Rogers – page 112 [plumber]; Alamy/Ian Caudron – page 152 [top]; Alamy/Imagebroker – page 74; Alamy/ImageState – page 105; Alamy/Jeff Morgan Environmental Issues – page 35 [flooding]; Alamy/John Sturrock – page 10 [brownfield]; Alamy/Justin Kase – page 204; Alamy/Kathy de Witt – page 4 [office]; Alamy/Leslie Garland Picture Library – page 101; Alamy/Martin Mayer –pages 49, 193 [top]; Alamy/Matthew Mawson – page 75 [beams]; Alamy/MasPix Backgrounds – page 147 [leather]; Alamy/Michael Jones – page 46; Alamy/Mike Booth – page 57; Alamy/Nick Kennedy – page 111; Alamy/Paul Bradforth – page 159 [blowlamp]; Alamy/Paul Glendell – pages 9, 183; Alamy/Peter Griffin – page 39; Alamy/PhotoDisc – page 3; Alamy/Photofusion Picture Library – page 112 [painter], 174; Alamy/Robert Brook – page 187 [refurbishment]; Alamy/Robert Morris – page 98; Alamy/Simon Rawles – page 21; Alamy/Stan Kujawa – page 45; Alamy/Steven Poe – page 117 [respirator]; Alamy/Tim Graham – page 189; Alamy/Tom Broadbent – page 172; Alamy/Trip – page 196; Alamy/Visions of America, LLC – page 10 [greenfield]; Alamy/Woodystock – page 116 [cream]; Arco – pages 116 [hat/goggles/gloves], 117 [vest]; Art Directors and Trip – pages 116 [trainers], 117 [mask]; Construction Photography/David Potter – page 171; Construction Photography/Xavier de Canto – page 157 [building]; Corbis/Comstock Select – page 104; Corbis/London 2012/Handout/Reuters – page 69 [Wembley]; Corbis/Paolo Fridman – page 14; Corbis/Steven Vidler/Eurasia Press – page 169; Crown Copyright/Forestry Commission/John McFarlane – page 30; Dreamstime.com/Andrzej Tokarski – page 132 [cross cut saw]; Fancy/Punchstock – page 24 [turbines]; Getty Images/PhotoDisc – pages 4 [Carrie], 119; Ginny Stroud-Lewis – page 116 [ear defenders]; iStockphoto/7nuit – page 35 [Earth]; iStockphoto/Chris Crafter – page 13 [drains]; iStockphoto/Dean Tomlinson – page 208; iStockphoto/filonmar – page 58; iStockphoto/Garry Hampton – page 121 [block]; iStockphoto/Ivanov Valeriy – page 159 [spanner]; iStockphoto/Jonathan Ling – page 40 [Thames barrier]; iStockphoto/Karl Kehm – page 4 [school]; iStockphoto/Karim Hesham – page 190; iStockphoto/Kiris Hanke – page 205; iStockphoto/Krzysztof Slusarczyk – page 24 [pylons]; iStockphoto/Lisa F. Young – page 112 [electrician]; iStockphoto/Lukasz Laska – page 191; iStockphoto/March Richter – page 99; iStockphoto/Margaret Cooper – page 4 [house]; iStockphoto/Margo van Leeuwen – page 177; iStockphoto/podfoto – page 159 [test meter]; iStockphoto/rfwil – page 209; Maria Joannou – page 138 [band bolt]; Pearson Education Ltd/Gareth Boden – pages 125 [all except rod], 132 [all except combination square/cross cut saw/mitre square], 133, 138 [all but band bolt], 148, 149, 153, 159 [all but spanner/tube cutter/test meter/blowlamp]; Peter White, BRE – page 39; Photographers Direct/Claudio

Bacinello – page 159 [tube cutter]; Photographers Direct/Darrel Gresbrecht – page 63; Photographers Direct/David Haggertont – page 157 [wall]; Photographers Direct/Graham Dunn – page 87; Photographers Direct/ Peter C Amsden – page 122; Photographers Direct/Photofusion – page 47; Photographers Direct/Rainer Raffalski – page 102; Photographers Direct/ Robert Clare – pages 121 [bricks], 147 [lincrusta]; Photographers Direct/ Robert Down – page 125 [gauge rod]; Photographers Direct/Shaun Perrin – page 188; Photographers Direct/Sid Frisby – page 100; Photographers Direct/Stuart Paul Sime – page 29; Photographers Direct/TBC – page 152 [bottom]; Rex Features/Jason Bye – page 202; Science Photo Library/ Shelia Terry – page 163; Shutterstock.com/Chris Green – page 4 [shops]; Shutterstock.com/Mark William Richardson – page 27; Shutterstock. com/Volodymyr Kyrylyuk – page 203; Simon Topliss – page 170; Steve Manley – pages 33, 51, 60, 72, 75 [site], 79, 85, 88, 89, 90, 91, 108; Toolbank – page 132 [combination square/mitre square]; Topfoto/HIP/Museum of London – page 17

Introduction

In this unit you will be introduced to the design of the built environment. This is often a challenging task for the architect or designer. Many builds are designed to be around for a number of years in the future. To do this architects and designers need to take several external factors into consideration. These can include the needs of planners and clients, size, height, aesthetics, materials and sustainability as well as several other factors.

Sustainability must now be carefully considered in any design. Raw materials need to last long into the future and key sustainable concepts need to be incorporated into the buildings structure and energy systems.

Buildings systems need utilities and these need to be often hidden within a structure and the surrounding environment. Electricity, gas, water and drainage are utilities that have to be accommodated into a project. This is often below ground level. The impact of this provision on the environment is explored within this unit.

The building project specification can often be a complex document. In this unit you will explore what a specification contains and work towards development of part of an external building envelope specification that meets the required criteria for the local climatic conditions.

How you will be assessed

This unit is assessed around a real life scenario where you will act in the role of a planning consultant who has to undertake some research. You will be given three tasks which match the learning outcomes. Your tutor will supply all the drawn and written information that you require to undertake this task. In all cases the sustainability and environmental impact of the design must be carefully considered.

On completion of this unit, you should:

LO.1.1 Know about factors that influence the design process

LO.1.2 Understand how the nature and availability of utilities affect the design process

LO.1.3 Be able to understand and apply technical information

THINKING POINTS

Where does the clients design come from? There are many factors that influence design. These can be internal or external. Internal factors could be corporate image. Look at McDonald's; their corporate image means every branch looks like another. External factors are those imposed by legislation, namely planning and building control, design influences with local materials and colours, objections from the local community, and the national needs for example a new motorway or by-pass.

The use and production of energy presents its own problems. Pylons have to be kept away from domestic housing due to electro magnetic radiation which can affect health. Gas, water and drainage all have to be buried below ground for distribution. Drainage waste water requires treatment before discharge to the sea which leads to disposal environmental issues. Fresh water requires reservoirs to capture the raw source then treatment to make it fit for human consumption.

The specification of materials can be a complex task because of the large variety of choice that the UK suppliers industry provides along with the ever changing technology that is incorporated into material manufacturer. Specifications have to be correct so that they meet the design criteria for the maintenance free life span of the building and its structure.

1.1 Definition of the built environment

This book is all about construction and the built environment – but just what is the built environment? How do you describe it? What should you include? What should you leave out? By looking into these questions, you will lay good foundations for going on to think about the many issues associated with construction in the modern world.

One definition

Everyone has their own ideas about what makes up the built environment, but here is one definition that you could use.

The built environment is that part of our surroundings created by humans for residential, commercial, retail, industrial, educational, health and entertainment purposes, together with the provision and distribution of transport infrastructures and primary building services.

What does it mean to you?

Think about yourself. Where do you live? Where do you study? Where do you go in your spare time? Without the built environment, where would you be? Practically everything you do is dependent on it.

This is Carrie.

This is where...

... she lives.

... she goes to school.

... she shops.

... her Mum works.

4

The construction cycle

The built environment doesn't build itself! That is what the construction industry is all about – creating an environment that meets the needs, concerns and sometimes the dreams of the people who use it. As you can see when you look around you, there are many different sorts of buildings and structures. However, most go through something like the 'construction cycle' illustrated below.

> **Client** – the person or organisation for which the building is designed and built
>
> **Conservation** – work carried out on any important or historic building or structure to keep it in its original state, often using special materials and techniques

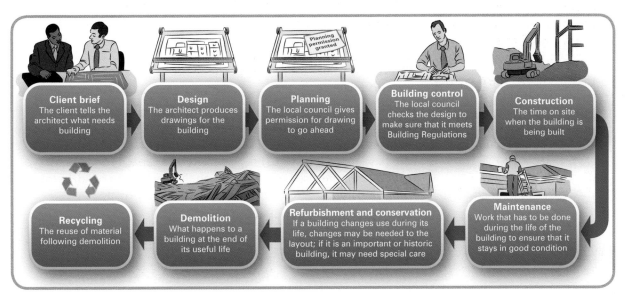

Client brief
The client tells the architect what needs building

Design
The architect produces drawings for the building

Planning
The local council gives permission for drawing to go ahead

Building control
The local council checks the design to make sure that it meets Building Regulations

Construction
The time on site when the building is being built

Recycling
The reuse of material following demolition

Demolition
What happens to a building at the end of its useful life

Refurbishment and conservation
If a building changes use during its life, changes may be needed to the layout; if it is an important or historic building, it may need special care

Maintenance
Work that has to be done during the life of the building to ensure that it stays in good condition

Activity 1.1

1 Discuss in groups or pairs what you think the built environment is. Make a list or a mind map of all the groups thoughts on this.

2 Write your own definition of the term 'the built environment'. How does it compare to the one given earlier? How might it change in the future? Write down your thoughts.

3 Create a collage of the built environment in your local area. Find images from the Internet or perhaps take photographs for your collage to remind you what the built environment can include.

Personal Learning and Thinking Skills

Discuss with a partner what the built environment means to you. What are the differences in your understanding?

Just checking

* What is the built environment?
* What are the usual stages of the construction cycle?
* There are many different types of buildings and structures, name some of them.

1.2 Infrastructure

The availability and capacity of infrastructure has a major effect on any development, and helps shape many of the design decisions that are made when creating a development. But just what is infrastructure? And how does it affect what the construction industry can build?

Types of infrastructure

The term 'infrastructure' refers to a whole range of different basic services which society depends on to function properly. Infrastructure means the basic services required for a development to take place. Look at the spider diagram opposite to see some of the main types of infrastructure.

If you think about building a house or a residential development, there are many of these types of infrastructure that need to be in place before the build can start. If there is no access to services infrastructure, this has to be addressed. The availability and capacity of different types of infrastructure also has an impact on the decision to build, because providing infrastructure from scratch can be very costly.

Availability and capacity

Considering the availability and capacity of infrastructure on development is incredibly important when planning a development. For example, think about how important transport infrastructure is. It can have an impact on a development in lots of different ways. Imagine you were considering building a residential development outside a city centre. For such a project, good transport infrastructure would be vital. Rail corridors with easy links to city centres are crucial to residential development. Or, if you were part of a distribution company looking for a new site, your development would have to be built near good transportation links such as motorways and ports.

When considering a new development, it is important not just to consider the availability but also the *capacity* of existing infrastructure. If a development is being considered near an existing road, key questions must be asked. What is the maximum capacity for this road? Can it take any more traffic flow? In the planning stages, it is important to liaise with government departments to find out what the current flow rates are, what the maximum capacity is, and what the likely flow rates would be if the proposed development were to happen.

HOW DO YOU GET THERE?

Consider the different things you did before you got to school or college this morning. Did you have a wash or shower? Did you boil the kettle or make some toast? How did you get to school or college? Make a list or a mind map of all the ways in which you depended on things such as electricity, phone networks, roads and transport this morning.

Functional Skills

The local authority announces that they are giving planning permission for a residential development near to an existing main road. Consider what effect the build would have on the existing road infrastructure. See if you can find information on the maximum capacity of a suitable road for this development in your own area.

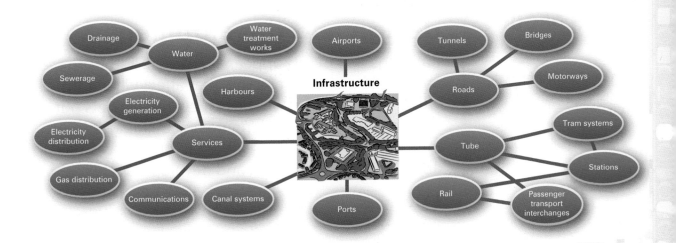

Case Study

A major haulage company is considering expanding and looking for a suitable site on which to build.

* What factors would they need to consider in locating to an area?

* Why would they need to consider transport infrastructure?

* Would they need to consider being near rail links? Why?

* Would they need to consider having good airport links? Why?

Activity 1.2

1 Write up your findings from the discussion in the Case Study as a short report.

2 Work in groups. Each group should take a different type of building from the following list. Pick someone to be the company head. In a role-play, the head leads a discussion on where you will build your new development. The others in the group discuss the advantages and disadvantages of building in the area you are suggesting.

Factory, residential development, supermarket, cinema complex, restaurant, shopping centre, bus station.

3 Make a list of all the types of infrastructure in a table. Next to this list, write how this impacts on you, personally: for example, 'water – being able to have a bath/shower'.

Personal Learning and Thinking Skills

Reflect on the different types of infrastructure that you use in your day-to day life. Discuss in teams any differences in these.

Just checking

* What are the different types of infrastructure?

* When planning a build, what factors regarding infrastructure would you have to consider?

* What does 'water' mean in terms of infrastructure?

Affordable housing – housing available to rent or buy at a lower rate

Services – electricity, gas, water supply and drainage and telecommunications to a property

1.3 Factors influencing design and development 1

Buildings do not just appear at random. Rather, there are a huge number of factors that affect what is built, where it is built, and what use it eventually gets put to. At the very start of planning any building, it is important to consider all of the factors that will have an influence on its design and development.

Influences

Many things can affect the design and development of buildings. For example, in the UK, there is currently a severe shortage of 'affordable housing', especially in areas of high employment. **Affordable housing** is classed as housing available to rent at a lower rate (such as council housing), as well as housing made available to buy at the sort of rate that young people or first-time buyers can manage. In many areas of the country, the demand for this type of housing is higher than the supply available. This demand is a strong influence on the types of buildings that are planned, and on the locations they are put in.

- Consumer demand
- Local planning regulations
- Transport and access infrastructure
- **Influencing factors**
- Government incentives
- Availability of services and resources
- Workforce skills

Many other factors come into play too, including the following:

* **Consumer demand** Do the general public want it or not? This does not just mean housing but also industrial buildings, for example the demand for industry to locate to a particular area.

* **Transport and access infrastructure** Are there roads, railways and other public transport to and from the site being developed?

* **Availability of services and resources** Are **services** available to support the buildings, such as electricity, drainage, gas, water supply and telecommunications?

* **Workforce skills** Are people available with relevant skills? If a building is being created with a very specific use – such as a hospital – are there enough skilled people in the area to run it? Industry may start up in (or relocate to) an area where labour is available.

* **Government incentives** Grants and support schemes are available in particular areas to support certain sorts of building. Some areas of the country have funding from the European Union to encourage building.

* **Local planning regulations** Different areas of land may be designated for buildings of different kinds, including certain areas for housing, other areas for industrial structures, and Green Belt land where no building is allowed at all.

Affordable housing like this can encourage first-time buyers

Case Study

Anna runs a construction company called *Build It!*
She is investigating a piece of land about five miles from a busy town centre. The company is looking into building a housing development there. What type of questions might Anna need to ask about the land to be developed? What do you think will affect whether *Build It!* decides to build there?

Activity 1.3

1 A company would be unlikely to build a factory in a remote part of the Scottish Highlands. Why do think this would be? Write a list of your reasons.

2 Where would be a good place to locate a factory? Identify what the positive aspects of a good location might be.

3 What government grants and schemes are available in your local area for funding building? Carry out some research to find out.

Just checking

* What factors affect the design and development of a building?
* How do government and local authorities affect things?
* Why are some areas of land protected from any building work at all?

1.4 Factors influencing design and development 2

'Sustainability' is at the forefront of modern construction. These days, good design means producing something that is **sustainable** and, at the same time, fits the demands and needs of the local community.

We need to look after the environment we live in. Legislation helps with this, offering local communities, and important green and natural spaces, some form of protection. However, those involved in the construction industry can do more to help the environment than simply staying within the law. By behaving responsibly and with the environment in mind, you can help to make sure that the areas we live in do not end up having development which is unsuitable or made up just of buildings!

Sustainability

Sustainability is now an essential consideration for any build, as being concerned about sustainability helps to minimise the bad effects of any build on the environment. One of the many ways that the construction industry can promote sustainability is by considering the use of **brownfield sites** over **greenfield sites**. The use of brownfield sites is usually better in sustainability terms – the land has already been developed, so less impact is likely to be made. However, using brownfield sites is usually the more costly option: there are often demolition costs, and more complex and expensive excavations are often needed because of things like existing foundations and services or ground contamination.

Sustainable – created and maintained in a way that lasts, without using up more and more resources, protecting resources for use by the communities of tomorrow

Brownfield sites – sites that have previously been developed or built on. This may require the demolition of existing buildings and is likely to contain drainage, services and foundations, that will require special attention during design and construction

Greenfield sites – sites that have never previously been developed, or built on, and forms part of the natural environment

Brownfield site

Greenfield site

Communities

When any build is being considered, it is important to take into account the needs and concerns of the local community. The construction industry often engages with the local community through community consultations, where local people can express their concerns, and industry representatives can respond to them.

Legislation

There are many Acts of Parliament that affect the construction industry. Buildings and developments have to follow these rules. One Act that is extremely significant is the Town and Country Planning Act 1990, which is overseen and enforced by the Government. Local authorities are responsible for processing any applications for planning developments in their own areas.

In the previous topic, we talked about local planning regulations. It is important to recognise that the regulations can put obstacles in the way of building. However, legislation exists to protect local communities against inappropriate development or over-development. Imagine what it would be like to be living near to a beautiful park and then for it to be turned into an industrial estate, or imagine living in a place where there are far too many buildings and no open spaces. How would you feel?

Activity 1.4

1 Compare the pictures of brownfield and greenfield sites opposite. Divide a page into two sections. In one section, describe a brownfield site and justify why you should use it. In the other section, describe a greenfield site and justify using it.

2 Imagine that you have to make a presentation on sustainability in relation to planning a building. Write an outline of the main points you would make. If you have time, develop this into a full presentation, and present it to your class.

Personal Learning and Thinking Skills

Carry out an independent investigation into the impact of the Town and Country Planning Act 1990. What processes happened before this Act was passed?

Case Study

A new development is proposed on a greenfield site in your local area. It is proposed that the development will be made up of homes, a shopping area and a small business park. Think about what may be of concern to the local community. Draw up a list of concerns under the following headings: traffic, pollution, local services, crime, housing, infrastructure, health and safety, and business units.

Just checking

* What does 'sustainability' mean?
* Why is it vital to consider local communities when planning a build?
* What are planning procedures and legislation there for?

1.5 The impact of infrastructure and utility provision on development

The infrastructure of our country is an important element of our economy. It involves the transport network of roads, railways, airports, rivers and canals, and how they attach and interact in the areas that we live in. Infrastructure also includes the services that we need to live: for example, electricity, gas, drainage, water supply and telephone communications.

Types of infrastructure

There are many different types and varieties of infrastructure. All of them provide a building or a community with something unique and essential in order to function correctly. The key aim for many new buildings and projects is to have as easy access as possible to as many of these as possible. Types of infrastructure were explored on pages 6 and 7.

Feasibility

The first thing that must be considered before a development is commenced is the *need* for that project. Will the local community require such a facility? This is a valid point, and is something that the local authority planning department must consider before allowing any development to commence. Once the decision is made to proceed, a lot of facilities have to be provided to service the development.

The scale and size of infrastructure

With new developments, there are many potential problems regarding infrastructure. These must be considered carefully at the planning stage, as solving them later may add a considerable amount to the development budget. Here are just a few examples of what must be considered.

* **Drainage** The existing drain capacity, plus flooding capacity, must not be exceeded, or the consequences for the new development could be disastrous

* **Electric supply** What will the electricity needs be? Is the existing cable large enough?

* **Services** Will the new development require land setting aside for a new school, police station or hospital?

* **Communications** Will a new link road or bypass be required as a result of the development?

Problems exist where you have to develop infrastructure around existing developments. For example, with road bypasses, compulsory purchase orders often have to be served to property owners, so that their houses can be demolished to make way for the new road. Similarly, drainage systems often have to be tunnelled in order to prevent disruption to the buildings that may lie over their path.

Can you see the infrastructure around the houses and offices?

What damage did these overflowing drains cause?

Case Study

Your local district council is considering a planning application for development of a new housing estate just round the corner from where you live. This will be a mixed development of social housing and elderly based community sheltered housing. This development will take place on a brownfield site that the council is keen to develop due to disuse and vandalism. This will involve the partial demolition and clearing of existing residential properties and the formation of a new infrastructure to service the new housing development site. The development will contain forty low cost houses, four sheltered accommodation blocks and a community centre. You need to carefully consider what are the implications for the existing infrastructure in order to identify what issues would be a cause for concern on the already stretched existing infrastructure. For example, the existing bus provider might not extend the route into the new development!

After carefully considering this, identify at least three infrastructional issues. Discuss this in a group with your peers, putting yourself in the shoes of the residents. Ensure you identify what you need to make this a pleasant place to live!

Functional Skills

Using IT skills, identify a local project that has just been completed. Use the web to find as much information as possible on this site, or interview those involved. Then identify five needs for this project and community.

Just checking

✳ What's the first thing to consider before starting a development?
✳ What does 'communications' mean, when talking about infrastructure?
✳ Why is good planning of infrastructure important?

WHY CARRY OUT PLANNING?

Have a look at the photograph below of a major city in a developing country. Look at the way houses are laid out and buildings have developed. What do you notice? What could be the consequences for the local population?

Functional Skills

Draw a proportioned sketch plan of the area surrounding your house and use colour to mark the different development areas that are permitted.

1.6 Town and country planning

In the UK, any major development has to be approved under the planning laws, applied by the local authority. There are some exceptions, but these are small in nature. **Planning** developments have to be undertaken so that the local authority has some control on what, where and when **development** takes place.

Look at this photo of Delhi. What do you see?

Planning – the controlled development of buildings in the community

Development – the construction of housing, factories, shops, roads and retail units

The local plan

This is the first stage of the development process. Under planning laws, the local authority sets out the local development in the form of a map. This shows what is allowed in certain areas: for example, housing only in one area and shops in another, or a mixture of both. This plan is produced with consultation, so that the wishes of the community and any developers are listened to.

The planning process

There are several stages in the planning process before you get permission to undertake your development. For a simple building project, the process would be broadly as follows.

1   Check with the planning department if development is allowed.

2   Commission a designer who can produce the drawings and specification.

3   Submit an application.

4   Details of the development are advertised to the general public for comment.

Functional Skills

Write a short, numbered, logical list of the documents that you have found that are required for a planning application.

5 Copies of the proposal are sent to water, highways and any other interested bodies for comment.

6 After eight weeks, a decision is made which may be subject to conditions.

7 You have the right of appeal if your application has been rejected.

An artist's impression. What does this show to the planning officers?

The future of planning

The government's Department for Environment, Food and Rural Affairs (DEFRA) is looking at planning, and trying to find ways to ease the process for people and developers and their projects. In 2007, the areas that they were considering included:

* removing the need for planning permission for some commercial developments

* streamlining minor domestic applications (for example, loft conversions) while still protecting neighbours

* improving the appeals procedure by speeding it up.

In such a rapidly changing area, it is important to keep yourself up-to-date with the latest developments.

Just checking

* Why is planning important?
* What are the key planning stages for a simple building project?
* What is a 'local plan'?

1.7 The need for building regulation

THE GREAT FIRE OF LONDON, 1666

Think about this historic event, with the loss of life, buildings and property that it led to. What reasons can you think of for why it happened? What do you think could have been done to prevent it at the time?

In the UK, formal building regulations have been in existence in some form since the Great Fire of London, when a fire at a bakery spread through the timber houses, until over two-thirds of the city burned to the ground. After destruction on such a scale, measures had to be put in place to prevent such a disaster happening again.

The Building Regulations

The current Building Regulations were established as a result of the Building Act of 1984. These set national standards throughout the UK.

Issues	What the regulations do
Fire safety	Fire barriers are required in the structure to prevent the spread of flame
Structural safety	Ensure that buildings do not weaken and collapse
Foundations	Ensure that the foundations are adequate for the load of the building
Insulation	Set the level of isulation against heat loss in winter
Sound	Cover the transmission of sound from one property to another
Sanitation	Deal with toilets and associated drainage
Ventilation	Cover the removal of moisture from a property
Drainage and waste disposal	Cover drainage to remove effluent and wastage
Conservation of fuel and power	The reduction in energy loss from a building
Disabled access	Ramps and wide doors required to enable wheelchair access
Electrical safety	Safe use of electrical wiring in and around a property

Issues covered by the Building Regulations

The Building Regulations are laid out in a series of documents – from Part A to Part P – each of which contains the sets of rules on a given issue. These rules have to be followed when designing and constructing buildings and doing alterations. These regulations have to be followed because they are for people's safety when occupying both commercial and domestic buildings. It is the responsibility of the designer initially to ensure that the drawings meet the Building Regulations, then of the client to ensure that they are built to this standard.

Enforced – made to work, usually through the threat of some sort of penalty

16

How might you prevent this happening in London today?

How are the Building Regulations enforced?

The Building Regulations are **enforced** through:

* the checking of plans and specifications submitted to the local authority building control, and

* the inspection of the work by building inspectors on site.

This enforcement has developed from the Great Fire of London through several other channels. The major cities that grew started to develop health problems because of inadequate drainage, which meant that sewage was not dealt with appropriately – it stank! The Public Health Acts produced regulations that today cover the sanitation and drainage elements of the Building Regulations and our modern day sewage system.

Case Study

You have started work on a small kitchen extension at home and have notified the building control officer of the start date. You have just completed the pouring of the concrete foundations when the building inspector turns up and stops the work, saying: 'You did not inform or contact me so that I could inspect the suitability of the depth of foundations.' Can the building inspector ask you to remove the concrete and excavate deeper foundations?

Activity 1.7

1 The Great Fire of London is not the only factor that affected the development of building regulations. Can you identify any other factors? To help you, try an Internet search on '*history of building regulations*'.

2 Taking a typical house construction, identify four items that the building inspector would inspect on site (for example, that the foundations have been taken down to a suitable depth).

3 What piece of documentation is handed over at the completion of the project by the building control officer, if requested by the owner? Do some research to find out (tip – you are looking for a particular certificate).

Functional Skills

Using the Internet, undertake some research on the structural part of the Building Regulations. You will find these on a government website. Part A is the building regulation you need to start with. How high can you build a structure? What factors have to be taken into consideration?

Just checking

* How did the Building Regulations come into being?
* What essential functions of a building do the Building Regulations cover?
* Who enforces the Building Regulations?

1.8 Community consultations

Any large project has to go through a planning process. Within this process is a consultation period, when members of the local community have the opportunity to view the proposals and pass comment or formally object to the scheme. Any responsible developer will endeavour to take into account any reasonable opinions and views of the local community.

Here we will look at various concerns that may be raised in response to planned development. These have been classified as community or environmental concerns, but they might well overlap: the community will naturally be concerned about their local environment.

Community concerns

Local communities are understandably concerned when construction projects are proposed for their local area.

NOT IN MY BACK YARD!

Imagine how you and your family might feel if a large construction project – a new housing estate, a shopping centre or a new factory – was to be built near your own home. You might quite naturally have worries and concerns. Write a list, in order of importance to you, of the things that might concern you.

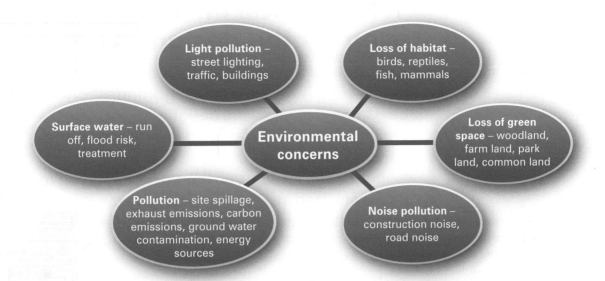

Environmental concerns

All construction projects impact on the natural environment. However, the impact is likely to be greater on greenfield sites. There are incentives and pressures for developers to develop brownfield sites: this is known as **regeneration**. Town planners are more likely to grant planning permission for developments on brownfield sites.

Personal Learning and Thinking Skills

Carry out an independent enquiry on issues in your own community. What regeneration ideas could help to solve these? For example, bus lanes and cycle paths to reduce traffic.

Activity 1.8

Look at the spider diagrams. The effects of all of the identified concerns can be minimised or even eliminated by either good design or effective site management. In addition some of the concerns are about the building work during the construction period or long-term issues related to the completed project.

1 Make a list of the concerns that you think can be reduced by good design.

2 Make a second list of the concerns that you think can be reduced by effective site management.

3 Which of these issues do you think are long-term concerns that relate to the lifetime of the building?

4 Which of these issues are short-term concerns that relate only to the period of construction?

Regeneration
– the redevelopment, or improvement, of an existing site or area to bring it up to modern standards and enhance the quality of life of local residents

Just checking

* What is the point of community consultation?
* What two categories could concerns about a development be put into?
* What sorts of issues are likely to be raised?

1.9 Technical information used by the designer

A designer will need a range of technical information to successfully design a building. Information might be gathered to allow the designer to visualise the project or to initiate design ideas. The size of the building or materials used could all be factors alongside the location/environment it is going to be constructed in. Designers may use the British Standards Institute (BSI) or Barbour Index to help their decision-making and communication.

LET'S GO!

Why do you think that 'technical information' is needed when designing buildings? Write down your thoughts.

This British Standards Institute logo, known as the kitemark, is an indication of certification by the BSI

Technical information

The designer of any building must be thoroughly trained and have a good knowledge of all aspects surrounding construction design, but they also need a great deal of technical information to create a successful design.

Standards of design are often taken from the British Standards Institute, whose codes of practice ensure that all parties involved understand the design and information shown. The table below lists a few of the British Standards used in the construction industry.

The designer will have other resources to hand, such as the Barbour Index (see opposite), and will draw extensively on their own knowledge, gathered through experience in the profession.

The designer also needs to know the location of the proposed project, the size of the building needed and the nature of the surrounding

British Standard	Description
BS 476	Fire resistance of building materials/elements
BS 1363	Mains power plugs and sockets
BS 1192	Construction drawing practice – Part 5 (BS 1192-5 – 1998) gives guidelines for structuring and exchange of CAD data
BS 4902	Sheet/tile floor covering colours used in building construction
BS 4800	Paint colours used in building construction
BS 5499	Graphical symbols and signs in building construction, including shape, colour and layout
BS 5950	Structural steel
BS 6312	Telephone plugs and sockets
BS 8110	Structural concrete

All this material is needed by the designer to complete their task

BSI – British Standards Institute

Standards – an official way of making or keeping something all the same

Product library – contains details on building products available for use on projects

environment. Materials will need to be considered, and various standards taken into consideration when producing designs.

Materials and tolerances

The designer may need information on specific materials. They may need to know the sizes available, or the way the materials react or work when put into a particular environment. The designer will also need to take into account the materials' tolerances, as this will provide information on how far the materials can be forced under particular stresses before failing. This will affect the design of the building, as only certain materials will be able to be used.

New materials are constantly being developed and released into the market; the designer must have a good knowledge of these to ensure that the building required is using the most up-to-date, reliable materials. Information on all possible materials must again be to hand, to allow the designer to create the most successful design. For buildings that are designed with individuality in mind, the designer may stretch to using unusual materials for certain features, but these must still be suitable for the job, so information must be gathered to ensure that they will work successfully.

Barbour Index

This service can be accessed through web services, directories and email briefings. The Barbour Index can provide information on standards, regulatory and guidance documents, as well as technical products and supplier information. The Barbour Index is a product library used by architects and designers to provide detailed information on materials and components suitable for inclusion in other designs. It is also used by quantity surveyors and other construction professionals in the production of specifications.

Activity 1.9

1 Why do designers use standards when communicating information?

2 What could happen if a consistent standards code of practice were not followed in the construction industry?

3 Research in pairs and try to find ten British Standards codes that are not shown in the table.

Just checking

* What sort of information does a designer need?
* Why are standards important when communicating?
* What does the Barbour Index offer?

1.10 Technical information sources

When we transfer an idea from a client into reality – the process of feasibility and design – we need standard information to build the project to. Here we will investigate the technical information that is available and how it helps in producing a quality product.

WHAT INFORMATION DO WE NEED?

Can we just turn up and commence a construction project? What information would we need to start? How would the client ensure that the project is been built to a quality standard? Make some notes before you read on.

Construction specifications

The designer needs to know what types of materials the client requires for the finished construction project. These are specified in the project specification that accompanies the construction drawings. The specification enables the main contractor to identify what types of materials are required and where they are to be incorporated. These materials often have to meet a stated budget. More expensive materials are specified in areas where they may be seen; less valuable materials are used in areas that will remain hidden.

Various organisations produce standard specifications that a designer can use to achieve the right quality product for the client. Here are some of the appropriate sources.

* In-house within the designer's practice

* British Standards

* British Board of Agrément certificates (BBAs)

* Technical indexes of suppliers

* National Building Specification (NBS), which is owned by **RIBA**

* Building Research Establishment (BRE) research and European Union standards

Different types of building materials will have different specifications; a designer needs to specify which ones are to be used

RIBA – The Royal Institute of British Architects

British Standards (BS) and Codes of Practice (CP)

The British Standards Institution (BSI) has been in existence for over 100 years. It provides a quality standard that is identified on a product by a kitemark symbol (see page 20) and develops and tests a technical standard, with a formal document for publication. This BS number that is given to a product is recognised throughout the world, so a designer knows that a product obtained from another country meets this agreed standard. Codes of practice are produced from the standard, often covering the use of a product in more detail.

Product libraries

These are suppliers' libraries that are produced by commercial organisations. Here are just some of the ones available in the UK.

* IHS Technical Indexes online

* Barbour Index

* NBS Specification Library

* RIBA Product Selector

* BRE research and EU standards

These provide the designer with suppliers' guides to construction products produced within the UK and Europe. They provide an easy one-stop shop for finding products for a particular design application. None of the above services is free: they all have to be subscribed to for a fee.

Suppliers' databases

Many UK construction material suppliers have databases of detailed information on the products that they manufacture. These are often contained within their websites, and you may have to register to use the information.

Design specifications

When a designer is producing a design for a client, they have to take into account the environment in which the completed project will be located. For example, a hot climate will require different design specifications from a colder climate.

The climate is changing, owing to human impact on global weather systems. This now has to be carefully considered at the design stage, and previously adequate specifications may have to be changed to take into account new extremes of weather. For example, in areas prone to flooding, we should start using solid floors instead of timber suspended floors.

Robust details

As the name suggests, these are construction specification details that meet a known standard and will meet the requirements of any testing. For example, local authorities use them for sound insulation construction, with details of how to construct floors and walls to reduce the level of sound disturbance to a neighbour.

ABOVE OR BELOW?

We have to use many methods to distribute our electricity around the UK, from the power station to the domestic house. In the UK, we use many pylons carrying electricity in cables in a network called the National Grid. Why do we not just bury this method of distribution in the ground? Think about the reasons for this.

1.11 Utilities

Buildings today require heating, lighting, communications and power in order to function in this modern technological world that we live in. To achieve this the necessary utilities have to be distributed around the UK, and locally, into commercial and domestic buildings. These utilities cover gas, water, electricity and communications.

Utilities and the design process

There are a number of utilities that a designer must consider, as they have to be incorporated into a construction project's structure.

We need energy to function – not just at home, where, for example, we need electricity to run an electric shower, but also at work, where a factory might use an electric arc furnace. Most utilities have to be hidden within a design, to make it acceptable to the end user. Would you want to buy a house with wires running all over the inside walls?

Energy reduction

The process of feeding a building with energy is changing and evolving with the reduction of our carbon footprint on the built environment. Energy reduction is now the key idea applied to building services design. This can mean the incorporation of several features into modern housing, such as: small wind turbines, solar power, increased thermal insulation, waterless toilets, energy-efficient boilers, micro combined heat and power plants and **district heating system**.

Pylons are a key part of the National Grid

Environmental impact of utilities

The UK's large inner cities require large amounts of services. Work to maintain these service distribution systems is often continuous. Streets have to be continually excavated and resurfaced, which has an environmental impact as well as causing traffic disruption. The amount of space services and utilities take up needs to be taken into account when planning new and refurbished services. Electricity supply also has an impact on the environment, in its main form of distribution – pylons. These carry electro magnetic waves and have to be kept away from residential areas on safety grounds. They can be buried but this is expensive and damaging to the environment. With new power stations, distribution systems may have to be placed across open fields and the countryside to link supply with the national grid. Telecommunication phone masts have become a focus for protest when sited near to buildings such as schools and houses. Wireless communication is now a modern and current method of communication but it does require aerials and routers to function.

UK wind turbines are becoming more common

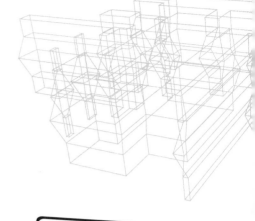

Distribution

Utility supplies do not just include water for drinking, washing and cleaning, gas as a cooking or heating fuel, electricity for power and lighting, telephone and cable TV: they can also include district heating schemes and warden call services.

Drainage

Water and waste products are removed from buildings by drains. Drains connect in with a local area's sewer system and transport this excess and waste away from buildings. Water can be recycled in sewerage treatment plants and other sustainable methods, and returned to the water supply to be returned to the building for use in the future.

Electricity

The main supply distribution from the power station is by pylons, then via transformers to utility meters in homes on the National Grid.

Gas

The main gas distribution in the UK is via buried pipelines that carry the gas in a nationwide grid. Gas also arrives in the UK from pipelines under the sea from Russia. It can also be stored as liquid propane fuel under pressure in separate residential storage tanks, that are filled by a visiting tanker when empty.

Water

This is again distributed via pipelines that are buried deep enough not to be affected by extreme cold. Water has to be treated before it can be pumped to the consumer.

Telephone

This can be either wireless or wired. Timber poles, cables and telephone exchanges are used to distribute the latter.

The major point of distribution is often within the footpath adjacent to the road network. This is the easiest option to install, and one that causes the least disruption when repairs are necessary. The whole distribution of electricity and gas now comes under the National Grid. Visit their website to obtain more information.
http://www.nationalgrid.com/uk

District heating system – a heating system that uses factories' waste heat and takes it in pipes from house to house

---

Activity 1.11

1 Services have to be colour-coded for health and safety reasons. The following are the main colours used for the four main services when placed under footpaths. Identify which colour goes with which service.

Blue, Green, Yellow, Black with marker tape or blocks

2 How deep must the services in question 1 be placed and why? Take a look in a building services textbook to find this information.

3 What does an electrical transformer do? You will need to research this by using the web or a building services textbook.

Just checking

✳ What colour are the different underground pipes?

✳ What is the National Grid?

✳ What is the environmental impact of energy distribution?

Introduction

In this unit you will be introduced to the materials and structures in the built environment. Construction materials have developed alongside technology and within the constraints imposed by the building regulations on energy saving measures over the past 50 years. Materials are now combined into composites that are used to clad the external envelope of a structure. You will learn that the function of a material in such a position includes: water resistance, freezing properties, thermal expansion, durability and strength as well as many other factors.

The properties of the material in its final state need to perform well to meet both the design brief and the planned life span of the structure. The details of how the material is fixed and finished are examined in both the specification and in drawn information. The introduction of sustainability into material use is examined for a range of materials used in modern construction. You will consider the advantages and disadvantages of each within this sustainable context.

The final outcome in this unit identifies the common forms of structural framework that supports the loads of the building down to the foundations. These are frameworks, shells, cellular and crosswall construction techniques. You will learn to apply this knowledge when identifying a suitable framework.

How you will be assessed

You will have to produce a technical report based on a local construction project, details of which are supplied by your course tutor. There are three elements to answer to this task that match the three learning outcomes. The report needs to be word processed and contain all the research you have undertaken for this project.

On completion of this unit, you should:

LO.2.1 Know about materials and their function within structures

LO.2.2 Understand how to use materials in a sustainable way

LO.2.3 Be able to evaluate and use different structural forms

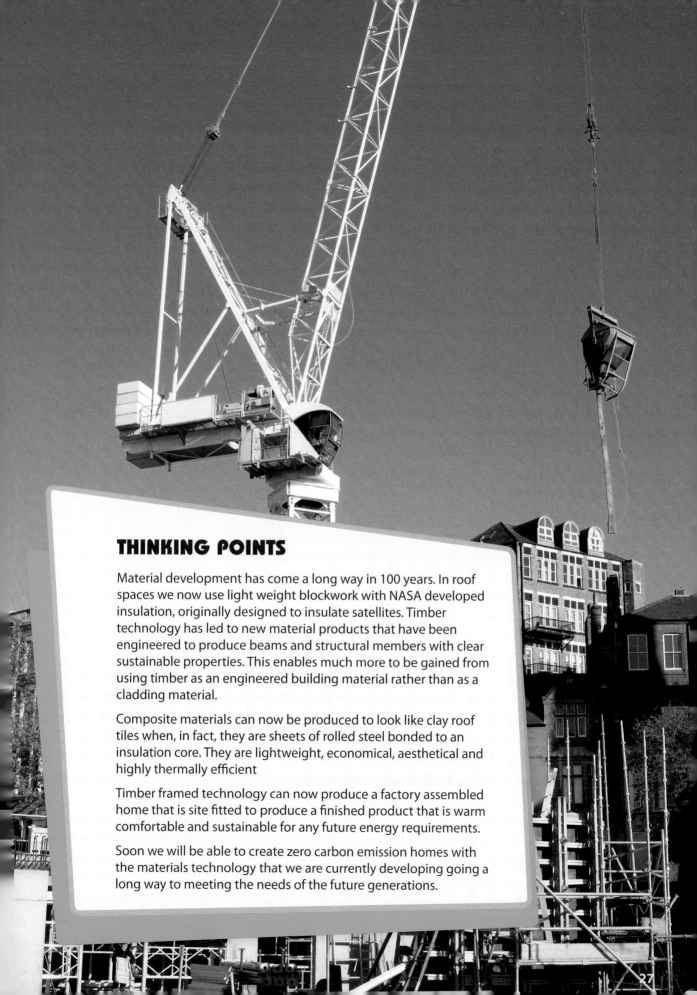

THINKING POINTS

Material development has come a long way in 100 years. In roof spaces we now use light weight blockwork with NASA developed insulation, originally designed to insulate satellites. Timber technology has led to new material products that have been engineered to produce beams and structural members with clear sustainable properties. This enables much more to be gained from using timber as an engineered building material rather than as a cladding material.

Composite materials can now be produced to look like clay roof tiles when, in fact, they are sheets of rolled steel bonded to an insulation core. They are lightweight, economical, aesthetical and highly thermally efficient

Timber framed technology can now produce a factory assembled home that is site fitted to produce a finished product that is warm comfortable and sustainable for any future energy requirements.

Soon we will be able to create zero carbon emission homes with the materials technology that we are currently developing going a long way to meeting the needs of the future generations.

2.1 Sustainable design practice 1: Energy conservation

Good design should minimise the **carbon footprint** of a building to help in the battle against global warming. This has other benefits for both the building users and the wider community. The building user will benefit from lower energy costs. Also the reduction in use of fossil fuels due to lower energy demand will benefit society in the future.

The architect, or building designer, is required by law to design energy-efficient homes. Energy efficiency relates not only to the insulation of the **external envelope**, but also to equipment and appliances. Sustainable design encourages designers to design 'greener', more environmentally friendly buildings than those required by the regulations. Here are some areas where an architect might attempt to make buildings more energy efficient. It is likely that a combination of these methods will be used in the design of a modern building.

Insulation

Insulating buildings reduces the amount of heat lost through the external envelope. The Building Regulations require a **U-value** of 0.4:3:5 for new dwellings, but sustainable design should attempt to achieve a much lower U-value. The use of very high standards of insulation can mean that a building has little, if any, need for heating, provided that the building is able to maintain a high indoor air quality within a draught-free, airtight environment.

Timber-framed construction offers opportunities for high levels of insulation, because the voids between the structural members provide space for insulation of substantial thickness. In fact, developers in the UK were achieving U-values of 0.3 as long ago as the 1980s, when timber-framed construction gained in popularity. Typical insulation materials include fibreglass, expanded polystyrene, styrofoam and vermiculite.

Building orientation

Buildings oriented to face south can benefit from 'solar gain'. Opposite you can see how winter sunlight can be harnessed to provide heating for the building. The **thermal mass** of parts of the structure heats up during the day and contributes to the night-time heating of the building. On top of the heating benefits, this minimises the need for artificial light during the daytime.

SAVING FOR THE FUTURE

How can we save energy in our buildings? Think about the typical buildings that you use – your home, school or college, sports centres, cinemas, etc. Make a list of ways of saving energy in these buildings. Try to rank them in order of importance or effectiveness.

Carbon footprint – the total amount of CO_2 emissions produced by an individual, building or even industry

External envelope – the building elements (e.g. walls, roof etc.) that enclose the internal space of a building

U-value – the rate of heat lost through a wall in watts per m^2 per °C difference in temperature between the inside and outside air temperature ($W/m^2/°C$)

Thermal mass – a dense, heat-retaining material

Biomass – organic matter, e.g. trees harvested as a source of fuel; can also include recycled waste

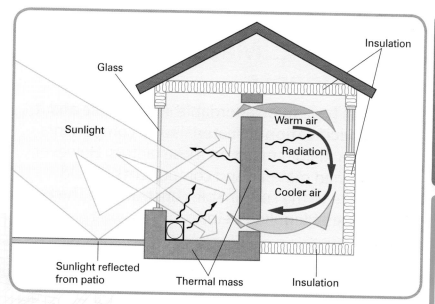

How 'solar gain' works

Alternative energies

The design could incorporate the use of 'alternative energies' such as solar heating or photovoltaic cells, which produce electricity from sunlight. Other sources of energy include wind and water power, geothermal power (ground source heat) and **biomass**, but these sources are dependent on the location or exposure of the site.

Energy-saving appliances

Modern electrical appliances are rated for their energy-efficiency from A to G on a colour-coded scale. The building designer should specify equipment with a high energy-efficiency rating; such equipment will consume less electricity and will lead to lower CO_2 emissions from power stations.

The specification of a modern, high-efficiency condensing boiler, which has secondary heat exchangers, provides positive benefits by reducing emissions when compared to traditional central heating boilers.

For your project

Remember – for your project, you will have to recommend good sustainable design practice. Look at the examples in this topic and decide which would be relevant and appropriate for your site report.

Personal Learning and Thinking Skills

Conduct an independent enquiry into the energy efficiency ratings, and the meaning of these, found on electrical goods such as dishwashers, washing machines and tumble dryers.

Activity 2.1

1 Write a list of the advantages of high levels of insulation. Can you think of any disadvantages?

2 Produce a poster to advertise the energy-saving features of a modern dwelling.

3 Do some research to find out the meaning of the term 'interstitial condensation'. Does this affect the way that buildings are designed and detailed?

Use of photovoltaic cells to generate electricity

Just checking

✳ What impact can the architect, or building designer, have on the energy-efficiency of a building?

✳ In what ways can energy be saved?

✳ What alternative energy sources are there?

2.2 Sustainable design practice 2: Materials and components

Buildings have to be affordable and durable and it is the **specification** of materials and components that has a major impact on these factors. However, the specified material and components should contribute to the sustainable construction. The key features are identified below.

Sustainable buildings

* are designed for minimum waste during use
* use lean, minimum waste construction
* minimise energy in construction and use
* do not pollute
* preserve and enhance biodiversity
* conserve water resources
* respect the local environment.

Local materials

By specifying locally produced materials and components, the environmental costs of transporting materials will be reduced. This will bring about a reduction in congestion on the road systems within the UK and reduce the amount of CO_2 emitted while transporting goods to the site.

Sustainable softwood

Softwood should be specified in preference to hardwood. When softwood is sourced from a managed forest, it is considered to be a renewable resource. This generally applies to forestry operations in the northern hemisphere, where a planned programme of planting and tree felling ensures that there will be a continuous supply of material. The relatively fast growth of softwoods makes this possible; softwoods reach maturity, depending on species, in approximately 30 to 45 years, while hardwoods can take up to 200 years to mature. Hardwoods are not considered a sustainable material as their use is leading to mass deforestation in some parts of the world.

Sustainable development can be defined as

'development that meets the needs of the present without compromising the ability of future generations to meet their own needs'.

The Bruntland Report 1987

Landscaping and planting

The use of appropriate planting and landscaping can help to enhance the biodiversity of the site. This can be planned to minimise the impact of the development upon wildlife and it may be possible to provide animal habitats within the scheme to compensate for the loss of natural habitat brought about by the project.

Sustainable forestry is a way of ensuring a constant supply of materials

Security

Fear of crime has been identified as an issue that concerns communities. The architect, or building designer, is able to design and specify security measures to counteract such fears. This may mean the incorporation of security locks, alarms, fencing and CCTV within the overall scheme. Careful design of the layout and locality is vital to reduce the number of potential crime hotspots and escape routes, such as alleyways linking streets.

Minimising waste

While you may think that waste is just a site management issue, the design of a building also has an impact on the waste produced on site. The building designer, or specifier, can help to minimise waste in two ways.

✱ The building should be dimensioned to reduce the cutting of materials. This may include ensuring that walls are dimensioned to match modular brickwork sizes, and structural supports are positioned to accept full panel sizes.

✱ Materials specified should be durable, fit for purpose and not easily prone to damage during handling or storage.

Energy-efficiency and emerging technologies

The architect, or building designer, should specify materials and components that are energy-efficient, so it is essential that they keep up-to-date with new and emerging technologies. The most notable product currently under development is the fuel cell, which produces electricity; it is fuelled by hydrogen, and the only by-product is water.

Demolition and recycling

The architect should consider how the building will be demolished at the end of its useful life, and how to recycle or reuse construction materials for use on other projects. It is also important here to consider the project's complexity, cost and pollution implications.

Sustainable urban drainage systems (SUDS)

The use of SUDS techniques should be considered for specification on all new projects. This will include the specification of materials such as pervious pavings considered in more detail on page 32.

Specification – when an architect creates a specification, they are saying which materials or components have to be used on the project; it will list all the project requirements as decided by the architect on behalf of the client.

Activity 2.2

1 Look at the concerns raised on pages 18–19. See if you can link any of the good practice detailed here to minimise these concerns.

2 You are working as a sustainability expert and have been asked to produce a leaflet that will encourage building designers to specify sustainable materials by explaining the advantages of using them. Use information from the Internet to create this leaflet.

Just checking

✱ How can the right choice of material affect a building's sustainability?

✱ How can design help reduce waste?

✱ Why should an architect keep up-to-date with new developments in materials and components?

2.3 Sustainable urban drainage systems (SUDS)

You have no doubt heard about the flooding that regularly occurs in certain areas of the UK. The areas worst affected are often adjacent to rivers or on flood plains. The built environment can be a contributory factor to these flooding problems, so special systems must be put in place to minimise the bad effects.

The problem

The problem of surface water **runoff** from rainfall has historically been solved by collecting the water and discharging it to the drainage system, in order to move the water rapidly away from the site. As the built environment continues to expand, the area of land covered by **impervious** surfaces continues to grow. The additional surface water runoff is directed into a drainage system that is struggling to cope with the volume of water.

The modern approach is somewhat different, and relies on a combination of a delay in the discharge of surface water runoff and natural **infiltration**. This reduces the burden on the drainage system during peak rainfall, and therefore reduces the subsequent flood risk.

With a traditional combined drainage system the foul waste is mixed in with the surface water and can have an impact on health. This is due to drain contents contaminating property and water supplies.

SUDS techniques

Filter strips

These are wide, gently sloping areas of grass or other dense vegetation that handle the runoff from adjacent impermeable areas. Runoff flows across the filter strip at a slow rate, allowing infiltration and sediment and pollutants to be filtered out. This makes filter strips a good pre-treatment method for other SUDS techniques.

Swales

These are broad, shallow channels covered by grass or other suitable vegetation. They are designed to convey and store surface water runoff, and allow natural infiltration into the ground. They can be used alongside roads, or within landscaped areas, in place of conventional piped drainage.

Infiltration basins, extended detention basins and wet ponds

Infiltration basins are depressions in the surface designed to store runoff and infiltrate water to the ground. Extended detention basins are similar, but have an inlet and an outlet and are designed to detain a certain volume of surface water runoff. Wet ponds are basins that have a permanent pool of water. They provide temporary storage for additional surface water runoff above the normal water level.

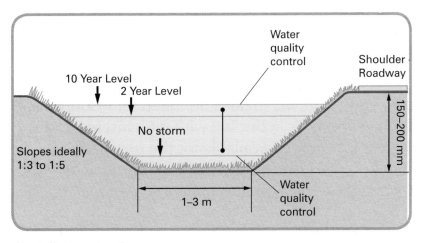

How infiltration takes place

Runoff – the water flowing off an impermeable surface

Impervious – not allowing water to pass through

Infiltration – percolation of water into the ground

Porous – with small holes that allow water to pass/percolate through

Permeable – allowing water to pass directly through

Biological action provided by plantlife and reed beds assists with the removal of pollutants. Wet ponds also provide amenity and wildlife benefits, although safety issues may have to be considered.

Porous and permeable surfaces

One way of reducing runoff to sewers is to allow infiltration through surfaced areas. **Porous** surfaces such as grass, gravel, porous concrete and porous asphalt allow water to infiltrate across their entire surface area. **Permeable** surfaces allow water to pass through voids in the surface even though the material itself may be impermeable: for example, some types of block paving.

An infiltration system being installed

Infiltration systems or devices

Infiltration devices temporarily store runoff following periods of heavy rainfall, then allow it to percolate into the ground.

Green roofs

This is when the roof of a building is covered with vegetation. This is laid over a drainage layer with additional layers providing protection, waterproofing and insulation. The use of green roofs reduces the water volume and runoff rate.

Just checking

* Why are SUDS techniques necessary?
* What are the main SUDS techniques?
* What are the benefits of SUDS?

2.4 Financial and economic sustainability

The UK is the fifth largest economy in the world. As our country grows, so does our need for resources. If the economy is in decline with high interest rates, there is less money available for the population to invest in housing and other buildings – and development growth slows into a recession.

Considerations

More and more, we now have to consider the construction of a building from three angles: the sustainability and environmental effect of the development, the human social effect of the development and the realisation that we often have to make a profit on construction developments to reinvest in future sustainable development.

'Externalities'

Behind every economy are factors that affect our development. These are what economists call 'externalities'. They have a direct impact on our financial wellbeing and can reduce or increase the see-sawing of our **financial markets**. Here are some examples of externalities and their effects.

As you can see, externalities can link together in ways that have important long-term effects.

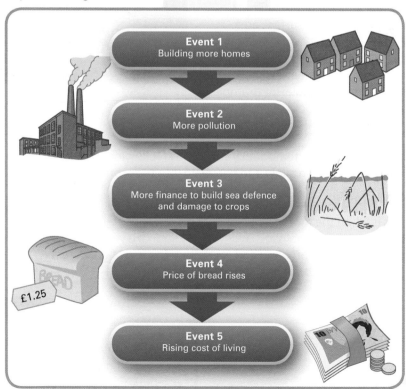

Externalities can cause each other leading to a final financial impact

The Stern Review

The Government asked Sir Nicholas Stern, Head of the Government Economic Service, to investigate the effects of climate change on the UK's financial future. He spent over a year on this task, and came to some important conclusions. Here are some of the main recommendations from the review.

✳ There is still time to avoid the worst impacts of climate change, if we act now.

✳ Climate change could have very serious impacts on growth and development.

✳ The costs of stabilising the climate are significant but manageable; delay would be dangerous and much more costly.

✳ Action on climate change is required across all countries.

✳ A range of options exist to cut emissions, but the government must state policy.

✳ Climate change demands an international response.

In essence, Stern said that we must act *now* to avoid severe financial losses in the future.

Do we have to act now to prevent severe financial losses in the future?

The issues that must be addressed

Wastage	We must reduce the level of wastage, as this uses valuable energy and materials, increasing the effect of CO_2 and global warming. The more we can get out of a given resource, the longer that resource will last.
Energy	We must change our economic reliance on oil as a principal energy source and develop sustainable energy sources such as wind, water and solar power, which are more sustainable sources. This will create growth in the sustainable energy market and help to reduce global warming.
Design	We need to design our buildings to make maximum use of daylight, infrastructure and recyclable and sustainable resources. This will reduce our CO_2 footprint.
Education	We must educate future generations to rethink the way we live and the way we treat our environment and resources.

We only have one earth – should we spend now to save it?

Financial markets – where stocks and shares are traded between companies and individuals, commonly known as free trade

Just checking

✳ What will be the effect on our economy if we ignore climate change?

✳ What are the sustainability issues that must be addressed?

✳ What were the recommendations of the Stern Review?

2.5 Types of structure

A structure is something that has been built or has been made of parts joined together. Many different forms of structure are used in modern construction. Think of all the different structures that surround us: as well as famous buildings like the London Eye and Blackpool Tower, in every city or settlement there are houses, flats, factories, schools, sports halls, churches … the list is endless!

Structures

There are three main types of structure: solid, framed and surface structures. The structure of any building is very important. The structure is what holds everything up or together. Different types of structures are used depending on various factors. For example, does the building have to span a large area? What is the purpose of the building? What is the building to contain, who is it for and who will use it?

Solid structures

This type of structure is usually used for low-rise buildings or buildings with a short span. Solid structures include cellular and cross wall structures.

✳ In cellular structures, the walls divide the buildings into cells. The walls transfer loads down to the foundations.

✳ In cross wall structures, the party walls are the structural elements and transfer the building loads down to the foundations. The front and rear elevations are then completed using a non-loadbearing cladding system.

Framed structures

These include structures with **rectangular, triangulated and portal** frames. This type of structure is used for a range of buildings from low-

Cellular

Cross wall

Cellular and cross wall structures

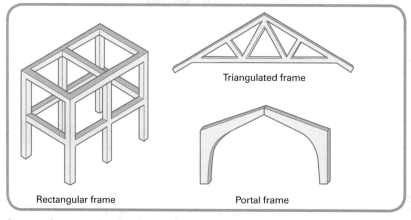

Triangulated frame

Rectangular frame

Portal frame

Rectangular, triangulated and portal frames

rise to high-rise, and also for civil engineering structures such as bridges.

Steel is widely used for constructing framed buildings. The design, method of construction, and erection procedures are all usually carried out by a steelwork specialist. The steelwork is connected to a foundation pad, which is then cast into the foundations.

Surface structures

These are sometimes called shell structures or open-span structures, and are used to span large, clear areas with a minimum of structural support. They are made of a thin material that has been stretched, curved or folded to gain strength. One well-known example is the Millennium Dome (now just called 'O2'), which has several steel structural supports with a stretched material spanning the gap between them. Another well known example is the Eden Biodomes. These can be either slab or gusset based. A gusset base has a thinner base plate and transmits a high bending moment to the foundations.

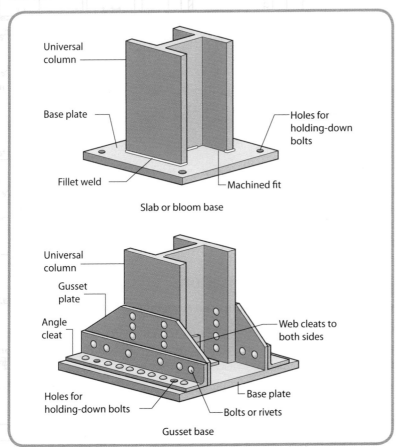

Surface structures

2.6 The use of prefabrication in modern construction

Prefabrication is a method of construction where the majority of the building structure is manufactured in a factory environment, off the construction site. With the rising cost of land and the drive to make houses affordable, prefabrication is becoming more and more effective as an economical method of production.

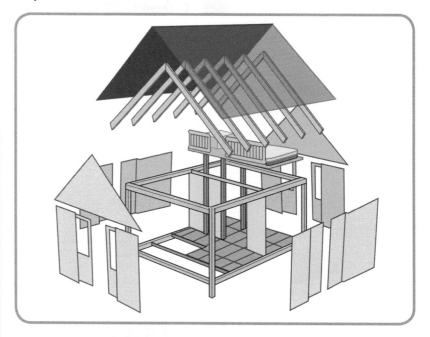

In this house each part is assembled on site and then cladded

Main types of prefabrication

Many types of prefabrication are used to construct buildings.

* **Timber-framed** – these use timber studs clad with external plywood to form panels. The panels are nailed together, insulated and clad externally in a finish such as brickwork or timber cladding.

* **Steel channel framed** – this uses steel channels to form panels which are clad in architectural styles to form a building. This type of prefabrication is useful for office-type construction.

* **Bonded brickwork** – there are now modern methods of construction that employ brickwork bonded together using resins in a factory to form solid brick panels. The panels are placed and bolted together to form a structure.

* **Module prefabrication** – many hotels are now formed by bolting together modules that have all the services connected (for example, a bathroom module).

Case Study

Recently there has been a drive to prefabricate off site a development which has included producing prefabricated schools. Issues include the reduction of noise in classrooms (acoustics), the shading of glare from the sun, the provision of natural lighting and the quality of the air in the rooms. This photo shows a school manufactured from timber off site and assembled on site using a crane and lorries. The advantages of this system include:

* time savings on site

* less disruption to an existing school

* constant internal summer temperatures – it does not get too hot!

* reduced foundation costs and installation

* it can be taken down and relocated.

As you can see this is an innovative method of modern construction. To be able to relocate a school without having to demolish it is a remarkable feat of engineering. This will save valuable resources that could be spent on education for the students. The time saving on site also reduces the costs for the contractor who assembles the schools, and this saving can be passed on to the client through project savings.

Advantages of prefabrication

There are many advantages to using prefabrication to construct a building.

* It saves time on site – a building can be delivered more quickly and can be watertight in less than two weeks, allowing trades such as electricians to start earlier.

* It reduces the need for 'wet' trades, where a building has to be allowed to dry out before it can be finished.

* It uses less skilled labour and thus saves costs.

* Prefabricated units can have better insulation properties.

* Factory-produced quality is maintained.

* Prefabrication uses sustainable materials and is environmentally friendly.

* Prefabricated units can be recycled after their useful life is over.

* It can be clad in a variety of materials.

With its many advantages and benefits, prefabrication is now taking over from traditional methods of construction. Seventy per cent of the world's homes are now of timber-framed construction.

Here the timber frame is constructed first and is clad afterwards

Just checking

* What does the term prefabrication cover?
* What types of prefabrication are available?
* What are the advantages of prefabrication?

So far this century we have had the warmest April on record, and the wettest June and July, with extensive flooding in parts of the UK. Our world's climate is changing – and construction must take this into account in the way it plans, builds and responds to climate change.

Causes of climate change

The earth is slowly warming up – and several factors may be contributing, including the intervention of humankind, by burning fossil fuels and releasing large quantities of CO_2 into the atmosphere. Scientists believe CO_2 has caused a 'greenhouse effect', warming up the earth significantly and changing the planet's natural balance. The consequences of this may be the melting of the ice caps and adverse alterations to our weather systems.

Building design up to today

Historically, we have undertaken decisions in our building design that now, because of an increased awareness of climate change, have become a cause for concern. These include:

* connecting the rain water drainage to the main sewers instead of to a soakaway

* building on river flood plains and low-lying areas

* building near to coastal high tide areas

* paving over grassed areas

* using materials that are not environmentally friendly.

We must act now to create a built environment that enables the key areas of sustainability to be improved.

MEASURING THE CHANGE

Can we predict what the consequences of our rapid increases in population and the resulting use of **finite** resources will be? Think of some ways we may be able to measure the impact.

Finite – with a definite limit or end, not everlasting

Personal Learning and Thinking Skills

Climate change is a very controversial issue – why is this? Working in teams, research the arguments on climate change using the Internet. Reflect on the two sides of the argument – which do you think is most convincing and why?

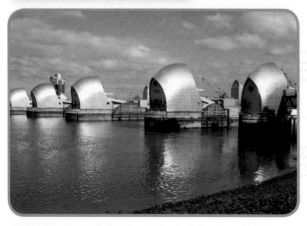

Precautions, such as the Thames Barrier in London, are being taken to help prevent dangerous flooding

The crucial areas the Thames Barrier is protecting

The changing climate of the UK is going to have a great affect on the way in which we approach building design. This table shows the potential impact on different elements of design, and the potential consequences if changes are ignored.

Possible change	The impact for building designers
Increased temperature	Buildings will expand and contract more, causing wear and shorten the life of plastics and mastic sealants Use of air conditioning systems that can potentially spread disease Buildings may overheat in summer, causing difficult conditions for the occupants Less heating may be required for buildings in winter
Increased rainfall	Rainwater disposal systems may become overloaded Increased risk of mould growth to internal finishes and furniture Possible damp problems Flooding to buildings at ground floor level
Drier summers	Shrinkage of clay soils and damage to foundations
Low pressure weather systems	Tornadoes and storm damage to buildings
Increased sunshine	A need to shade windows to prevent heat gain
Humidity	Uncomfortable internal conditions
Rise in sea levels	Destruction of coastal buildings by erosion of the soil

The construction industry is becoming aware of its own role in tackling climate change and promoting sustainability. The industry has responded positively in some of the following ways:

* changes in designs to incorporate green and sustainable construction techniques

* a broad move towards using recycled materials

* greater use of timber engineered products that use and extend timber resources

* a reduction of building wastage

* the promotion of modular building design, where houses are constructed off site and assembled in situ

* Building Regulations now demand increased thermal insulation for houses.

All of these methods reduce the 'carbon footprint' of the construction industry on our planet.

Activity 2.7

1 Imagine yourself in a room within your college or school at the height of the summer term. Is it comfortable? Consider this carefully, and then produce a table. On the left, put items that affect your comfort and, on the right, what happens when these factors are increased or decreased.

2 You have been asked to design a luxury hotel on the banks of the Thames in London, on the seaward side of the Thames barrier. How could you cope with the potential impact of flooding on the ground floor? Think of different uses for the space. Is there anything that could be done to reduce the level of the river, such as special maintenance? What other elements of the hotel would have to be redesigned for the changing climate? Think about heating and lighting.

3 A luxury hotel is considering the use of green energy and energy saving systems to promote itself as a 'green hotel' which will appeal to a wider market. The building services engineer has been asked to look at different types of renewable energy that could be used for the hotel. After undertaking some research identify and list at least three areas of energy reduction and three renewable energy sources that could be used on this development.

Just checking

* What does the term 'climate change' cover?
* What is global warming caused by?
* What are the consequences for building designers?

Introduction

There are many different people involved in the construction process. From the designer, the structural engineer, the contractor to the client who receives the finished project. Each of them has a very different role to play within the process. Some of these are defined by their professional organisations such as the Royal Institute of British Architects (RIBA) through the Plan of Work or facilities managers through their Professional code of conduct. In this unit you will explore a range of roles from design to construction, as well as the team work between them and the role of the professional organisations that support them.

The second learning outcome examines the clients brief, its interpretation, evolution into a final design solution and the processes involved in achieving this. You will learn to use and produce drawings that provide details of the design solution against the clients brief. You will also learn how to evaluate this against the clients requirements.

How you will be assessed

This unit only has two learning outcomes but they cover a wide range of depth of knowledge. The assessment is split into two tasks. For the first you will produce a design solution from a given clients brief which should be feasible and realistic against the clients expectations. The second task asks you to place yourself in the role of a recruitment consultant. This is so you can explore the roles and responsibilities of the various parties involved within a typical construction contract.

On completion of this unit, you should:

LO.3.1 Understand job roles and occupational structures, and the importance of teamwork, in construction design and related activities

LO.3.2 Be able to create from a brief and evaluate a realistic design solution for a typical modern building or structure

THINKING POINTS

Could one person produce a construction project? Well yes if it was very small! In reality large complex construction projects require more than several people, all with very different skills, to produce the final building as a team. It can take years of training within each profession to reach the professional status that the industry expects for a high quality design and construction team.

Interaction is essential and teamwork plays an important part in achieving a successful project for all the different people who are involved within it. A strong leader is essential to ensure that the project runs smoothly and efficiently.

A client's brief can be as simple as a small sketch or as complicated as the Getti Museum in America. This took seven years to design and agree the brief! We don't always get the design right and several mistakes in the early 1970's, especially in high rise housing, have only recently been demolished. There are several factors to consider when producing an acceptable solution. The primary consideration is does it meet the clients needs within the requirements of the legislation we have to build to?

3.1 Classification of buildings and structures

There are many types of **buildings** and **structures** within the built environment. You only have to look around a city to see the very different types that exist. There are tall, short, wide – all shapes and sizes of buildings. In this topic we will look at how buildings are categorised in different ways.

Classifying by height

All around us there are buildings! Schools, houses, museums, railway stations, shopping centres, sports centres, castles, warehouses, factories, and cinemas are all types of buildings. We can classify all buildings into three main categories according to their height:

* low-rise – one to three storeys
* medium-rise – four to seven storeys
* high-rise – over seven storeys.

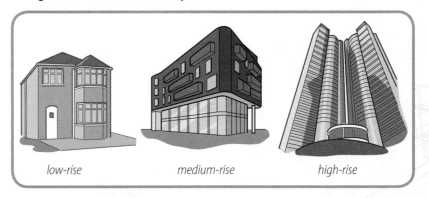

low-rise   *medium-rise*   *high-rise*

Classifying by style

One of the main ways that we think about buildings and structures is according to their style – how they look, and what fashion or historical period they fit into. For example, a *detached building*, which is not connected to any other building; a *semi-detached building*, which shares one dividing wall and is joined to only one other building adjacent to it; and a *terraced building*, which is part of a row of three or more buildings – the inner buildings of a terrace will share two dividing walls.

When you look around a city, you can see the different styles of buildings that exist. Some are old; some are new. There are buildings that appear to be made almost entirely of glass, and those which are unconventional in their shape, such as the Swiss Re building in London, known affectionately as 'The Gherkin'. When you are next in a city, take a good long look around at the vast array of different styles, which can be truly inspirational!

BUILDING BLITZ

Before reading on, think about all the different types of buildings and structures you have seen in the nearest town or city, for example factories and bridges. Make a list of every different type that you can remember seeing.

Buildings – any structure with a roof that can provide shelter from the weather, for things, or for people to carry on activities such as living, working or spending leisure time

Structures – the frame or fabric of a building that holds everything up: the walls, floors and roof of a building are part of the structure

Detached and semi-detached houses

Classifying by purpose

Buildings can also be categorised by their purpose. This table shows the main categories we can use.

Residential	Where people live, such as houses, apartments and bungalows.
Commercial	Where people work in offices, such as banks, publishing and insurance companies.
Retail	Where goods or services are sold, such as shopping centres, shops, restaurants and hair salons.
Industrial	Where things are manufactured or repaired – factories, warehouses and workshops.
Educational	Where we can go to learn – schools, colleges and universities.
Health	Where we can go for people to look after our health – doctors' surgeries, hospitals and health centres.
Entertainment	Where people can go to relax and do leisure activities – cinemas, football stadiums and theatres.
Leisure	Where people go to take part in sporting activities – sports centres and gymnasiums.
Religious	Where people go for spiritual reasons, for example to worship – churches, mosques, synagogues and temples.

Activity 3.1

1 Check your understanding of the way in which we classify buildings and structures. Collect a range of images of different types of buildings and structures. Separate them into categories, first by height, then by style, and lastly by purpose.

2 How might you tell what purpose a building has? Think about what features the following types of buildings have: residential, commercial, retail, industrial, educational, health, entertainment, leisure. Are there any common features across the categories? Note them down.

3 Using the collection of images you gathered in question 1 as inspiration, sketch a design for an unconventionally shaped building, for a use determined by yourself.

Just checking

✳ What is the definition of a 'building'?

✳ How many storeys are low-, medium- and high-rise buildings?

✳ What categories might you use when classifying buildings and structures by purpose?

3.2 Building design

Lots of different types of information is needed to successfully design a building or a group of buildings. Designers are required to use information from the British Standards Institute to ensure that designs are accurate and within agreed guidelines. The appearance of buildings has changed dramatically over time, aided greatly by the use of new materials and construction methods.

Design considerations

Initial designs and concepts are usually generated using freehand sketches, but as building designs become more detailed and complex, 3-D design software is usually used. Different types of drawings will be produced, between them containing all the information required to construct the building. Dimensions are included in the drawings alongside required relevant standards. **Technical information** will be needed to create a successful design, such as knowledge of materials, structures and fabrication techniques.

The design team also have to consider the Construction Design Management (CDM) regulations which place an obligation to design a project that can be safely built, used, maintained and demolished/decommissioned.

Blend in or stand out?

Many buildings are designed to fit within, and blend into, the surrounding environment, although new materials and construction methods are constantly being applied. In other cases, designers try to be controversial and produce work that stands out against the local landscape, using materials and designs that are completely different from those used on neighbouring buildings. Buildings that 'make a statement' like this may come in the form of luxury lakeside apartments, or in a building like 'The Gherkin', which stands out against the backdrop of central London.

Some old factories and disused buildings have also been redeveloped, modernised and made into apartments or rental workplaces, to meet the rising demand for modern style living accommodation over the past 10–15 years.

The designs of buildings are constantly being updated and developed. New materials are being used to improve the quality of the building and to create designs that may not have been possible previously. Buildings may have a range of new features or structures that increase the speed of construction or reduce cost. Buildings are also being designed with the thought of saving as many natural resources as possible. These days, contractors may be asked to use more recycled materials or materials with a longer lifespan. The Internet provides the consumer with a quick, easy way to find out about the most recent, cost-effective and suitable materials to be used for any building.

The Swiss Re building ('The Gherkin'), considered to be a fine example of modern, inspirational construction

No limits

Some buildings can have the luxury of having no limitations when being designed, and this can allow the designer vast scope for creating remarkable, grand designs. Material choice can become very open, and the cost of the building may be insignificant as long as the building appeals to its owner. Buildings can become very personalised, with features and decor suited to the occupier/owner's individual taste and interests.

Modern luxury apartments show how new housing can be designed and constructed

Activity 3.2

1 Why have luxury apartments become so popular over the past ten years, for both the contractor and the owner?

2 Find an example of a recently constructed building that highlights modern minimalist styling. Make notes about the characteristics of this building.

3 Find a range of different buildings, from different countries within Europe, and comment on their appearance. What are the similarities and differences?

Functional Skills

Carry out research, using the Internet, into a well known building project, such as The Gherkin – what makes this building unique?

Sustainability

Many buildings are now designed to take account of the fact that they will one day need to be demolished. The aim is that most of the materials will be able to be recycled or reused on future projects, and thus save valuable natural resources.

New materials are being used in the construction industry all the time and, with new methods of construction being developed, this can also have a big impact on the amount of natural resources that are used.

Just checking

✳ What different types of information are needed to successfully design a building?

✳ How has building design changed over time?

✳ How are buildings designed to relate to their surroundings?

Bills of quantities – a set of descriptions of the work needed together with the measured quantities of everything needed to complete a project – they are produced using a Standard Method of Measurement (SMM7)

Activity 3.3

1 Investigate two of the job roles listed opposite and find out what they do in detail. Use the Internet and printed resources, as well as information from site visits and speakers, to collect information.

2 Design your own dream house using notes to explain where different job roles mentioned in the table would be deployed.. Outline what they would do individually and investigate how long it may take to complete the work that is to be done. Try to think about costs this could relate to, such as wages or materials used.

3.3 Job roles and responsibilities: The design team

There are many job roles within the design team. Almost all work that is undertaken by the design team is office based, although visits to potential sites are used as well. All these jobs are very important and form the backbone of the built environment.

The design team

Architect

The architect leads the design team, dealing with the sketches, initial concepts and ideas surrounding the building design. All professional architects are Royal Institute of British Architects (RIBA) qualified to ensure that standards are met. The initial design and concept of the building is produced by the architect.

Architectural technicians

The role of the architect technician is to produce all the technical drawings, plans, sections and any other relevant details that will be used during the build. This team member also produces any construction drawings detailing information about the buildings, and they may have a small contractual role to fulfil. Architect technicians often use CAD to help with any drawings of the building.

Quantity surveyor

Quantity surveyors are the cost consultants of the construction industry. Before a tender, they play a crucial role in offering cost advice and cost planning, producing specifications and **bills of quantities**, preparing tender and contract documents, analysing tenders and advising on the appointment of contractors, etc. Then they will value the ongoing work that is being completed on the build and also produce the final cost of the overall building, after any alterations have been made.

Structural engineer

The structural engineer's role is to design the structure and foundations of the project and to ensure that the design concept will work technically. The main areas of design are to make sure that the building is both stable and capable of supporting the weight or loadings above the foundations. The structural engineer also has to consider any impact from the weather, especially wind and snow, to ensure that the building can withstand both static and dynamic loads.

Other construction professionals

Other construction professionals that may get involved with the design process are listed in this table, along with the roles they perform.

Landscape architect	This is a person involved in the planning, design and sometimes oversight of an exterior landscape or space.
Interior designer	Interior design is the process of shaping the experience of the interior space, through the manipulation of spatial volume as well as surface treatment.
Electrical engineer	This person designs the circuitry that will be used internally and externally throughout the build. They must follow all the regulations that are in place.
Heating and mechanical engineer	This engineer will incorporate a central heating system to the whole interior of a building, (or portion of a building), from one point to multiple rooms. When combined with other systems to control the building climate, the whole system may comprise an HVAC (heating, ventilation and air-conditioning).
Kitchen designer	Kitchen designers are used to optimise the use of space within a kitchen and to ensure that all key appliances are included. This is usually supported by the use of 3-D software, to allow the client to have a virtual view of the room before any work is completed.
Civil engineer	Civil engineers play a key role in relation to any roadwork or bridges that are to be built.
Lighting engineer	The lighting engineer ensures that all lighting levels that are required are controlled.
Highway engineer	Highway engineers advise on impact on road systems and consult on any street lighting. They are also criucial when working on new road network designs.
Permanent way engineer	These professionals are consulted on impact on rail track and are involved in any design undertaken on rail systems.

Sustainability

For most new buildings, it is considered best practice to use the services of a landscape architect and an ecologist, in order to ensure that environmental impact is taken into consideration throughout the planning and build.

The design team need to work together effectively

Health and Safety

All jobs have health and safety issues to consider, professional training in using the correct tools and machinery, and the use of protective clothing. A site manager and health and safety officer will ensure that all health and safety issues are dealt with appropriately. The CDM Regulations influence the design of a building by compelling the design team to produce a design that can be built safely.

Just checking

* What information might be gained on a site visit?
* What qualification must architects have?
* What areas might an architect consult with another professional on?

Traditional drawing techniques have been used for many years and are an important part of any design work. Equipment is used to ensure that the drawings are accurate and to enable the designer to draw the buildings and landscapes to scale. Computer Aided Design (CAD) has now virtually taken over for use with design work, but it is important to know about the traditional drawing techniques that are still used.

The drawing board

Architects use drawing boards to generate accurate, scaled, detailed drawings relating to the building to be constructed, and to give an idea of the overall design though several 'views': for example, ground floor plan, elevations, etc. Typical equipment used with a drawing board includes 2H pencils, drawing pens, eraser, T-squares, compasses, dividers, parallel motion boards, adjustable set squares and protractors, scale rule, French curves, flexi curves and stencils. A drawing board should be maintained, and equipment used properly, to ensure that the drawings produced on it are always accurate.

The drawing board is designed to ensure that the user is comfortable and is able to use the equipment with ease. The drawings can be time-consuming, depending on the amount of detail that is involved and the expertise of the user. Before CAD was introduced, this was the only way that drawings of buildings could be created. Designers had to be thoroughly trained, having a good eye and a superb knowledge of building design techniques. The idea that your plans could get a long way, but then be scrapped, meaning that you had to start all over again, led to the term 'back to the drawing board'.

Here are some of the advantages of using either drawing boards or CAD.

Isometric projection – a method of showing a 3-D object in two dimensions. One corner is closest to the viewer with horizontal lines drawn at 30 degrees to the horizontal

Orthographic projection – a drawing created using detail from one view. Different views are generated – plan view and elevation view – to allow the designer to see all the important information

Advantages of using drawing boards	Advantages of using CAD
Low capital outlay for equipment. No computers are needed, so investment is minimal.	Can have a virtual, realistic view of the building. The materials used can be shown through rendered views. A virtual tour can also be presented.
Can be done anywhere; there is no designated workplace for the drawing boards.	Can make changes easily: at the click of a button the design, or a particular feature of it, can be altered.
Can be easy to use. Once trained, they are straightforward and certainly not as complex as 3D-design used with computers.	Files can be emailed to associates to provide details of the design.
If maintained, they can be used over a prolonged period of time.	Can produce very accurate designs; the building can be designed to the nearest mm.
Can have a more 'personal touch'.	Files can be saved and reused in the future.

A typical drawing board and range of drawing equipment as used by an architect

Orthographic projection

Orthographic projection works as if parallel lines were drawn from every point on a model of the building onto a sheet of paper held up behind it (elevation view), or laid out underneath it (plan view).

There are then different ways that we can display the views on a drawing. Drawings in construction would usually concentrate on one particular element of the building: for example, a ground floor plan or a first floor plan. This is to provide as much detail and information as possible.

How the front and side elevation of a house would appear when drawn in an orthographic projection

3.5 Computer aided design

Computer Aided Design (CAD) is regularly used to create realistic 'virtual' views of buildings, showing both interior and exterior details. Rendered designs can allow the designer and potential owner to visualise how the building will look when it is completed. There are advantages and disadvantages of using this technique, as you will see.

Designing has typically been done using hand-drawn sketches, but over the past few decades, major advances have taken place in the design industry, with the development of a range of new computer-based design tools. Architects still use freehand sketches to provide detail of concepts and initial designs, but CAD has replaced the traditional drawing techniques used for much of the designer's work.

The introduction and development of CAD has had a dramatic effect on design itself. Individuals and companies are now able to design properties with realistically rendered views and virtual 'walk through' tours. These virtual designs can encompass the whole of the building or focus on a particular feature, such as a bathroom or kitchen. Changes to design work can be done at the touch of a button, making it incredibly easy to alter and play with designs. Designers can also test how the proposed design would look or fit into the intended surrounding environment by creating a virtual view of any completed constructions.

Computer aided design can also be very accurate; this is important when designing structures that will be constructed to defined dimensions. CAD allows provisional materials to be tested in a virtual format: for example, the tolerance of materials put under particular pressures or constraints can be recorded, and decisions made accordingly.

VIRTUAL BENEFITS

What do you think the benefits and drawbacks would be to a company of using software that allows them to design buildings in 3-D? Write some notes before reading on.

Walk through – a virtual simulation of how a person would view the property in 3-D if given a guided tour

Virtual testing – seeing how materials, components and structures will perform under different pressures and constraints by using a computer program

Advantages of using CAD	Disadvantages of using CAD
Can be very quick to produce designs	High capital investment in hardware (computers)
Is incredibly accurate – good for defined measurements	High capital investment in software and upgrades
Can render the designs in realistic-looking materials	Cost of employees needing training with the software
Can be modified immediately	Does not always have a 'personal touch'
Can send design files electronically	Files can be corrupted or lost
Can provide 'walk through' to illustrate design	
Virtual testing of products can take place	
A change to one drawing is automatically made to all other views	

Rendered camera view using Autodesk Revit

Here are two typical examples of the sorts of images that CAD software can achieve. The first image above shows the building in a 3-D format, with rendered features, to allow the designer to have a realistic virtual view. The second image (below) comes from a different software program, Autocad, which many design companies use.

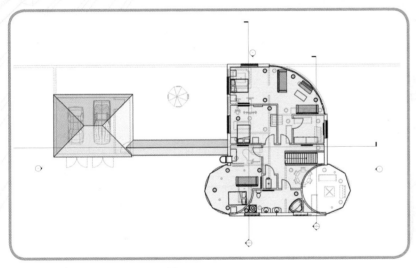

Floor plan of a house using Autocad Revit

Personal Learning and Thinking Skills

Reflect on how CAD can help lead to creative solutions to design issues. What are the benefits of designing this way?

Activity 3.5

1 Draw a plan drawing of the ground floor of your house. Include details such as walls and doors. A key can be added. Record how long it took to generate the piece of work. Would it be quicker using a CAD system? Explain your answer.

2 Why is a 'walk through' simulation useful to both the designer and the future occupier of a building? Write up your answer in the form of a table, showing the benefits for the designer on one side, and those for the future occupier on the other.

3 Explain how initial investment in CAD software can be recouped in the long run.

Just checking

✳ How has the equipment that a designer uses changed in recent years?

✳ What does 'virtual testing' mean?

✳ What are the main drawbacks of using a CAD system?

3.6 Construction drawings

Construction drawings are used to communicate technical information to the different parties involved in the building process. Designers and architects use standardised methods, symbols and language to make sure that everyone clearly understands the information that any drawing conveys.

Location drawings

Location drawings include both block plans and site plans. Block plans identify the proposed site through a bird's eye view. They show the site in relation to the surrounding area. Block plans are drawn at a scale of 1:500 or 1:1250.

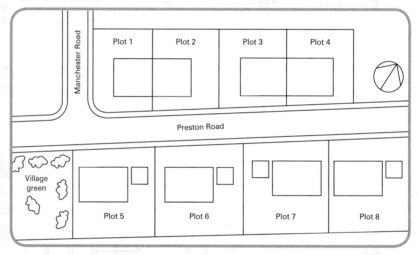

Block plan

Scaling

In order to draw a full-size building you must scale the drawing in order for it to fit on the drawing sheet. The table below shows how different types of drawings can be scaled in different ways. **Scaling** rules are used to ensure that there is never a need to convert dimensions to scale mathematically.

On a scale of 1:50, 10 mm represents 500 mm.

On a scale of 1:100, 10 mm represents 1000 mm.

Drawing scales

Drawing type	Scale
Detail drawings	1:5
Setting out drawings (including plans and elevations)	1:100, 1:50
Section detail drawings	1:20

NEAT AND TIDY

Drawings produced by designers and architects are always very neat and clear. Why do you think this is important?

Construction drawings – a drawing used to communicate technical information to different parties involved in the building process

Scaling – creating an exact copy of an area or item to a different, usually smaller, size

Symbols – figures or drawings used to represent a material that is to be used at that point of the build

Abbreviations – shortened versions of key terms, used so that all parties are clear on what is being drawn or explained

Functional Skills

Details in construction drawings must follow the guidelines set by the British Standards Institute: BS 1192 Construction Drawing Practice.

Identifying materials

These are the **symbols** used to represent different materials and components in a building drawing. They are used alongside **abbreviations**.

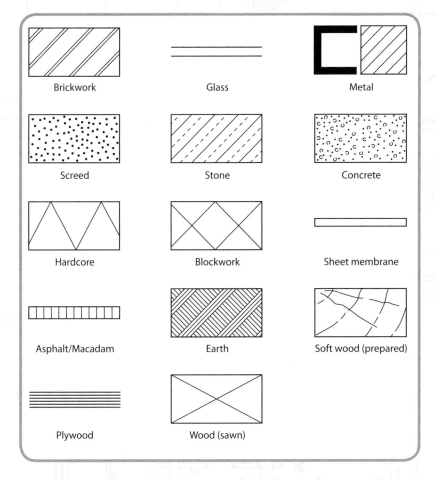

Brickwork

Glass

Metal

Screed

Stone

Concrete

Hardcore

Blockwork

Sheet membrane

Asphalt/Macadam

Earth

Soft wood (prepared)

Plywood

Wood (sawn)

Activity 3.6

1 Using the scale 1:50 draw a plan of the ground floor of your home.

2 Working in a team of three, produce a scale drawing of your classroom or a room you work in. Make sure that you choose the correct scale for the site, and include any important features in a key. Write a report on how it was done, e.g. what role did you play, how did you start the task, how difficult it was, etc.

Graphical symbols

These are the symbols used to represent different materials and components in a building drawing.

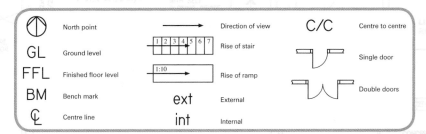

North point

GL   Ground level

FFL   Finished floor level

BM   Bench mark

CL   Centre line

Direction of view

Rise of stair

Rise of ramp

ext   External

int   Internal

C/C   Centre to centre

Single door

Double doors

Just checking

* Who uses construction drawings?
* Why do construction drawings need to be so accurate?
* What is the point of using symbols and abbreviations?

4 CREATE THE BUILT ENVIRONMENT: STRUCTURES

Introduction

Structures are an important element of a building. They hold up the roof, walls and upper-floors and safely transmit the loads down to the foundations. In this unit you will explore the various foundation options to suite ground conditions and learn how these are constructed using appropriate plant and equipment. The detailing of the external envelope that wraps the structure is explored looking at the various options that are available using modern construction techniques.

The modern technique of prefabrication is investigated within the second learning outcome and compared with traditional insitu construction techniques such as brickwork and blockwork or concrete frameworks. Prefabrication does require site fixing techniques and the various options for this type of construction are also examined.

The last outcome looks at the communication that takes place in construction, namely graphical and written. Drawings, specifications and instructions play an important part in the development and construction of a project and these resources need to be controlled and managed efficiently to avoid any delays. Communication is vital on construction projects so that everyone involved is aware of what is required, when and in what sequence.

How you will be assessed

This unit is the only unit at Level 2 which is externally assessed. This will take the form of an examination containing a number of questions which will require responses from the learner.

On completion of this unit, a learner should:

LO.4.1. Know about the methods used in the construction of the main structural elements of a new building or structure

LO.4.2. Understand how buildings and structures can be built entirely in-situ or be part fabricated off site

LO.4.3. Be able to explore different formats of graphical and written communication relating to the construction of the built environment

THINKING POINTS

How you hold up a building or structure is important, especially when it conflicts with the designer's brief which may contain an impossible feature structurally. There has to be a balance between current technology and the materials available. For example the roof on the Sydney Opera House has a unique concrete shell construction. Structural engineers often have to compete with design aspirations in order to produce an acceptable solution for the client that is both structurally sound and aesthetic.

The ground conditions that the building sits upon also have to be considered and there are various foundation designs that can be used to overcome weaker load bearing soils that will not support the building loads. Lighter structural concepts now enable slimmer foundations to be designed that carry these loads safely.

Prefabrication is now available as a tool in producing an energy efficient home and several manufacturers produce kits that can be self assembled for the self build project. Timber framed prefabrication technology now incorporate composite panel construction where complete walls and floors can be built within a factory and assembled on site using a crane.

Communication is vital. Get it wrong and this can be a costly mistake to absorb. Getting the correct drawing and specification is vital to ensure that the client receives a quality product at completion. Record keeping also forms part of this traceable process.

4.1 Excavations and groundworks

Many years ago, all excavation work was carried out by hand using shovels and pickaxes. Now, hand excavation is rare, thanks to the appearance of **tracked mini-excavators**.

Equipment

These days only small, inaccessible jobs are excavated by hand. Excavations to strip **topsoil** and reduce level are normally carried out using a tracked excavator with a front shovel, while trench and isolated pad foundation base excavations are dug using a back actor.

GETTING A GROUNDING!

Think of a plot of land in your local area that could be developed in the future. Make a list of things that need to be done before excavation work commences. Can you see any potential problems (e.g. poor access or waterlogging)?

Complexity

The complexity of excavations will vary from site to site. Before work commences, a series of bore holes and trial pits will be surveyed to find out the soil type and condition, and the water table level. Ground conditions on greenfield sites are much more predictable: brownfield sites may be riddled with old basements, foundations, drains and services. However, developing brownfield sites is considered good practice, as it reduces the impact on the natural environment.

The JCB 3C has long been a popular general-purpose excavator. It has both a front shovel and a back actor.

Stages of an excavation

First, the site is cleared of vegetation and other surface features. Then the topsoil is stripped and is usually reused during landscaping – any surplus can be sold on. The site is then excavated or filled to achieve the required level, or cut and filled as shown opposite.

Crushed and graded rock, known as hardcore, is compacted in layers to bring the site up to the correct level and to help distribute the building load on the ground. Recycled demolition rubble can sometimes be used as a fill material – this is good sustainable site practice.

Tracked mini-excavators – small excavator that runs on tracks, so it is easy to manoeuvre on small sites

Topsoil – the top layer of soil, usually 150 mm to 300 mm thick, capable of sustaining vegetation

Bearing capacity – the load the ground can carry (measured in kN/m^2)

Subsoil – the soil below the topsoil

Plant – any type of mobile construction machinery

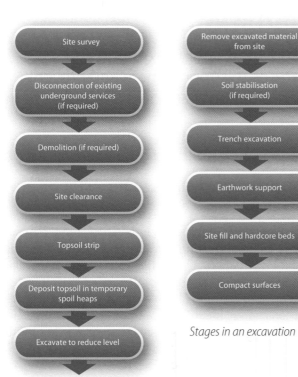

Stages in an excavation

Stabilising the ground

When the **bearing capacity** of the soil is limited or variable, you may need to stabilise it. This is often needed on brownfield sites where there are unknown underground obstacles or empty spaces, such as cellars.

Grouting

Here a cement grout is pumped in to fill any gaps, to improve the bearing capacity of the **subsoil**. It is hard to work out in advance how much grout will be needed or exactly where it should go.

Vibro-compaction

With vibro-compaction, a crane-mounted vibrating probe is lowered into the ground, and vibrates its way down through the subsoil, leaving a cylindrical hole. Hardcore is then gradually introduced into the hole and the probe compacts it to form a dry stone column. The probe's action causes a 'bulb' to form at the base of the column. Eventually, the site is covered by a grid of dry stone columns passing down into the subsoil, and this substantially improves the bearing capacity of the subsoil.

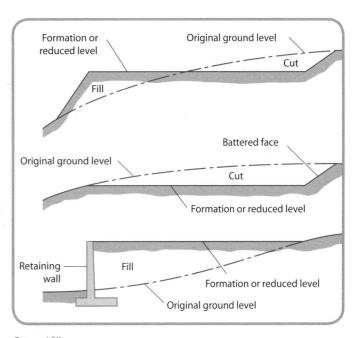

Cut and fill

4.2 Foundations

Buildings exert a **load** onto the ground and need **foundations** to support them and prevent **settlement**. Foundations can solve the problems in two ways. They can:

* spread the load of a building over a larger area, or

* transfer the load to a deeper, more suitable **bearing stratum**.

Subsoils can be of many different types including rock, sand, clay, silt and peat. Each has a different bearing capacity and needs a different type, size or depth of foundation. A lower bearing capacity generally means that foundations have to be wider or deeper, or must transfer loads to a suitable bearing stratum. Clay is a special case; because it's moisture content can change meaning it can be affected by seasonal weather changes to a depth of 1 m. This leads to shrinkage in summer and swelling in winter. Foundations in clay subsoils have to be a minimum of 1 m deep. Normally, foundations have to be 750 mm deep – the depth to which frost can penetrate. Subsoils can contain water which expands when frozen, leading to 'frost heave' – an upward pressure which can damage a building if the foundations are of insufficient depth.

The bearing capacity of subsoils	
High	**Low**
Rock	Loose sand
Granite	Soft clay
Chalk	Silt
Compact sand	Peat

Strip foundations

This type of foundation is used in most types of low-rise housing up to three storeys. The concrete strip spreads the load of the heavy walls. The width of the strip depends on the load of the building and the bearing capacity of the soil. Also, if the width of the strip exceeds the thickness of the wall plus twice the thickness of the concrete strip, steel reinforcement has to be put into the concrete.

Strip foundations

Deep strip foundations

How does this diagram differ from the foundations shown in the picture opposite? What do you think are the advantages and disadvantages of this type of foundation?

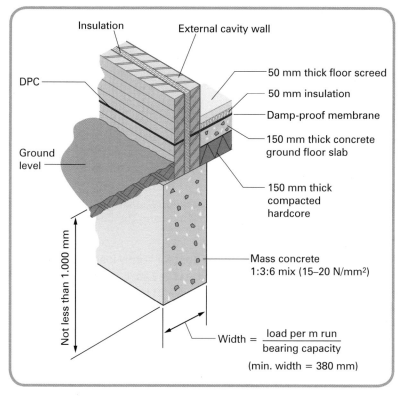

Deep strip foundations

- Insulation
- External cavity wall
- DPC
- Ground level
- 50 mm thick floor screed
- 50 mm insulation
- Damp-proof membrane
- 150 mm thick concrete ground floor slab
- 150 mm thick compacted hardcore
- Mass concrete 1:3:6 mix (15–20 N/mm²)
- Not less than 1.000 mm
- $\text{Width} = \dfrac{\text{load per m run}}{\text{bearing capacity}}$ (min. width = 380 mm)

A deep strip foundation, sometimes known as a trench fill, is a more economical alternative when the foundation is relatively narrow (typically 450 mm). It reduces the amount of brickwork, blockwork and backfill needed in the substructures, thus cutting costs.

Health and Safety

The sides of trenches can collapse if the ground is not supported, putting construction workers in great danger. It is important to use earthwork supports, sometimes known as 'timbering' or 'planking and strutting'.

Activity 4.2

1 In pairs, discuss the dangers of trench excavations, then produce a safety poster for use on site. (Remember that workers from other countries may not be able to read English.)

2 Both of these foundations use concrete in their construction. Why do you think this is a suitable material? Discuss in groups, and research further.

Steel reinforcement – steel rods incorporated into the concrete to resist tensile and shear forces

Load – the weight of the building that is supported by the ground

Foundation – the base on which a building sits

Settlement – movement in the ground, usually caused by the building's load compressing the soil below, or volume changes in the soil caused by seasonal weather changes

Bearing stratum – a layer of soil or rock with greater bearing capacity than the soil above

Just checking

* What is the main purpose of foundations?
* What is the difference between strip and deep strip foundations?
* When and why is earthwork support important?

A FIRMER GROUNDING

In the previous topic, we looked at strip foundations, which support the walls of a structure. Strip foundations are often used for traditionally constructed buildings, to a height of up to three storeys. But what kind of foundations do you think would be needed for a building that was much higher, such as Canary Wharf?

4.3 Raft and pile foundations

We have already looked at some ways to increase the surface area of a foundation or to transfer the load to a deeper soil of better bearing capacity. We will now consider other ways to do this, which are suitable for taller buildings.

Raft foundations

Raft foundations spread the load over the entire area of the ground floor of the building – effectively the ground floor slab becomes the foundation of the building. Rafts are usually reinforced with steel mesh reinforcement and laid on a damp-proof membrane (**DPM**). A layer of sand, called a **blinding**, is used to protect the DPM from damage that could easily be caused by the stones that form the graded hardcore bed. As you can see from the diagram below, rafts are usually 'thickened' under areas of loading such as along the line of walls or underneath columns.

Raft foundations can be used on poor soils for lightly loaded buildings, or where subsidence may be expected, as they are considered capable of withstanding small settlements in the soil. Raft foundations provide an early, level working space during the construction phase of a building.

Activity 4.3

1 After reading this topic and 4.2, list the advantages of using a raft foundation.

Personal Learning and Thinking Skills

Foundations often include basements. Think about the mass of the soil removed in the construction of the basement and the load imposed by the building on the subsoil. What are the implications?

DPM – damp-proof membrane, a barrier (e.g. polythene sheeting) that prevents damp or moisture entering the structure

Blinding – a compacted sand-bed

Auger – a large diameter drill capable of boring holes into subsoil

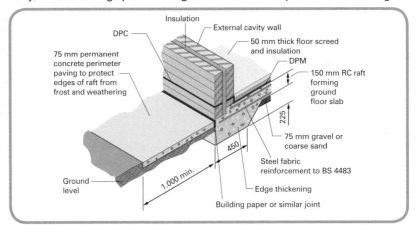

Raft foundations

Pile foundations

Pile foundations transfer the load of the building to a much deeper subsoil level that has a higher bearing capacity. They are effectively concrete or steel columns passing through the ground to connect with a firm subsoil or rock. Pile foundations can also be in the form of a 'friction pile', which makes use of the friction between the pile and the surrounding soil to help support the building. Solid piles can be driven into the ground, using either a vibration driver or a pile driver (which 'hammers' the pile into the ground), or they can be bored using a large vehicle-mounted **auger**. A common approach to pile foundations in tightly loaded structures is to use small bore piles, which can be laid out in a grid or clustered at, or under, main load points of the building.

Types of pile

Bored	Cast in situ	A cylindrical hole is bored using an auger and is then filled with concrete. These piles are often reinforced by placing a cage of reinforcement into the hole before pouring the concrete.
Driven	Cast in situ	A hollow steel tube is driven into the ground, and concrete is poured and compacted through the tube, forming a 'bulb' of concrete at the base.
Driven	Solid	Steel or pre-cast concrete piles are driven into the ground and left in place, to transfer loads to high bearing capacity subsoils.

Piles are arranged in patterns or grids designed by the structural engineer, then are linked together using reinforced concrete ground-beams to support loads imposed by the walls. For larger buildings, clusters of piles (normally between two and four) are joined together by a reinforced concrete pile cap underneath the load-bearing columns.

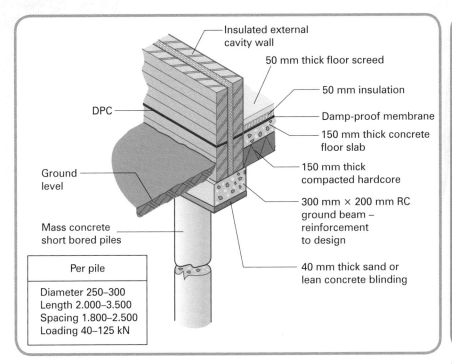

Insulated external cavity wall
50 mm thick floor screed
50 mm insulation
DPC
Damp-proof membrane
150 mm thick concrete floor slab
Ground level
150 mm thick compacted hardcore
300 mm × 200 mm RC ground beam – reinforcement to design
Mass concrete short bored piles
40 mm thick sand or lean concrete blinding

Per pile
Diameter 250–300
Length 2.000–3.500
Spacing 1.800–2.500
Loading 40–125 kN

Short-bore pile foundation

Piling rig

Health and Safety

Before building on a site, a survey is needed to find out if there are any underground services such as gas or electricity that would need diverting. In some cities, the routes of underground railway systems need to be carefully plotted before piling work begins.

Just checking

* What are the two options if traditional strip foundations are unsuitable?
* When is each type of foundations used?
* Are they ever used in combination? When?

4.4 Reinforced concrete

Concrete is a mixture of **cement**, fine **aggregate** (grit or sharp sand), coarse aggregate (gravel or crushed rock) and water. Its strength depends on the mix proportions, the crushing strength of the aggregate, the water to cement ratio and how well it has been compacted.

Concrete mixes

Mixing on site is done by machine and is batched by volume of cement to fine aggregate to coarse aggregate. Common mix proportions are:

1:3:6 – weak general-purpose concrete mix

1:2:4 – strong mix used for reinforced concrete

When ready-mixed concrete is used, this is batched accurately at the plant by weight, ensuring consistent high quality. This concrete is usually ordered by strength in N/mm^2 (Newtons per square millimetre) – the minimum crushing strength after 28 days. There are 12 grades, from Gen7.5 (7.5 N/mm^2) to Gen60 (60 N/mm^2).

The water:cement ratio is:

total weight of water in the concrete ÷ weight of cement

This ratio is normally between 0.4 and 0.7. If the ratio is higher than 0.7, the concrete will not be strong, but if the ratio is below 0.4, it will be difficult to compact the concrete effectively, again resulting in weak concrete. Always wear gloves when concreting as cement can burn the skin. Wash off any splashes immediately.

Reinforcement

Concrete has a high compressive strength but is not strong in tension. Steel reinforcement is introduced when tensile strength is required. Generally mesh reinforcement is used in walls and floor slabs, and bar reinforcement is used in beams and columns.

Formwork

After mixing, depending on the amount of water added, concrete is in a semi-liquid state and will 'flow'. This flow is more evident when the concrete is being vibrated to aid compaction. Concreting is therefore essentially a 'casting' process, and the wet concrete needs to be poured into a mould or former. This is where formwork (also known as shuttering or falsework) is used. It

Distance piece (remove as concrete is poured if it reaches this level)

75 mm x 100 mm soldier at 600 mm c/c

50 mm x 75 mm

Form panel 50 mm x 100 mm framing 18 mm ply

Sole plate

55 mm x 75 mm struts at 600 mm c/c

50 mm square stakes

75 mm x 150 mm sole plate

Folding wedges

Blinding concrete

Column pad base formwork

may only be to a perimeter – for example, a concrete slab at ground level, where the hardcore bed forms the bottom of the mould and the top surface is tamped and screeded level before trowelling smooth – or it may be complex and to many faces, such as a concrete staircase.

Concrete finishes

Finish	Description
Tamped	Ribbed effect achieved by tapping a long, straight batten in a parallel motion across the surface.
Steel float	Very smooth, even surface. A powerfloat finish is produced by a push-along petrol-powered rotary float.
Wood float	Produced with a wooden float. Finish not as smooth as with steel float, so useful as an anti-slip surface.
Patterned	Could be a surface finish to give the appearance of stone setts or could be applied to the internal face of, e.g. board-marked formwork, where sawn softwood boards of variable thickness imprint a pattern onto the surface of the concrete.

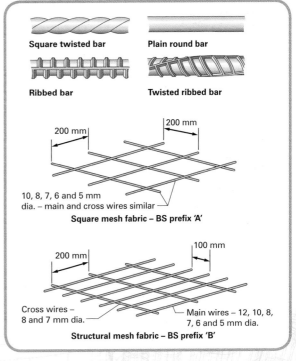

Reinforcement

Testing

There are two main types of test used on concrete:

✳ *Compression test* – cubes of concrete are produced in a 150 mm metal mould and covered by a damp sack for 24 hours, then cured by submersing in water until testing. After 7 days, samples cubes are crushed to see if they have the desired strength. If not, further tests are conducted at 28 days.

✳ *Slump test* – this is a test for the workability of the concrete and may give some indication of the water:cement ratio (the higher the water:cement ratio, the greater the slump).

This testing is important to ensure that the actual strength and properties of the concrete match those required by the design team, i.e. that it matches the specification.

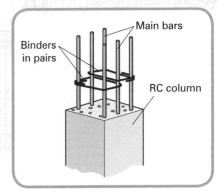

Column with 6 main bars

Cement – a grey powder-like substance that reacts with water and hardens to bind aggregates together

Aggregate – pieces of crushed rock or stone, gravel and sand

Activity 4.4

1 Have a look around your school or college. How many things can you name that are made out of concrete?

2 List three factors that affect the strength of concrete.

Just checking

✳ What things go into a concrete mix?

✳ When is concrete strong, and when is it weak?

✳ How can you test concrete?

4.5 Substructures

The substructure is all parts of a building or structure below ground floor level, including: the foundations, walls below ground floor level, hardcore fills, under-floor insulation, service entry ducts and the ground floor construction. You will normally view a substructure via a cross sectional drawing.

Solid ground floors

The diagrams below show a cross-section through two different solid ground floor substructure details. You will see that both details have a damp-proof course (DPC) in the walls and a damp-proof membrane (DPM) under the floor. These prevent damp or moisture rising from the ground into the building. They are commonly a plastic material, such as polythene or PVC, in sheet form. Below the DPC, the inner leaf of blockwork will be a dense aggregate block, and below ground level,

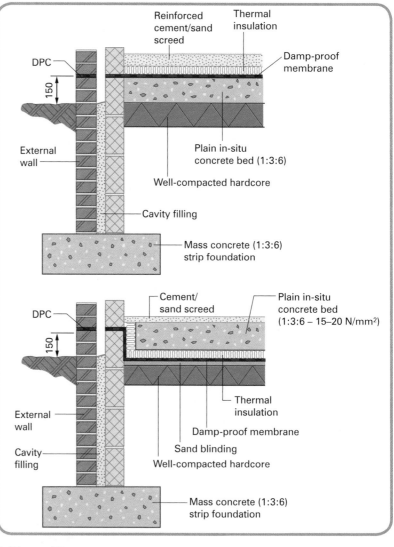

Solid ground floors

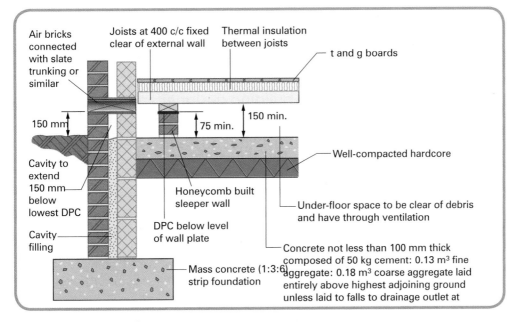

Air bricks connected with slate trunking or similar

Joists at 400 c/c fixed clear of external wall

Thermal insulation between joists

t and g boards

150 mm

150 min.

75 min.

Well-compacted hardcore

Cavity to extend 150 mm below lowest DPC

Honeycomb built sleeper wall

Under-floor space to be clear of debris and have through ventilation

DPC below level of wall plate

Cavity filling

Mass concrete (1:3:6) strip foundation

Concrete not less than 100 mm thick composed of 50 kg cement: 0.13 m³ fine aggregate: 0.18 m³ coarse aggregate laid entirely above highest adjoining ground unless laid to falls to drainage outlet at

Suspended timber ground floors

the brickwork will be in commons, or will be blockwork like the inner leaf. Up to ground level, the cavity is filled with concrete to resist pressure from the ground and to prevent the cavity filling with groundwater. (Note: see page 79 for an example of substructure construction with an insulated, beam and block, suspended concrete floor.)

The position of the insulation in the top diagram opposite leads to this being known as 'cold slab' construction, because the insulation is above the structural floor. Even **non-load bearing** partition walls should not be built directly off this floor. The bottom diagram opposite shows a 'warm slab' construction, as the structural floor is above the insulation. This is capable of withstanding light loadings from non-load bearing walls. In warm slab construction, the floor slab acts as a thermal mass and retains heat during the heating season, providing a warmer surface than cold slab construction.

Suspended timber ground floors

The diagram above shows a substructure detail with a suspended timber floor. Softwood floor joists span sleeper walls and rest on a **wall plate** that is protected by a DPC. The sleeper wall is built in a **honeycomb** pattern to allow air, which enters the under-floor void via the air bricks, to circulate and maintain the level of ventilation needed to prevent decay of the floor joists.

Sometimes the depth or detail of a substructure may change, even after the project has started, because the ground conditions might not be as good as expected, leading to changes in the substructure design.

Activity 4.5

1 It is important to be able to identify the materials shown on construction drawings by recognising their fill pattern. Sketch the fill pattern for the following materials found within substructures: concrete, hardcore, subsoil, brickwork, blockwork and sawn softwood.

2 Explain why you think that the damp-proof course has to be a minimum of 150 mm above ground level.

Just checking

✱ What is a substructure?

✱ What elements does a substructure include?

✱ How are the different types of ground floor substructure different?

4.6 Superstructures

When you say 'Think of a building', what most people think of is actually the superstructure of the building. To the building designer and end users (the people who will occupy and use the building), the superstructure is the most important part of a building project.

Construction projects are split into **elements**, such as substructures, superstructures, external works and drainage. These major elements can be sub-divided into sub-elements; for example, substructures may be sub-divided into excavation and earthworks, concrete works, brickwork and blockwork and service entries. We are going to define a superstructure and consider the elements that may be included within a superstructure.

What is a superstructure?

A superstructure is that part of a building that can normally be seen because it is above ground. In industry, the superstructure is normally considered to be that part of the structure above the level of the ground floor of the building (i.e. not from the level of the surrounding ground, which is normally a minimum of 150 mm lower than the ground floor level).

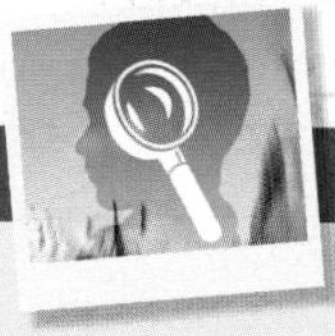

The superstructure can be built out of many different materials including brick, concrete, stone, steel and glass. The main function of a superstructure is to provide a safe, secure shelter to allow the occupants to go about their business, leisure or domestic activities in a comfortable environment.

SUB OR SUPER?

Think back to what a substructure is. Does this give you any clues about what a superstructure might be or include? Jot down your thoughts before reading on.

Elements – part of a project such as a floor, wall or roof, that performs a function within the building or structure

Contract programme – the plan of the works, usually a Gantt chart, showing when each part of the project will be completed

Functional Skills

Using the scale 1:50, draw an aerial view of the classroom you are working in. Get someone else to use your plan to work out the actual measurement of some key features – the door, a window, etc. Do they get the answer right? If not, check your drawing!

Case Study

Parul is a trainee site manager in an international construction company. She is gaining experience in different parts of the company, including the new housing and major contracts departments. Opposite, you can see two different projects that she might have worked on. Describe the superstructures that you can see in the photographs. Try asking yourself the following questions:

1 What materials can you see used on the project?

2 What skills are required to complete the project?

3 What plant and equipment are required in its construction?

4 Comparing the two projects. What do you think the organisation and management challenges will be?

Elements within a superstructure

Not all buildings and structures are the same. However, these are some elements commonly found in superstructures:

* Painting and decorating
* External walls
* Internal partitions
* Floors
* Roof
* Windows and screens
* External doors
* Internal doors
* First fix
* Second fix
* Floor, wall and ceiling finishes
* Suspended ceilings
* Electrical installations
* Plumbing installations
* Heating and mechanical installations

These elements will be described in detail in the topics that follow.

A modern sports stadium

A modern dwelling

Why are buildings split into elements?

There are several reasons:

* The quantity surveyor may organise the ***bills of quantities*** into elemental sections, so that the cost of each element can be easily identified. This makes it easier to evaluate the work completed by the contractor each month, and to report on the cost implications of any changes to the specification.

* The site planner uses the elements to identify the main parts of the project in the **contract programme**.

* The architect uses the elements to organise the specification and drawings into appropriate sections.

* The buyer can identify which materials are needed for the various elements and, working in conjunction with the site planner's Gantt chart, can ensure that the materials are delivered to site at the correct time.

Activity 4.6

Now that you know about the different elements that form a construction project, take a look around your own home – how many elements can you identify? Can you think of any parts of the elements that are hidden or unseen?

Just checking

* What does 'superstructure' mean?
* What elements make up the superstructure of a building?
* Why is it useful to split a building up into elements?

4.7 External walls

Here we look at the external walls of a typical modern dwelling – often known as a 'domestic construction'. While this form of construction is very traditional, modern materials are now widely used to improve the performance of the wall. In particular, there has been a vast improvement in the insulation incorporated into new buildings.

Functions of an external wall

Structural

In most domestic construction, cellular techniques are used – your own home is likely to be of this type. Here the walls act structurally to transfer loads to the foundations from the floors and the roof, as well as the **superimposed loads** from the users of the building. The diagram below shows how loads are distributed through a building down to the foundations.

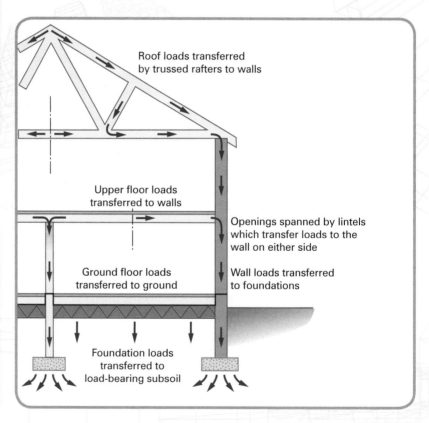

Distribution of loads through the building superstructure

Weather protection

A major function of the external wall is to provide protection from wind, rain and snow. This is achieved in three ways:

WHAT ARE WALLS FOR?

We all take our own homes for granted. What functions does your home have to perform? Think about what the external walls do – apart from keeping the roof up!

Activity 4.7

1 Think about the external wall of your own home. Make a list of the things that a wall has to do or control (not forgetting the types of weather encountered in the UK).

2 Produce an artwork that illustrates the functions of an external wall.

Functional Skills

Sketch the elevation of an external wall including openings for doors and windows. Do you think that the size and positioning of openings has any effect on the strength and stability of the wall? Write a few paragraphs to explain your thoughts.

* by using a dense, impermeable material for the outer skin of the cavity wall: for example, ordinary quality bricks for normal conditions, or special quality bricks for conditions of extreme exposure

* by the incorporation of a cavity, a minimum of 50 mm wide, so that moisture cannot transfer to the inner skin of the wall

* by using vertical damp-proof courses at all positions where the cavity has to be closed: for example, around openings for windows and doors.

Thermal insulation

The Building Regulations require all buildings to be well insulated: for example, external walls should have a U-Value of 0.35 W/m²/°C. This is normally achieved by fitting insulation into the wall cavity, either as a partial fill (where an air space is maintained) or a full fill (where the entire cavity is filled with insulation). An alternative, or additional, method is to use insulation blocks. These have insulating properties, through the use of a lightweight aggregate, aeration (where air bubbles are introduced into the concrete) or by the inclusion of insulation such as polystyrene or fibreglass.

Sound insulation

The wall must prevent excessive transfer of sound from the outside of the building, e.g. traffic noise from a busy road. The most effective way do to this is by using dense materials, such as concrete blocks.

Security

The external walls of a building provide security against burglary and unwanted intruders.

Lighting

Most walls in traditional construction do not allow the transfer of light. However, in modern construction, glazing systems and **curtain walling** mean that, in some buildings, the external wall can have the function of providing natural light.

Section through an external cavity wall

Labels: Block inner leaf; Facing bricks (102.5 mm); Galvanised steel lintel with insulation; UPVC window frame; Window board; Wall tie; 50 mm insulated cavity; DPC; Solid insulated ground floor; DPM over sand blinding hardcore; 150 mm min.; Loadbearing concrete blocks or bricks below ground; Weak concrete cavity filling; Concrete strip foundation

Superimposed loads – the load applied to a structure: for example, the weight of furniture or items stored in the building, or the load imposed by snow on the roof

Curtain walling – a glazed cladding system used on some high rise structures

Just checking

* How are external walls constructed in most houses?
* How can external walls protect you from the weather?
* What other functions do external walls perform?

4.8 Openings in external walls

In this section, you will need to learn that in buildings there are not just 'openings in walls'! There is much more to it than that. From the construction point of view, the key issue is the detailing around openings: this must ensure that no moisture or damp can penetrate and must protect against the creation of 'cold bridges'.

Head

The head is the part of the opening, such as a door or window, that has the task of supporting the load of brickwork above it. As well as carrying the load, the head has to transmit the load to the jambs at the sides.

Lintels or beams are used for the construction of such heads (see page 123 for details). Different types of material are used depending on the type of opening involved.

Type of material	Type of opening	Characteristics
Steel	Small spans	For outside skin of cavity wall, with other skin supported by another steel or concrete lintel.
	Medium spans	Joist section or a channel can be used.
	Large spans	Here a universal beam to set calculations is needed. If there is any exposure to weather, the beam will need protection from corrosion. For small/medium spans preparatory galvanised steel lintel can be used.
Concrete	All spans	Pre-stressed lintels are available for small and medium spans, or there are pre-cast beams reinforced with steel, which can be used for all spans.

Material used for the heads of different openings

Jamb

This is the vertical part of the wall opening. On a single door or window opening, one side is known as the hanging jamb, and the other is the closing or shutting jamb.

There are several different types of jamb treatment, depending on the type of wall. On a solid wall, the jambs are bonded to give them their shape and strength; in cavity walls, the area where the opening is can be closed by a timber frame, incorporating a damp-proof course (DPC)

A lintel being installed

as required by the Building Regulations. The detailing of the vertical DPC, cavity closure and insulation is particularly important. If this is not done correctly, 'cold bridges' could be created, and moisture or damp could penetrate. Here are some examples of what jamb treatments to openings might look like.

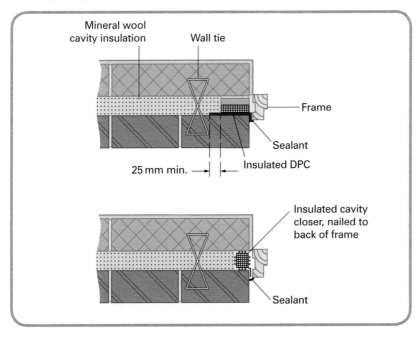

Typical jamb treatments to openings

Arches

An arch is made from special types of brick called voussoirs. These bricks are wedge-shaped, designed to support each other and carry a load over an opening. However arches can also be constructed from standard bricks where the radius of the curvature is quite loose. When an arch is being constructed, it is important that the arch is given a temporary support until the mortar is set and the arch is able to carry its own weight.

Sills

Look at any window or door, and you will see that it has a piece of material below it – plastic, concrete or timber. This material is shaped to allow rainwater to run off, away from the opening. This is called a sill or threshold. It does not have to carry any load, but is simply there to get rid of the rainwater that runs down the surface of the door or window.

Activity 4.8

1 Investigate the different types of arch that are used in construction. Look for details of the following types: soldier, rough and gauged arches.

2 Using the information you found in question 1, draw sketches for each of the three types of arch. Put in as many labels as you can to describe the parts and functions of each arch. Mark all the key differences between the three types.

Just checking

* What is the function of a 'head'?
* What materials can lintels be made of?
* Why do all doors and windows have sills?

4.9 Steel-framed structures

Structural steelwork has been used for many years for developments such as offices, retail units and factory units. It provides a high strength-to-weight ratio, carrying all the loads of the building down to the foundations. Steel can be moulded into many shapes and can be used to great effect in modern architecture.

The steel-frame

Steel-frames consist of two key elements: columns and beams. Columns are the upright or vertical elements that carry loads down to the foundations. Beams are the horizontal members that transfer the loads from the floors to the columns. When this framework is complete, it is known as a skeleton framework.

The portal frame is a further modern development which uses a portal shape with columns and rafters. The portal shape is symmetrical and has a sloping roof (see page 36 for a diagram).

Here you can see the supporting steel framework of a covered walkway

Steel-frame details

All steel-frames require foundations to hold the steelwork and to transmit the loads safely to the ground, without settlement. A typical foundation for a steel-frame is known as a pad foundation. This is a solid block of concrete cast into the ground, in which holding down bolts sit to anchor the steelwork. The bases of the columns have a base plate welded to them, onto which the bolts grip as they are tightened down onto the concrete.

Once the steelwork is checked for verticality, the bolts are filled with a grout that sets solid. Beams connect columns to columns, and these are bolted together using plates on the end of the beams, or cleats. The picture shows typical details of these connections.

HOW HIGH?

Cities demand ever taller and more important and unique buildings. Steel-frames play a major part in keeping these tall structures safe and secure as this is the only material that is capable of doing so. Is there any limit to how high we can build? Is the mile high structure possible/inevitable?

Activity 4.9

1 Identify a multi-storey building near to where you live. Establish that it is constructed with a steel frame. Then answer these questions.

   * How old is the structure?

   * What measures have been used to fireproof the steel-frame?

   * How has the building's envelope been fixed to the steelwork?

2 Identify and describe the advantages and disadvantages of using steel structures for the building you have found.

3 Are there any alternatives to using steel as a material for the structure? Find out, and write a brief report.

Sequence of construction

The foundations are constructed before the steelwork arrives on site. The steelwork is loaded onto lorries for transport to the construction site, where it will be put up. A crane has to be used to erect the steelwork safely as individual pieces are very heavy. The crane starts at one end of the structure raising columns and a beam, working down a building until it is complete. The steelwork is then plumbed level and grouted in. Work can then begin on intermediate floors, the roof covering and the wall coverings.

Steel framework being erected

The envelope

The steelwork has to be covered in order to make the building secure against the elements. The most common form of steel-framed buildings (especially portal frames) is cladding.

Cladding consists of steel-profiled sheets fastened to sheeting rails that span from steel beam to steel beam. The panels are lapped and have flashings to cover all the joints. Normal rainwater gutters catch the water and direct it to downpipes. The cladding of the roof often contains roof lights. These let natural daylight into the building. Modern cladding materials are a sandwich construction of insulation bonded to inner and outer sheets of steel panels, forming what are known as composite panels.

Doors and windows are detailed by forming framed openings through the panelling cladding. These frames can then accept UPVC or aluminium windows and are finished using flashings.

High specification steel-framed buildings are often covered with glass panels. This is very specialised work, undertaken by glazing subcontractors.

Steelwork has to be encased to finish a building to provide fire protection. The casing protects the steelwork from the high temperatures of the fire that could cause it to weaken and fail.

The bolts used are high strength and have to be tightened correctly

Just checking

* What does a holding down bolt do?
* Why does steelwork need fireproofing?
* What is a portal frame?

4.10 External cladding

In traditional domestic construction, the walls of the building transfer loads to the foundations. However, there are other forms of construction where the walls do not perform a load-bearing function. Cladding is a non-load-bearing external 'skin' that provides protection from the elements and contributes to the aesthetic appearance of the building.

Types of cladding

There are two main types of cladding: cladding fixed to a structural backing, and cladding on framed structures.

* Cladding fixed to a structural backing tend to be used when the structural wall cannot provide an adequate barrier to the elements, or because it is not aesthetically pleasing in its uncovered form.

* Cladding fixed to a structural frame has to provide protection from the elements, including wind, rain and snow, as well as dealing with extremes of temperature. In addition, the cladding contributes to the security of the building.

Tile hanging

This is often used as an aesthetic feature. Plain roofing tiles are usually used, hung on and attached to treated softwood battens fixed to the structural wall. This method is sometimes used in renovation works, to extend the life of a building when an external wall has deteriorated and no longer provides adequate protection from the elements, or to prevent further deterioration of the structural wall.

Timber cladding

This can be wooden tiles known as 'shingles' or overlapping or interlocking boarding. Western red cedar is one of the best materials to use for external timber cladding because the natural resin that is present in the wood resists decay. The timber may be treated with a decorative **microporous** coating.

Profiled steel cladding

Most modern industrial buildings are clad in profiled steel cladding. This is made out of mild steel and is plastic coated or galvanised. A factory-applied paint system protects it from the elements and prevents rusting. The 'ribbed' profile provides rigidity and prevents bending and flexing of the material.

A typical modern steel clad factory unit using profiled steel sheeting

IN THE FRAME

Have a look at the buildings in your locality and make a list of the ones you think are framed buildings. What are their external walls like? Can you tell how thick they are? What materials are they constructed of?

Activity 4.10

Use the Internet to investigate some of the cladding systems. Find out about the materials and components used, and how they are fixed on site. Write a brief report on your findings.

Microporous – with small holes; in cladding, a microporous coating allows the timber to breathe

Brick cladding

Brickwork is normally associated with cellular construction, where the brickwork is structural and transfers roof and floor loads to the foundations. In a framed structure, brickwork is non-structural and is, in fact, just a cladding. This is usually a half-brick thick skin of brickwork that is supported by and tied to the structural frame at each floor level.

Concrete cladding

This was widely used in the 1960s and 1970s, but is once again gaining popularity. Storey-height cladding panels, incorporating window openings, are prefabricated off site and then bolted to the structural frame. The joints between panels incorporate water bars and sealant joints. A variety of surface finishes can be applied during manufacture including 'exposed aggregate', 'board marked' and patterned.

Glazed cladding

This is often known as patent glazing or curtain walling. Take a look at the modern buildings in your nearest city centre – you will see some where the outer skin of the walls is made up entirely of glass.

Membrane or fabric structures

This consists of a fabric material supported on steel columns and stretched to form a taut surface – a classic example is the Millennium Dome. Although essentially a form of roof covering, the fabric often extends down to ground level to form the enclosing walls. Tensile fabric can achieve greater spans than conventional materials with a minimal supporting structure. There are cost advantages to this form of construction, and because tensile fabric structures significantly reduce the volume of materials required in construction, the carbon footprint of the project is minimised.

A typical modern glazed high rise building

Functional Skills

Consider these cladding systems – think about the materials used and write a list of the advantages and disadvantages of each type.

Just checking

✱ What are the two main types of cladding?

✱ What coatings and external finishes can be applied to cladding?

✱ What does cladding do apart from changing the appearance of a building?

4.11 Floors

Floors within modern buildings come in many varieties. Each floor's specification will depend on the type of structure and the activities that the building will be used for.

Functions of a floor

The floors in a building may have to perform a number of functions:

* providing a level surface that can support people, furniture, partitions, finishes, equipment, vehicles (where appropriate) and other building contents
* reducing sound transfer between adjacent floors
* providing a fireproof barrier between floors
* accommodating services, including water, heating, electrical and telecommunications
* at ground floor level, providing environmental control against the passage of water and heat.

The floor may also incorporate an embedded under-floor heating system.

Types of floor

Here we will look at three different types of floor: solid floors, which are used at ground floor level only, and beam and block floors and suspended timber floors, both of which are used in either ground floor or intermediate floor construction.

Solid floors

Solid floors bear directly onto the ground from which they gain their support. Solid ground floors usually comprise a concrete bed on a damp-proof membrane (DPM), laid on **sand blinding**, on top of a compacted hardcore bed.

The damp-proof membrane is a plastic material – usually polythene or PVC that comes in a roll. The strips of DPM must be folded and lapped to make it continuous across the floor area. It is good practice to tape the joints with self-adhesive tape to ensure that the joints do not open up when the concrete is being laid. The DPM is linked to the DPC in the external and internal walls to give continuous protection against damp.

Solid ground floors have to be insulated to prevent heat loss. This insulation can be placed under or on top of the concrete slab. If on top of the slab, it is covered with a sand and cement **screed** or a 'floating' floor of **chipboard** with glued, tongued and grooved joints.

WHAT ARE FLOORS FOR?

We often take floors for granted – but what are they for? Look at the floors in your own home and write a 'performance specification' for the floor – a list of the tasks that the floor has to perform.

Sand blinding – a thin bed of sand, typically 25 mm thick, which protects the damp-proof membrane from the risk of puncture

Screed – a mix of sharp sand and cement (1:3) trowelled smooth in a bed 50–75 mm thick it provides a smooth surface for the application of finishes

Chipboard – a board made by bonding wood chips with synthetic resin

Bearing – a surface supporting a load

Personal Learning and Thinking Skills

Look at the photograph opposite of a suspended timber first floor and produce a 2-D sketch of the joist layout. Can you see why the double joist or trimmer joist is used? Discuss this in pairs and explain why these are used.

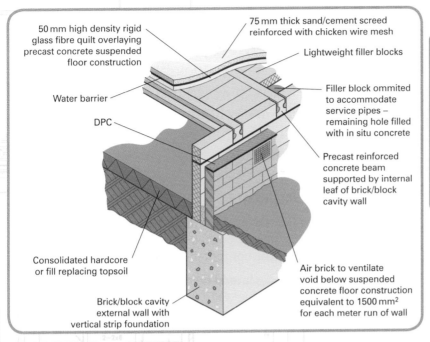

- 50 mm high density rigid glass fibre quilt overlaying precast concrete suspended floor construction
- Water barrier
- DPC
- 75 mm thick sand/cement screed reinforced with chicken wire mesh
- Lightweight filler blocks
- Filler block ommited to accommodate service pipes – remaining hole filled with in situ concrete
- Precast reinforced concrete beam supported by internal leaf of brick/block cavity wall
- Consolidated hardcore or fill replacing topsoil
- Brick/block cavity external wall with vertical strip foundation
- Air brick to ventilate void below suspended concrete floor construction equivalent to 1500 mm² for each meter run of wall

Modern beam and block ground floor

Activity 4.11

Look at the two types of floor illustrated in this topic. Write a list of advantages and disadvantages for each type. It may help if you think about the functions that a floor has to perform – these are shown at the start of this topic.

Beam and block floor

This is the modern alternative to the suspended timber ground floor. This type of floor comprises pre-stressed beams spanning between supporting walls, with an infill of lightweight concrete filler blocks.

The beam and block floor also requires an additional finish such as a screed or a floating chipboard finish. At ground floor level, the floor will also incorporate a layer of insulation.

Suspended timber floors

Look at the photo. You can see the joists **bearing** onto blockwork walls. Around the opening in the floor, known as the stairwell, a double joist or trimmer joist supports the trimmed joists. A trimmer joist may be a single joist 1½ times the thickness of the common joists (joists spanning the full width between supports). You can also see galvanised steel joist hangers providing support to the end of the trimmed joists. Strutting – either solid or herringbone – is positioned at mid-span to prevent twisting of the joists.

A typical modern 'engineered joist' suspended timber first floor

Health and Safety

Completed floors must be fully boarded at the time that the joists are installed, so that workers using them as temporary working platforms do not fall to a lower level. This is required by the Construction (Design and Management) Regulations 2007.

Just checking

* What functions do floors perform?
* What are the three main types of floor?
* How is each of these types used?

UNDER THE SURFACE

You know what a roof looks like from the outside, but what about the supporting structure? Think about the difference between a sloping (pitched) roof and a flat roof. Write a list of the possible advantages and disadvantages of each roof type.

4.12 Roof structures

A roof must span between supporting walls and be able to support its own weight as well as the superimposed loads to which it is exposed. These loads may include snow loading, **dynamic** loads imposed during maintenance, and the loads imposed by wind forces.

Types of roof structure

There are two basic types of roof: flat roofs, with an upper surface less than 10° to the horizontal, and pitched roofs, with an upper surface that is more than 10° to the horizontal.

The roof structure provides **lateral restraint** and stability to adjacent walls by linking the roof to the wall with metal straps. These straps also anchor the roof to the walls, to hold the roof in place during periods of high winds. Roofs need to be ventilated to prevent build up of moisture which can lead to decay.

Traditional roofing terms

This drawing shows the different parts of a traditional pitched roof. This is a roof that is entirely constructed in situ using individual structural members.

Trussed rafter construction

Trussed rafters are prefabricated, computer-designed, triangular roof frames that include the rafters and the ceiling joists, together with structural triangulation. Manufactured using **stress-graded** timber and steel-toothed plate connectors, they are hoisted into place and fixed, typically at 600 mm centres, resting on softwood wall plates.

Trussed rafters are tied together by longitudinal bracing, at right angles to the rafter. The bracing is positioned at the ridge and at the node points along the bottom structural member (the ceiling joist). Diagonal bracing is provided because the roof structure acts as a support to the gable end. When external and internal finishes are applied, the tile battens that are attached to the rafters, and the plasterboards that are fixed to the ceiling add to the overall structural rigidity of the roof.

Flat roof construction

Flat roofs are made up of horizontal joists that span between walls or elements of a structural frame. This is very similar to timber floor construction, but the joists are of a smaller cross sectional size because of the lighter loading.

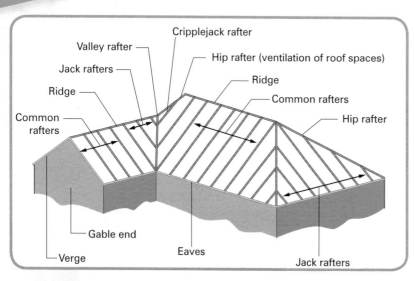

Parts of a traditional pitched roof

Activity 4.12

1 Look at the diagram of parts of a traditional pitched roof. This is shown in 3-D. Have a go at producing a 2-D drawing showing the layout of different parts or structural members.

2 Find out the differences between a rafter and a trussed rafter. Why are they different in these ways? Explain.

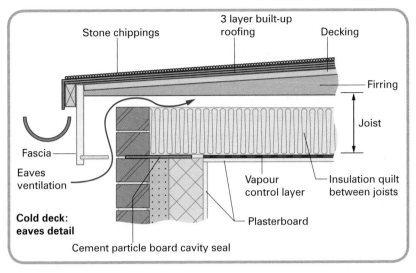

Stone chippings — 3 layer built-up roofing — Decking

Firring

Joist

Fascia

Eaves ventilation

Vapour control layer — Insulation quilt between joists

Cold deck: eaves detail

Plasterboard

Cement particle board cavity seal

Typical flat roof eaves detail

Dynamic – a dynamic load is a changing load, e.g. the workers moving about, carrying out maintenance

Lateral restraint – resisting a sideways force

Fall – a slope that allows water to flow from a higher to a lower level

Stress-graded – timber that has been visually checked to ensure that it is free of defects such as knots, shakes, splits, etc., that would reduce its structural performance

Purlin – a horizontal roofing member, parallel to the eaves or ridge, that provides support to rafters or roof sheeting

Although it is called 'flat', a flat roof must have a **fall** to force rainwater to move towards the drainage outlets. The fall is provided by a tapered timber on top of each joist known as a firring (see drawing). The structural deck, which is fixed to the firrings or joists, is normally a manufactured board such as plywood.

The flat roof structure incorporates a layer of insulation, which can be placed either above or below the structural deck.

Roofing to framed structures

Generally, framed structures can have any type of roof style or covering. A key feature of a framed structure is the provision of fixings, by which the traditional roofing system is attached to the structural steel frame. Fixings may include drilled rails or beams to which wall plates can be attached, or fixing lugs fixed to sloping structural members, to which **purlins** can be bolted.

Longitudinal ridge brace

Gable wall

Diagonal brace

Diagonal brace

Longitudinal tie brace

Toothed plate connector

Main ties as ceiling joists

Traditional cavity closer course

Trussed rafter roof construction

Just checking

✳ What is the difference between flat and pitched roofs?

✳ Can you name all the different parts for a traditional pitched roof?

✳ What is a key feature of a framed structure when considering roofing systems?

81

4.13 Roof coverings

A building's roof is more exposed to the effects of wind, rain, snow, atmospheric pollution and solar radiation than any other part of a building. Roof coverings provide a protective barrier against the elements through a combination of impervious materials and falls, which allow water to be quickly removed. Different materials and methods are needed for different roofs to perform effectively.

Flat roofs

Flat roofs do not shed water as quickly as pitched roofs, so there is a risk of 'ponding', or water accumulation, during heavy rainfall. Flat roof coverings need to be totally watertight.

Built-up felt roofing systems

These typically comprise three layers of polyester or glass fibre roofing felt, bonded using hot bitumen. The felt layers are laid at right angles to each other, with the first layer at right angles to the fall. The upper surface has a layer of reflective stone chippings bedded in hot bitumen, to provide protection from external fire, solar radiation and mechanical damage. You can see an illustration of this sort of roof on page 81.

Mastic asphalt roofing systems

Mastic asphalt is a mixture of bitumen and mineral fillers that can be spread with a **float** when heated. Applied in two coats, it provides a dense, impervious shiny black barrier. It is typically protected with a covering of solar reflective tiles or reflective chippings. The junctions of vertical upstands and the horizontal roofing need special attention, so a triangular fillet of mastic asphalt is used which protects against induced cracking.

Non-ferrous metals

Roofs can be made of non-ferrous metals such as lead or copper, which can be moulded into complex shapes. They are hard wearing, but very expensive. This type of covering is subject to thermal expansion and contraction, so the construction detailing must allow for this: sheet sizes are limited and joints are incorporated in the form of rolls running parallel to the fall of the roof.

Vapour control

Have you noticed how water forms on the inside of a window on a cold winter's day? Water vapour turns into liquid water when the temperature drops to a certain level – known as the dew point. With flat roofs, controlling water vapour is crucial, as the limited size of the roof void limits the effectiveness of ventilation. The difference in temperature between the inside and outside of the building creates a temperature gradient through the roof void. At the dew point

WHAT'S IN A ROOF?

Think about different roofs on different buildings. What materials are they made of? What properties do these materials have? Write a list of the relevant properties of the material, or the functions it performs.

Activity 4.13

1 More advanced flat roofing systems use 'torch on' technology such as **APP**, and felts with improved physical properties such as **SBS**. Find out more about the properties, uses and advantages of these materials.

2 Carry out an investigation into the difference between plain and interlocking tiles. How do the requirements for lapping tiles differ?

temperature, water will form in the insulation material, potentially leading to timber decay and staining on the ceilings. A vapour barrier, such as foil-backed plasterboard, is needed on the warm side of the insulation.

Pitched roofs

Pitched roofs shed water quickly and easily, so do not need fully sealed roof coverings. The typical tile and slate roof construction relies on the overlap to allow water to run down the outer surface of the roof. Felt placed under the tiling keeps out wind and dust that could otherwise blow through the lapped tile joints; it also acts as a secondary waterproof layer in the event of any tiles becoming damaged or displaced.

APP – atactic-polypropylene

SBS – styrene-butadiene-styrene

Float – a tool with a flat rectangular face that can be used for applying plaster, mastic asphalt or a surface finish to concrete

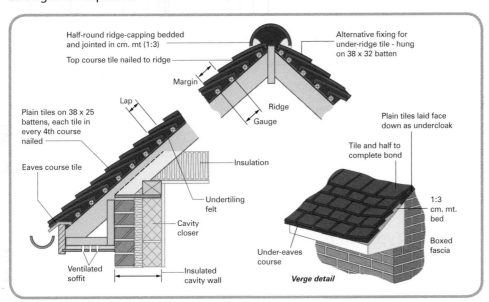

Typical plain tile roofing details

Materials

The most common materials for pitched roofs are clay and concrete tiles and traditional slate. With plain tiling, there should always be at least two layers of tile covering any part of the roof, and tiles should be staggered so that any vertical joint is over the centre of the tile immediately below.

Roof coverings to framed structures

In general, framed structures can have any type of roof from the wide selection available. However, portal framed industrial buildings mainly use profiled cladding systems, to match the wall cladding system on the building. This cladding is fixed to horizontal galvanised purlins or sheeting rails. Modern cladding systems also incorporate an insulation layer, sandwiched between the outer cladding and the inner lining, to speed up installation.

Personal Learning and Thinking Skills

Carry out an investigation into the meaning of the term interstitial condensation. How does this affect the design of roofs?

Just checking

✳ What is the purpose of roof coverings?

✳ What materials can flat roofs be covered with?

✳ What sort of coverings do pitched roofs usually have?

4.14 Internal partitions

Internal partitions are the walls that provide the physical space separation within the building. They divide the internal space into useable areas, providing privacy and security. They may also provide fire protection between the internal spaces, and an appropriate level of sound control. Partitions must be robust enough to cope with the everyday rigours of building use, and be able to take various fixings for furniture and equipment.

Key performance requirements

* Subdivision of space

* Structural support

* Lateral restraint

* Fire performance

* Sound reduction

* Future flexibility

* Routing and provision of services

Types of partition

The major factor determining the design of an internal partition is whether the wall is load-bearing or non-load-bearing.

Load-bearing

Load-bearing partitions help to distribute the **combined loads** of the building down to the foundations and supporting soil; they can also act as a buttress to provide lateral support and restraint to external walls. In domestic construction, this usually involves supporting the first floor loads, which include the floor's weight and the loads imposed by the contents, occupants and partitions.

Load-bearing internal partitions are generally constructed of bricks or blocks – a thickness of ½ brick (102.5 mm) or 100 mm blockwork is usually adequate. This construction also complies with performance requirements including fire protection, sound control and suitability to receive fixings for internal fixtures and fittings.

Non-load-bearing

Non-load-bearing partitions are designed to carry their own load (self weight) together with any attached fixtures and fittings. They must not carry any other loads from the structure, as they can be removed to allow the internal layout of the building to be changed without any structural work.

WHAT DOES AN INTERNAL WALL DO?

In previous topics we've looked at external walls and considered their functions, but what about internal walls? Make a note of the differences in function between an external and an internal wall.

Functional Skills

Look for details of demountable partition systems. List the advantages and disadvantages of such systems.

Combined loads – the dead, live and wind loads imposed on the structure

Dead loads – the fixed loads of the building itself

Live loads – the moving loads of the people and objects within the building

Stud – a vertical structural member in a framed partition

Noggings – a short horizontal timber cut to fit between studs in a framed partition

Brick or block walls can be used as non-load-bearing walls and they provide good sound and fire performance. However, more lightweight solutions are the norm, especially above ground floor level where they are built off intermediate floors.

The illustration opposite shows details of a timber **stud** partition, with 100 mm by 50 mm softwood studs. A head plate is placed at ceiling level and a floor plate at ground level. The studs are then spaced at 400–600 mm intervals – to suit the size of the plasterboard panels without the need for cutting – and are braced at the mid-point by timber **noggings** of the same cross section. The timber studs are usually planed to a regular thickness to prevent bumps in the wall surface. Galvanised steel cold-rolled profiles to BS7364 can be used instead of timber studs.

Completed studwork ready for the application of plasterboard

The fire and sound transmission performance of a stud partition can be improved by applying a second layer of plasterboard and including insulation material in the internal void of the partition.

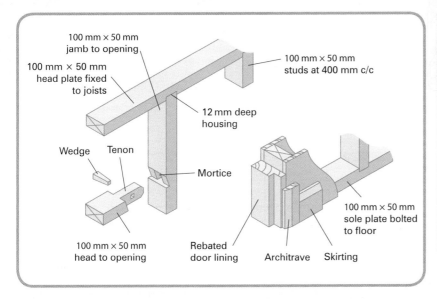

Stud partition details

Demountable

These are proprietary partitioning systems that are specifically designed to be easily taken down, modified or changed to suit differing user requirements. These systems are most often used for the subdivision of office space.

Activity 4.14

1 Measure an internal wall at home or in school and produce a scale drawing. Show the layout of the structural members as if the wall were constructed of studwork.

2 List the trades involved in the construction and final completion of different types of partition.

Just checking

* What functions does a partition perform?
* What can load-bearing partitions be made of?
* Why are non-load-bearing partitions different?

4.15 Services installations

Modern buildings need water, electricity, gas, drainage and telecommunications – things that the construction industry calls 'services'. To supply or connect services, a range of pipes, **ducts** and cables are necessary. You need to know what they are and how, when and where they enter any property.

Services

The following diagram shows the services usually installed for a house. Without these, you would not be able to wash your clothes, cook or even have a bath!

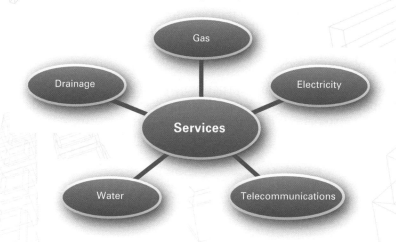

Types of services usually installed in a house

Water	Wash clothes
Electricity	Dry hair
Gas	Bath
Drainage	Brush teeth
Tele-communications	Watch cable television

Water – This is supplied at a pressure of between 30 and 70 metre head of water from the water main to the building's **stop and drain valve**. The supply from the main is through service pipes, which have to be at least 750 mm beneath the surface of the ground to protect them from frost damage.

Electricity – This is supplied at 240 volts to domestic buildings; other buildings need larger supplies for larger and more powerful equipment. Electricity is used to power many different kinds of appliances and products within the home including televisions, lighting and washing machines.

Gas – This is supplied to properties for heating and cooking. Gas is supplied to homes through service pipes, straight to the gas meter in your house, where it can be isolated for maintenance.

Drainage – This is to collect water, which is split into foul and surface water. Foul water goes to the treatment plant, while surface water drains into a watercourse, possibly via a sustainable urban drainage system (SUDS).

Telecommunications – This usually includes telephone lines and cable television.

Regulations

To protect the public, all the above services are governed by regulations and laws. Examples of such regulation are:

* IEE Wiring Regulations
* Electricity at Work Regulation 1989
* Gas Safety Regulations 1988
* Water Byelaws and Building Regulations

Make a list of all the services installations you can see in this picture

Activity 4.15

1 Extend the mindmap opposite. Add appliances or products that would need these installations to work. For example onto electricity you could add kettle, toaster, hairdryer and many more

2 Why are the installation of water, electricity and gas all governed by law? Write a paragraph to explain.

3 Why do services have regulations regarding the depths they enter properties? And what is the purpose of colour coding? Write brief explanations to both of these.

Just checking

* What are the five main types of service installation?
* How do the services supplied to homes and those supplied to larger buildings vary?
* Why are services governed by laws and regulations?

4.16 Plastering and dry lining

Plastering is a process by which **masonry** (usually walls) can be left with a smooth finish, ready to be painted or papered. Professional plasterers speed up the plastering process and ensure a quality finish. Plasterboard can also be used to create a dry lined wall.

Plastering

Plastering has been done for thousands of years but, in recent years, there have been major advances in the process. Cement plaster is still used to render external walls or damp internal walls, but gypsum-based plasters are more commonly used, and are a better choice. They are easier to work with, set a lot faster and produce a high quality, smooth finish. Earlier types of plaster, like lime plaster, are still used in restoration work.

An undercoat plaster is applied to help smooth out the uneven surface. Finish plaster, which has a finer grain, is then applied, usually in a 3 mm layer over undercoat, or a 5 mm layer over plasterboard. This layer is then smoothed to enable it to be painted or papered. One-coat plasters can be used, and do save time, but tend to be more expensive.

Plaster being applied using a trowel. The smoothness of the wall highlights the quality of the finish

Dry lining

Wallboards are a very popular material for lining rooms. They do not require the full skim coat, reduce the drying-out time and are easy to apply a finish to. Wallboards can be nailed with plasterboard nails onto the studs and noggings of a partition wall, or onto wooden battens fitted onto a masonry wall. They can also be stuck directly onto masonry with an adhesive. Wallboards are available in a range of sizes,

A CLEAN COAT!

What tools and materials do you think are involved in plastering? Try to think of what's needed throughout the process, from measuring up to cleaning up!

Activity 4.16

1 Create a step-by-step guide, or booklet, using notes and sketches to explain how plaster is both mixed and applied and how long it may take to dry out. Name tools and equipment that will be used and highlight any health and safety issues..

2 Carry out some research into how long it takes for plaster to dry out before any decorative work can be done, e.g. painting surfaces. Write up your results.

Dry lining – a lining (normally plasterboard) fixed, with an air space, to the face of a masonry wall

Masonry – built of blocks, bricks or stone

Functional Skills

Calculate how many square metres your classroom walls cover, to see the total area of plastering that would be need to be done.

but most commonly come in large sheets, enabling you to cover large areas quickly. A fine-toothed saw or a knife can be used to cut the wallboard to alternative sizes.

The 'dot and dab' method can be used to fix the wallboard to the wall. This simply means dabbing small blobs of adhesive onto the wall in various places with a trowel, then pressing the wallboard against the adhesive.

Plasterboard being attached to masonry

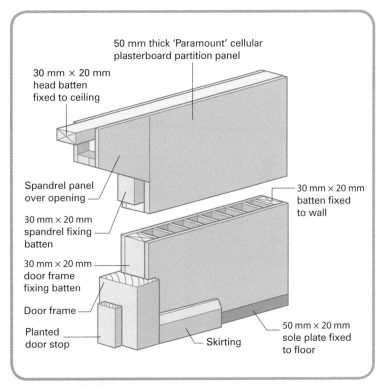

50 mm thick 'Paramount' cellular plasterboard partition panel

30 mm × 20 mm head batten fixed to ceiling

Spandrel panel over opening

30 mm × 20 mm spandrel fixing batten

30 mm × 20 mm door frame fixing batten

Door frame

Planted door stop

30 mm × 20 mm batten fixed to wall

50 mm × 20 mm sole plate fixed to floor

Skirting

Typical preformed partitions

Solid	Lath and plaster	Dry-lined	Partition
Common in old houses. Two to three coats of plaster would be applied to the masonry/brickwork. These walls are the easiest in which to secure fixings.	Used commonly until 70 years ago. Plaster would be laid on a framework of wooden laths. Heavy objects are difficult to attach and are therefore often uneven.	Plasterboard on masonry. Plasterboard started to replace plaster 80 years ago, and is more commonly used today. It is easier and quicker to use than plaster.	Plasterboard on stud. Stud frames are used to attach the plasterboards to both external and internal walls. The wall is hollow, which provides extra insulation.

Plastering methods

Just checking

* What is the difference between plastering and dry lining?
* What is the correct way to use undercoat and finish plasters?
* What is involved in the 'dot and dab' method?

4.17 First and second fixings

Fixing is the process of completing a building once the basic elements are in place. Buildings undergo two stages of fixing. The first stage is completed while the build is in skeletal form, before any doors have been hung, baths fitted or plastering completed. The second fixings can only be carried out when the first have been completed.

IN A FIX

What sorts of jobs may need to be done after first fixing has taken place after the building is in skeletal form? Mindmap your ideas before reading on.

Preparation and planning

There is a real need for careful planning and preparation before any work takes place. If planning and preparation of work or materials is not carried out properly, larger problems could be created later on in the build. Tools, materials, equipment and contractors all need to be organised in such a way that it does not create a detrimental effect on the quality or the overall time of the build. As one stage follows another, it is crucial that all aspects of the build are carried out correctly.

First fixing

First fixing consists of fitting any essential pipework and wiring, as well as constructing stud partitions and fixing doorframes.

Have a good look at the photo below of a first fixing. As you can see, all the wiring has been completed, before any ceilings have been fitted or plastering has taken place. With this example, the electrician would wire the house so that any lights, domestic appliances or

Personal Learning and Thinking Skills

What professionals are involved in the first fixing stage and what tasks do they perform? Investigate this and prepare a report.

First fixing – all work done before plastering has taken place

Second fixing – all work done after plastering has taken place: e.g. installation of kitchen units, sinks, wash basins etc.

An example of first fixing

power sockets could then be connected once the fix has taken place. Any back boxes would also have to be fixed throughout the house, as well as the pipework, which would generally be situated within the floor voids. The pipework will then be in place to be connected to sinks, baths, washbasins, etc. at the **second fixing** stage.

Second fixing

Second fixings include installation of interior lighting, connecting any bathroom facilities, plastering and many more such as: socket outlets, switches, consumer units, aerial sockets, radiators and bathroom suites.

From the picture opposite, you can see that the plastering has been completed, but note also that the doorframe now has an architrave, to finish off the joint between the plasterwork and frame. Other jobs involved in second fixings include: painting walls, fixing skirting boards, wiring any interior/exterior lights, connecting bathroom facilities, fitting sinks, wash basins, etc., connecting light switches, hanging doors, adding door ironmongery, fixing coving.

Because one stage follows another, the second fixing stage relies heavily on the first stage being completed on time and to a professional standard.

An example of second fixing, before and after painting

Types of first and second fixings	
First fixing	**Second fixing**
Back boxes for in-house wiring	Kitchen units
All wiring	Bathroom facilities
Studwork or stud partitions	Sinks/wash basins/taps
Doorframe	Coving/skirting boards
Floorboards	Doors/door ironmongery
Pipework	Plastering
Stairways	Windows

Activity 4.17

1 Explain why, within the construction industry, second fixing has to follow first fixing.

2 Produce a table, like the one opposite, linking job roles and responsibilities with the first and second fixing items given in the table.

Just checking

* Why is good planning and preparation important with fixings?
* What does first fixing involve?
* How is second fixing different from first fixing?

4.18 Windows and doors

A child's drawing of a house usually shows a square, with a roof and some windows and a door! Windows and doors may seem like simple components, but they come in many types, and their correct construction and positioning is crucial.

Windows

The basic function of a window is to let light into the room. Windows can also provide **ventilation** to help prevent mould, remove stale air and reduce **condensation**. Windows also provide a view of the outside world, and therefore should be given serious thought when considering their location within the building.

WHAT GOES WHERE?

Draw a 3-D drawing of your house, highlighting where all the windows are located. Why have they been located in those positions? Would you place any of them differently?

Activity 4.18

1 Take a tour round your house or school and identify the different types of doors and windows you find. Note down where you find each type. Draw the doors that have been used, naming materials and highlighting the difference between the internal and external doors.

2 Why was each type of door and window used in each location? Discuss with a partner, taking turns to explain in each case. This could relate to style or type of door used.

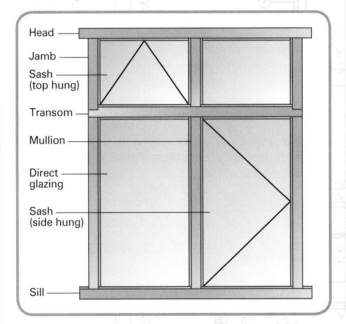

The parts of a window

Ventilation – letting air in and out, to improve air quality and prevent damp and rot

Condensation – water formed when warmer, damp air meets a cold surface

Window types	
Casement	Most popular window, in many styles and sizes.
Sash	Two wooden sashes slide up and down for good ventilation; can stick and rattle, and cords can break; aluminium versions available.
Pivot	Window swivels on a pivot so is easy to clean; provides good ventilation, but opened window projects into room.
Louvre	Horizontal strips of glass, which can be opened or shut using a lever; can be draughty; opening can obstruct view.
Bay	Very popular during Victorian times; several styles: square, splayed and curved; offer a more desirable view out of room but project from the building.
Sliding	Like a horizontal sash; split in two, windows slide for good ventilation; usually double glazed; do not project into room.

Double glazing is now used for new builds and provides better insulation than single glazed windows. It can come in the form of a sealed unit – two panes of glass joined by an airtight seal – or as a secondary window, where a sheet of glass or plastic is placed inside or outside an existing window. Double glazing also provides sound reduction.

Doors

External and internal doors

Aluminium or plastic (UPVC) are popular as they are weatherproof, although wooden doors are still common. An external door has a doorsill at the bottom, to keep water out of the building, and should have a weatherboard to stop water entering the gap between the door and the frame.

A greater variety of internal doors ensures that they fit into their surroundings. Flush and panel doors are often used as they can both be manufactured from hardwood or softwood, and are normally painted or stained. Louvred doors are more commonly associated with cupboards.

The parts of a door

Types of door	
Flush	Most popular type, typically painted or veneered to fit surroundings; basic in design but work well.
Panel	Consists of two vertical wooden stiles with three horizontal rails; typically softwood for internal use, and hardwood (or softwood with a hardwood veneer) for external use; more aesthetically pleasing than flush doors.
Boarded	Strong, simple door associated with cottages; made of tongue and groove boards; vee jointed, framed, ledged and braced door (FLB) is best.
Louvred	Wooden frame holding wooden slats set at an angle; air can pass through, so this type of door is normally used for cupboards.
Patio	Frame usually aluminium (plastic and wood also used); fully glazed from floor to ceiling; brings living room and garden together.

Sill details

The weatherboard, which is attached to the face of the door, forces water away from the door (water will run down the external face of the door during heavy rainfall). The top surface of the sill is 'weathered', i.e. it slopes away from the door to shed water away from the potential gap between door and sill. The bottom of the door is rebated and closes onto a water bar which prevents water flowing under the door and into the buldings.

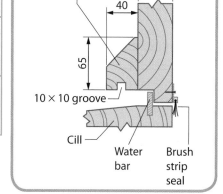

Standard weatherboard

Just checking

* What role do windows and doors play?
* What are the main types of window?
* What materials can you make doors out of?

4.19 External works, drainage and landscaping

ALL AROUND US!

Make a list of all the different features you can think of, that surround your house.

External works, drainage and landscaping are all aspects of construction that essentially makes up the exterior of the building. Drainage is a very important part of the building as it allows excess rainwater to be drained away and also provides a system to hygienically remove sewage. External works are used to provide such things as boundary walls, pavements, parking areas, footpaths and gardens to complete the surrounding area of a building.

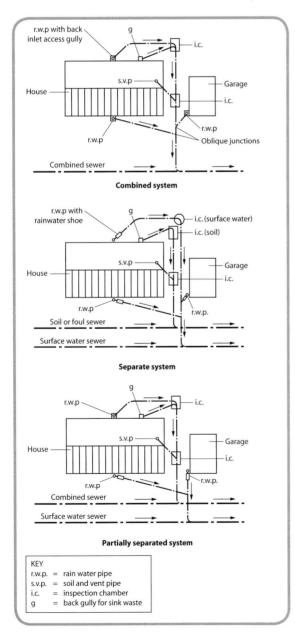

Combined system

Separate system

Partially separated system

KEY
r.w.p. = rain water pipe
s.v.p. = soil and vent pipe
i.c. = inspection chamber
g = back gully for sink waste

Drainage

Excess water and sewage needs to be drained away and removed from buildings that are constructed. This can be achieved through a system of pipes that take the unwanted substances to a local sewage treatment plant or, for rainwater that is not contaminated, back into the local water source (reservoir).

Combined system

This is a system whereby all rainwater and sewage that is taken away is removed through one single drainage system — therefore it is mixed. Although this is a cost-effective method and has been proven to be the easiest system to clean, all the substances that are drained go through to the local sewage treatment plant. This does not always need to happen with rainwater that is not contaminated as it can simply be returned to the natural water reserves. There is also a higher risk of flooding and flood damage.

Totally separate system

This is commonly used by local authorities, and provides two separate systems that are used to remove foul discharge or rainwater separately. Although not as cost effective as the combined system, it does allow the rainwater that is not contaminated to be discharged straight back into the natural water reserve. The foul discharge that is taken from basins, toilets etc. is carried to the local sewage treatment plant. Problems can occur if pipes are connected to the wrong system, and it is generally harder to maintain than the combined system because the rainwater helps to keep the pipes clear of sewage.

Typical examples of drainage systems can be seen in these three diagrams.

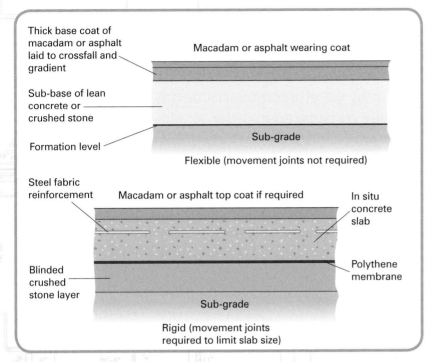

Thick base coat of macadam or asphalt laid to crossfall and gradient

Macadam or asphalt wearing coat

Sub-base of lean concrete or crushed stone

Sub-grade

Formation level

Flexible (movement joints not required)

Steel fabric reinforcement

Macadam or asphalt top coat if required

In situ concrete slab

Blinded crushed stone layer

Polythene membrane

Sub-grade

Rigid (movement joints required to limit slab size)

Cross section of a typical road

Partially separate system

This is sometimes favoured by local authorities and is a compromise between the other two systems. One of the sewers is used to take away surface water only, while the other deals with a combination of surface water and foul discharge. There is the flexibility, however, of altering the amount of surface water that goes into the combined sewer, and this is why it may be favoured by local authorities.

Soakaways allow rainwater to be drained into the soil via pits, which take the load off the drainage systems that have also been put in place.

External works

What areas are involved in external works? The diagram opposite shows just some.

Surfacing

Common types of surfacing that can be used in construction are concrete, block pave, tarmac, stone paving and gravel. The diagram above shows the cross section of a typical road and how it is constructed.

Paved areas
Landscaping
Bin stores
Boundary walls
Footpaths
Roads
Kerbs
Gates
External works
Driveways
Gardens
Septic tank
Fencing
Parking areas
Planters
Chippings
Patios
Planting

External works

4.20 Demolition

Demolition consists of breaking up an existing building or buildings, usually to make way for a new building. Careful removal of debris and materials is usually considered in order to allow for reuse.

Demolition is a dangerous trade that should be carried out by specialist contractors. Surveys might fail to find problematic areas, and any live gas, electricity and water that is located on a site has to be terminated or diverted. Temporary supplies may be needed for properties in the local area while the demolition work is being carried out. Shoring or underpinning for any adjacent buildings may be needed, and there may need to be special measures for the removal of asbestos.

Size matters

For most buildings, such as housing, that are only two or three stories high, demolition is a relatively simple process. The building can be pulled down either manually or mechanically. Large hydraulic equipment, elevated platforms, excavators, cranes and bulldozers can all be part of the demolition process at this level.

For larger buildings, a wrecking ball may be needed. This comes in the form of a large weight on the end of a cable, controlled by a crane. The wrecking ball is especially effective in demolishing materials such as masonry, but can be less efficient than other methods if used in an uncontrolled manner.

Health and safety

Safety should always be paramount during demolition. A site safety officer should be assigned to any project to make sure that rules and regulations are carried out. Many dangers surrounding demolition need to be investigated, including looking at the risks to site workers or to neighbouring structures.

Wrecking arm

The wrecking arm is often used on small-scale demolition. Buildings that are no higher than three stories can be demolished in this way. Using a wrecking arm is more controlled and does not carry the dangers of using a wrecking ball or explosives.

A wrecking arm in action

Wrecking ball

One of the most commonly used methods for building demolition is the ball and crane. The wrecking ball can weigh up to 6,000 kilograms and is used to demolish many types of structures. During the process, the ball is either swung onto or into the structure that is to be demolished. The ball and crane, however, is not suitable for all demolition applications. The process can be limited by the size of the crane, the working area and its surroundings, and other factors such as the position of any overhead power lines.

Highly skilled and experienced crane operators are used on ball and crane demolition projects. Controlling the wrecking ball is important, as missing the target may result in the crane tipping over. Dust, vibration and noise pollution can be caused by this process too.

Explosives

Tall chimneys, large buildings and some smaller structures can be destroyed by building implosion, using explosives. This method may involve a lot of set-up time but, once in place, takes only seconds to carry out. An expert can also determine where the collapsed material falls, either within its own footprint or missing any adjacent structures.

Recycling and sustainability

During the demolition process, many materials can be recycled. These may include slates or tiles from roofing, timbers, brickwork or other masonry, glass and stripped-out copper or lead piping. A lot of recycled masonry can be crushed and reused for general site fill on new builds.

Sustainability is now a major factor in building design. New builds are designed with ease of demolition in mind, and designers must consider what materials will be recyclable when the building comes to the end of its useful life.

Explosives are effective and dramatic but also very dangerous

Activity 4.20

1 Think of a building that is familiar to you. List all the materials that could be recycled before, during and after demolition. Go on to explain how the building would be best demolished. Highlight health and safety risks involved and any costs that need to be considered.

Just checking

* Why is demolition a dangerous business?
* What are the main methods used in modern demolition?
* What factors determine the type of demolition method used?

4.21 Construction plant: Details and application

The use of **construction plant** in modern construction work is widespread in the UK. The variety and range of equipment available extends from hand tools to large earth-moving vehicles.

The range of construction plant

In the construction industry we use a wide range of plant and equipment; here is a list of some of the common types that are in use on construction sites today.

* **Excavators** – which can be tracked or wheeled vehicles
* Dumper trucks – to transport loose materials
* Cranes – to lift items horizontally and vertically
* Scaffolding
* Concrete pumps
* Forklifts
* Breakers and compressors
* Small tools and plant
* Concrete batching plant or silos.

This excavator has two methods of excavation. What do you think they are?

Construction plant – mechanical machines used on construction sites

Excavator – a digging machine that can swivel its excavator arm 180° or 360°; the most common is the JCB 3CX

Mechanisation – the use of mechanical plant instead of manual labour

Tower cranes – a crane sitting on a mast, comprising sections bolted together, which can lift materials to great heights; these cranes tower over the project, and can climb up a structure as it is built

Case Study

Have a look locally for a construction project where some construction plant is being used. Look for one item of plant and, in small groups, list what factors you think would have to be considered before bringing it onto the site (e.g. for an excavator, you might have to think about how much earth you had to move). Groups should then compare lists, checking with the tutor to see if you are correct.

Four main reasons for use

Time	Clients require their buildings to be handed over, completed, earlier than originally planned; plant makes the job faster.
Safety	Some situations would be dangerous for manual working; for example, if you need to excavate to 2 m depth in loose ground, working by hand could cause ground to collapse in on the workers.
Efficiency	For many types of work, using plant is more cost effective than using manual labour .
Height	Particular building structures require specialist tower cranes to lift materials to great heights.

How does the operator get to the control cabin?

The effects of mechanisation

Mechanisation has brought many changes to the construction industry.

* Larger designed structures – Terminal 4 at Heathrow is a massive, open-span passenger terminal that would have been impossible to build without cranes. Cranes enable large loads to be moved safely into place enabling large span steel beams to be used for structures.

* Massive engineering projects – many items of plant were used at Wembley to create the arch over the stadium. Mechanical plant enabled the old stadium to be demolished quickly so that work could start on the new stadium.

* Infrastructure – dams producing hydroelectric power are created using large earth-moving equipment. Using manual labour, it would take a considerable time to construct a dam. Large excavators with huge buckets can shift large quantities of earth very quickly.

* Taller buildings – **tower cranes** have enabled us to build tall structures. We can now use climbing cranes where the crane climbs up with the structure as it is built. This reduces the restrictions on the height of buildings.

Activity 4.21

1 Taking a well-known excavator manufacturer, visit their website and look for a plant specification sheet. Find out how deep it can excavate, how much the front bucket holds, and how high it can reach vertically.

2 Now find out if there are any attachments that can be fitted to the rear arm of the machine and check what they can be used for.

3 Look closely at the specification of the excavator. What items are going to have to be maintained, and so will slow down the usage of the machine?

Personal Learning and Thinking Skills

During your visit to look at this site, make a short list that illustrates the range of construction plant being used. When you return, expand this list with short explanations of what each piece of plant is being used for.

Elect a team leader and debate the factors that affect plant choice. Choose one particular piece of construction plant to discuss. The team leader should ensure that each member is encouraged and able to contribute.

Just checking

* Why do people use construction plant?
* What sort of tasks is plant used for?
* What effect has the development of plant had on buildings?

4.22 Site management

Site management is a vital function on a construction site. Site managers have to have many skills, be experienced and suitably qualified, and be very efficient in what they undertake – mistakes in construction can cost a lot of money. A site manager can make a great deal of difference on site, but finding a good one can often be hard.

WHO IS INVOLVED?

A construction site is a complex and unique production line, involving many roles and responsibilities. What would happen if there were nobody in charge? Think about what could go wrong.

Groundworks – heavy works that are undertaken below ground

The site office – planning in progress

Case Study

You have just started work on site as a site manager.
The general foreman is complaining that there is not enough labour to undertake the concrete slab pour, and you don't have the correct equipment on site to finish the concrete. The concrete has been ordered. What are you going to do to sort this out?

Personal Learning and Thinking Skills

Working in a team, imagine that you need to put together a site management team. What would you look for in each role? What skills and abilities will be important for each type of person? Create a list for each role of these abilities and skills and write a few paragraphs explaining your decisions.

Activity 4.22

1 Using the types of site personnel explored in this topic, draw up a typical site organisational chart showing the chain of command (who answers to who on site), starting with the contracts or project manager.

2 On your chart, add a health and safety advisor. Where are you going to place them in the site set-up? Who is usually responsible for health and safety on site?

3 Taking a couple of the people on your chart, identify two items that they might interact about on site on a daily basis, through verbal or written communication. Write down what the communication would involve, from each person's point of view.

Site management team

The contractor undertaking the project on site typically employs the people listed below. These people work within a team on site to produce the finished project, on time, to budget and to the best quality. The contract or project manager heads the team and must ensure that it runs smoothly.

Construction team members

Contracts or project manager	Looks after all the company's current building contracts and tends to be office based.
Site manager	Is responsible for the whole of the site.
Site engineer	Is responsible for the dimensions and position of the project.
General foreman	Is concerned with the supervision of the day-to-day running of the project.
Craft operatives	Skilled employees such as carpenters or bricklayers.
General operatives	General labourers who are semi-skilled.

Site manager

This person works under the supervision of the contracts manager and is responsible for the day-to-day running of the construction site. On large construction projects, there may be assistant site managers or a resident project manager.

Site engineer

This person deals with the setting out of the building and associated external works in accordance with the architect's or designer's drawings. Their work therefore has to be accurate and regularly checked against the drawings. The site engineer uses surveying and measuring equipment to accomplish this task.

General foreman

This person supervises the craft operative gangs on site, to ensure that work progresses on time and is to the correct quality. Sometimes a general foreman is trade-specific, dealing only with brickwork, joinery or finishes. The general foreman reports to the site manager.

Craft operatives

These skilled employees undertake the craft work on site and cover aspects such as joinery, brickwork, plastering, services and finishes. They report to the general foreman.

General operatives

These employees may be semi-skilled in **groundwork** activities. They work on drainage and concrete works and any general labouring involving manual techniques. They may report to the senior craft operative within the labour gang, or to the general foreman.

Groundworkers installing a pipeline

Just checking

* What does site management mean?
* Who is involved in site management?
* How do the different roles interact?

4.23 Organisation and programming

THE CONTRACT PROGRAMME

Imagine that you are the main contractor on a project. All you have are the project start date and the date that the client wants the work to be handed over. How might you go about organising the work so that you can deliver on time?

The role of the planner

The planner has a role that is vital for large contracting companies. This should not be confused with a town and country planner who takes responsibility for development. This table shows a planner's main responsibilities.

Produce a master programme	This is a chart with activities and durations that visually represents the programme from start to finish.
Produce monthly and weekly programmes	These break down the activities from the master programme into much more detail.
Schedule delivery dates as required	These are critical dates for the delivery of materials and subcontractors.
Plan the layout of the site set-up	This often takes the form of a scaled drawing illustrating the complete site **set-up**.
Monitor and report progress	Progress reports are important because delays can be costly for the main contractor.

Functional Skills

Using suitable software, create the Gantt chart answer in a format using a table or spreadsheet

This construction site is very small and requires careful planning

Activity 4.23

1 Looking at the list of the planner's roles, why is it important to schedule delivery dates for suppliers and subcontractors? Write down a list of reasons.

2 Using the following information, draw up a simple Gantt chart for the five activities.

  ✳ Excavate foundations: **duration** 5 days, start day 1

  ✳ Concrete foundations: duration 3 days, start day 4

  ✳ Cast floor slab: duration 3 days, start day 5

  ✳ Backfill foundations: duration 1 day, start day 7

  ✳ Complete drainage – first stage: duration 1 day, start day 3; second stage: duration 1 day, start day 8

3 In the job in question 2, the subcontractor for the floor slab has just informed you that this will now take 7 days. Redraw your Gantt chart to reflect this.

The Gantt chart or contract programme

This is a useful way of monitoring the progress to date on site. At any time, you can easily see what should have been completed and when. Normally, the Gantt chart is placed on the wall of the site office, with a string line running from top to bottom to represent the current time. By colouring in the bars with progress as a percentage, you can keep track of which **activities** are running behind or ahead of schedule.

Take a look at the Gantt chart below. As you can see, the bars form a slope. This slope shows you how fast you will have to work on site: the steeper the incline, the faster the progress; the shallower the incline, the slower the job goes.

> **Contract programme** – a visual aid for planning and charting a project's progress
>
> **Site set-up** – the contractor's temporary services: for example, the cabins and fencing
>
> **Activities** – the items on a chart: for example, excavate foundations
>
> **Duration** – how long each individual activity takes to complete

Contract Activity — Factory extension Duration Week Nr

Contract Activity	Dur	1	2	3	4	5	6	7	8	9	10	11	12	13	14	15	16	17	18	19	20	21	22	23	24	25	26	27	28	29	30	31	32	33	34	35	36
Site set up	1	■																																			
Excavation	3		■	■	■																																
Concrete fnds	5					■	■	■	■	■																											
Hardcore flr slb	4				■	■	■	■																													
Erect steelwork	2											■	■																								
Clad roof	2													■	■																						
Concrete flr slab	2															■	■																				
Clad walls	3																	■	■	■																	
Brickwork walls	8																	■	■	■	■	■	■	■	■												
Doors and frames	1																								■												
Drainage	4/5		■	■	■	■	■																														
Painting	4																									■	■	■	■								
Electrical Instn	5																									■	■	■	■	■							
Heating Instn	2																																■	■			
External Landscaping	7																									■	■	■	■	■	■	■					
Clean & handover	3																																		■	■	■

A Gantt chart, also known as a bar chart

Other types of programme

There are other ways of illustrating the **contract programme**:

* arrow diagrams (sometimes called 'critical path diagrams'), which are a series of circles and arrows that interconnect to represent the sequences of the contract programme; however, these are very difficult to construct and operate

* computer software programmes that run and operate the programme.

> **For your project**
>
> Produce a small bar or Gantt chart for part of your project that illustrates a few items of activity over time.

> **Just checking**
>
> * What are a planner's main responsibilities?
> * How do you use a Gantt chart?
> * What can a Gantt chart tell you?

4.24 Information technology in project management

THE AGE OF THE COMPUTER

We are now receiving communications faster than ever before, drawings and documents can now be sent via email, and virtual project sites can now be set up. There is now a real need for computer-based specialists to coordinate the flow of information to all involved in construction. What training are they going to need?

The rise of information technology (ICT) has had a remarkable effect on the construction industry. The use of computing has grown in many areas, from programming to the calculation of payrolls. The paperless construction site has been trialled by companies wanting to get away from the vast array of documentation, from drawings to specifications. This can be achieved, but it does take a great deal of effort on the part of the design and construction teams.

Communication formats and standard ICT applications

There are many formats available in the modern construction environment. We shall now explore the more common forms of graphic and written communication.

Computer aided design (CAD)

This has been the main advance in ICT technology applied to the construction industry. No longer does a pencil and pen have to be used to produce working drawings for a project. It can now all be done electronically using a mouse and keyboard. Electronic drawing files are created, and these can be electronically delivered to other members of the construction team via the Internet.

Drawing boards are increasingly being replaced by computers

Various formats are available. AutoCAD is the 'industry standard' that dominates the graphical detailing market. This is a very complex drawing tool enabling 2-D and 3-D models to be constructed of a construction project. It is a very powerful tool, and operators require considerable training to use all the commands that are available in the software.

Electronic wordprocessing

Text documents can now be created and again passed to all concerned using the Internet, but there is still a need to initially write down information at certain points, for example a verbal instruction given to the contractor from the architect.

Email

This is now the most popular format for communicating with others involved within a construction project. It is fast and efficient, and allows documents to be attached to the communication.

Program software

There are many commercial software systems available that will manage a construction project. They differ in complexity and ease of use. Microsoft Project is just one such software system. This has the ability to produce a bar or Gantt chart (see page 103) from information which you put into the package.

These programs provide a very powerful tool to manage the time aspects of controlling a project, keeping it on time to the completion date agreed.

ICT and programming

The contract program has evolved from the humble bar chart that was manually drawn on paper and placed on the site cabin wall and used to track progress of the construction work by using a vertical string line stretched across the chart at the right time.

ICT has meant that the production of contract programs can be undertaken using proprietary software packages that draw the program on screen. This can then be manipulated to produce a complete contract programme.

The advantages of using this are:

* The contract programme can be resourced – details of labour and plant can be loaded into the program to produce a detailed report that can be used to manage the construction work.

* Real-time cash-flow and construction costs can be used within the software to monitor not only the physical progress on site, but also the financial profitability of the project.

* Information can be processed very quickly.

* Short-term details of the programme can be printed easily.

* Reports can be produced for managers.

Activity 4.24

1 On the Internet, do some research into the different types of work program software available. Make a list of the advantages claimed by the manufacturers. Can you see any disadvantages? List these too.

2 Download *Google sketch up*, a free CAD software package. By working through the tutorials, see if you can produce a drawing of a small building in three dimensions.

Designing on screen can speed up the designing process

Just checking

* What are the advantages of ICT?
* What is CAD?
* What ICT methods of communication are used on a modern construction project?

In earlier topics we considered how construction affects both local communities and the natural environment. Many of the concerns of the community can be reduced or eliminated by use of appropriate good site practice. Look back on some of the concerns that were identified in earlier topics – are there any solutions? Can the contractor make life more bearable for the local community?

Community liaison

Communication plays a key role in community relations. If the public is aware of what is happening on site, when it is happening and what the impact will be, they will be better placed to cope with any inconvenience caused by construction activities. Liaison is a two-way process, and should allow the contractors to consider the specific needs of the community. Good community liaison may include:

* providing information on how the contractor will minimise impact on the locality
* organising the timing of deliveries to site
* holding community meetings to agree on working hours
* taking care with car parking and site access routes
* offering information about the timing of activities that will produce high sound levels, create dust, etc.
* giving safety talks in local schools
* the appointment of a community representative to be a central point of contact.

Often, on a large project, the contractor will employ a community liaison officer to deal with these issues and to maintain contact with members of the local community. Remember that the local community will include residents, traders, local businesses, service providers and local schools.

Site management and sustainability

The site management team can make a large contribution to reducing the impact of a project during the construction period. Here are some of the techniques that can be used to respond to community concerns.

* **Appropriate site security**, such as fencing, alarms and having a 'site minder'. This minimises theft and contributes to health and safety, by preventing intruders and limiting inappropriate access by children at night and weekends.
* **Arranging times of deliveries and access routes** to have minimum effect on the local community: for example, ensuring that deliveries

Acoustic – concerned with sound/noise; an acoustic hoarding absorbs or reflects back the sound so that it is not transmitted

Hoarding – a solid security or safety fence around a building site. This is normally constructed of plywood and painted in the company's colours

do not occur when children are arriving at or leaving local schools.

* **Providing wheel-cleaning facilities** at site exits to prevent transfer of mud onto the road. This is especially important during the period of excavation work and before the site roads are surfaced.

* **Damping down** by spraying water onto surfaces to prevent dust being blown onto adjoining properties.

* **Use of acoustic hoardings and screens** to minimise sound transfer to neighbouring properties.

* **Reducing noise** by re-routing of vehicles, agreement of hours worked on site, and using off-site prefabrication.

* **Keeping the site clean** and tidy at all times and disposing of rubbish before it accumulates.

* **Maintenance of plant** to ensure that sound suppression is effective, and emission levels are within regulatory limits. This is governed by British Standard, BS5228 'Noise control on construction and open sites'.

Considerate Contractors Scheme

The Considerate Contractors Scheme is a national scheme that encourages contractors to be considerate to the environment, the workforce and the general public. The scheme centres around a 'Code of Considerate Practice' which covers eight different categories.

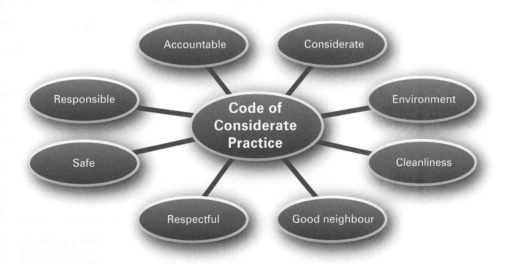

All sites registered with the scheme are monitored and assessed against the eight categories shown above. There are even annual awards for the best performing, most considerate sites and personnel.

Activity 4.25

1 Visit the Considerate Contractors Scheme's website at www.ccscheme.org.uk where you will find a section on how to be considerate, and examples of considerate practice in each of the categories. After investigating the website, write a short accout of the benefits of being a considerate contractor.

2 Produce a poster to encourage and promote good sustainable site practice.

Just checking

* What are the advantages of using community liaison?
* What are the consequences of not adopting good site practice?
* Why should contractors join the Considerate Contractors Scheme?

4.26 Sustainable site practice 2: Environmental issues

Site practice affects both local communities and the natural environment. Good site management can make a major reduction in the environmental impact of a project. In this topic we will investigate the methods and practices that minimise the impact of construction upon the natural environment.

Many of the environmental and community concerns that were identified in earlier topics are interlinked: an environmental concern is often also a concern of the local community. In particular, the recommended practices to reduce dust and sound emissions from the site can be considered both a community and an environmental solution. The following methods are considered to be good site practice both to protect and sustain the natural environment and to reduce a site's contribution to the emission of **greenhouse gases**.

✳ The use of proper on-site storage of materials limits damage during storage and reduces the amount of site waste. Remember: all waste has to be transported to a landfill site. Proper storage will include hard standings, racking, storage containers and protection from the elements.

Use of a bund wall to prevent ground contamination in the event of leakage

* The use of **silt traps** on temporary surface water drains prevents silt entering the main drainage system.

* Local sourcing of materials means that they do not have to be transported long distances. This lowers energy consumption, pollution from vehicles and congestion.

* Damping down by spraying surfaces prevents dust being blown onto adjoining property.

* The segregation of waste makes recycling materials easier. This will involve the use of different skips or containers for different types of waste material.

* Recycling materials such as crushed demolition rubble can be used as general site fill. Stone can be reclaimed and redressed for reuse. Road shavings can be used as a hardcore fill.

* Proper storage of fuels and chemicals prevents the risk of ground contamination. This will include the use of **bund walls** to avoid any leakage from storage tanks from spreading.

* Many sites, both greenfield and brownfield, provide important habitats for wildlife. The construction team should use specialist contractors to relocate animals to safe, suitable locations.

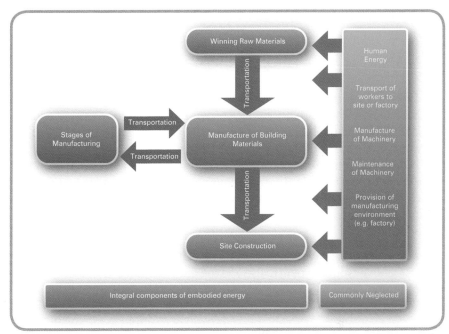

Sources of embodied energy

Embodied energy

These days, it's not appropriate to just consider the energy used by a building throughout its life. Indeed, the improvements in insulation standards and appliance efficiency mean that, by comparison with the energy used for running the building, the energy consumed in the production of materials and in the construction of a building have a much greater significance than ever before. **Embodied energy** is the total energy consumed in the production of a building. Above you can see all the sources of embodied energy within a project. These include the energy consumed during the extraction and processing of raw materials, off-site manufacturing of components, site construction and transportation at all stages.

Fossil fuels – non-renewable sources of energy extracted from the ground such as coal, gas and oil

Greenhouse gases – gases that contribute to global warming, such as CO_2

Silt traps – a series of settlement chambers to intercept silt before it enters the main drainage system

Bund wall – a wall that surrounds a storage tank to contain the contents of a tank in the event of a leak

Embodied energy – the total energy consumed in the production of a building

Just checking

* Which good environmental practices also solve community issues?
* How can the construction industry minimise waste?
* What does the embodied energy of a project include?

5 CREATE THE BUILT ENVIRONMENT: USING TOOLS

Introduction

In this unit you will be introduced to the practical aspects of construction. These are brickwork, carpentry and joinery, painting and decorating and the building services of plumbing and electronics. This will give you the opportunity to select the trade route you wish to take. Throughout you will also be introduced to the very important health and safety considerations, which you must remember at all times. You will have to identify the risks and hazards associated with the work you are going to undertake and assess their impact and implication for others.

Within each of the practical themes consideration has to be given to the materials you are going to use and the risks associated with these, especially Control of Substances Hazardous to Heath (COSHH). Each of the practical themes contains a realistic outcome that you will have to produce yourself to an acceptable standard. For example, in brickwork you will have to build a wall and point it.

The other part of this unit is a presentation. This is a team effort on the roles of the team within the construction industry from craft through to technical and management levels.

How you will be assessed

You will be assessed on the production of a practical exercise that will be given to you by your tutor and is contained in a descriptive form within the specification for the unit. Make sure that you obtain photographs of your progress and complete a portfolio including any witness statements or observation records required in preparing your task.

The second part of the assessment is in your contribution to a team presentation using the power point slide format which can be presented electronically as well as in paper format.

On completion of this unit you should:

LO.5.1. Know about, use and be able to extend own implementation of health and safety practices in a construction craft environment

LO.5.2. Understand the working characteristics and safe use of materials

LO.5.3. Be able to use tools safely and effectively to produce a practical outcome

LO.5.4. Understand the job roles, progression routes, occupational structures and importance of teamwork in the crafts and related activities

THINKING POINTS

This unit gives the learner an awareness of the skill levels that are associated with the craft based workforce that produce the projects for the client. There is a high level of skill and dexterity required in performing these tasks, and it is not easy for those of us who have not tried it. Over the years many specialised trades have disappeared as new materials technology has been developed. For example plumbers working in lead on roofs have now been replaced by glass reinforced plastics, as this method is quicker, more economical and lasts over 20 years without maintenance. The range of trades associated with constructing a complicated and heavily serviced building can extend into the hundreds on a large construction site, from the semi skilled right through to service professional engineers, along with the vast amount of sub contract trades that are required for specialist works. All of this has to be managed and organized, often by a project manager who has the responsibility for ensuring that the building is delivered on time, to budget and at the right quality.

5.1 Job roles and responsibilities: The construction team

There's a wide range of job roles available in the dynamic and exciting construction industry. Large companies offer many opportunities that you may not even have thought of: solicitors, accountants, sales staff, marketing personnel, administrators, training and HR (human resources) staff – the list goes on!

Job types

Here are some of the more traditional 'craft' jobs. These are often the ones that first spring to mind when you think about construction work.

Joiner	Carpenter	Bricklayer	Electrician

'I work in a joinery workshop manufacturing items out of wood – such as windows, doorframes and staircases – for installation on-site.'

'I'm the on-site woodworker, constructing formwork, floors, roofs and internal partitions, and fixing joinery items in place.'

'I lay bricks and blocks, and install other components associated with brickwork such as damp-proof courses, lintels, cavity wall insulation and wall ties.'

'I install electrical services, power distribution circuits, lighting services, control systems and alarms.'

Plumber	Painter & decorator	Building services engineer

'I install sanitary goods, hot and cold water systems, soil, vent and waste pipework, gas services and domestic heating systems.'

'I provide the final decorative coatings – usually painting and wallpaper hanging.'

'I install more complex mechanical and electrical heating and air-conditioning systems to larger non-domestic construction.'

Job title	Classification	Description
Architect	Professional	Acts as supervising officer during the construction phase. Is in overall charge of ensuring that the building is constructed to the required standards. Also deals with contract administration, issuing architect's instructions and authorising payment.
Quantity surveyor (QS)	Professional	The contractor's QS agrees monthly valuations and the final account with the client's QS. Produces budgets and forecasts of costs, and may be involved in the measurement and paying of subcontractors.
Project manager	Management	Leads the management team on large projects. Is accountable for completing the project on time, within budget and to quality standards.
Site manager	Management	Sometimes known as a 'site agent'. Manages the site as the contractor's representative.
General foreman	Supervisory	Organises and supervises operatives and craftspeople. Will be in overall control on small projects.
Trade foreman	Supervisory	Organises and supervises craft area, and may provide technical support, quality control and advice specific to the craft.
Ganger	Supervisory	Supervises a group of non-craft operatives such as drain-layers, concreters and ground-workers.
Planner	Technician	Produces contract programmes, often in the form of Gantt charts. Plans site activities to ensure that the project is completed on time.
Buyer	Technician	Schedules materials, obtains quotations and places orders for materials to arrive on site to meet the planner's programme.
Site engineer	Technician	Assists the site manager in establishing levels, setting out the works on site, ensuring that drains are to the correct falls, etc. Does quality control checks to ensure that work is within specified tolerances.
Clerk of works	Supervisory	Acts as the architect's on-site representative to ensure that the construction is to the architect's design and specification.
Construction operative	Operative	General site worker, such as drain-layer, forklift driver, concreter or general labourer.
Safety officer	Technical	Deals with all aspects of health and safety, including inductions, training, safety briefings and inspections.

The table above explains some of the other job roles available during a construction project. Often the size of a project will determine the exact nature of the job role, with some being combined on smaller projects.

Activity 5.1

1 Conduct some research about any of these jobs you might want to do, writing down the qualifications you would need, and the advantages and disadvantages of each job. You may wish to use the school careers library or to carry out some Internet investigations. Produce a brief report on your findings.

2 Find out more about the role and purpose of the professional institutions involved in construction, such as **RIBA**, **CIOB** and **RICS**.

CIOB – Chartered Institute of Building
RICS – Royal Institute of Chartered Surveyors

Did you know?

Construction is one of the largest industries in the UK, employing over two million workers.

Just checking

✱ What sorts of jobs would you find in a construction team?
✱ Which jobs need specialist qualifications?
✱ Which jobs have supervisory or managerial responsibilities?

5.2 Health and safety legislation

Construction work can be very hazardous. Projects could involve: deep excavations, confined spaces, working at height, temporary works, power transmission, cranes, construction plant, hazardous chemicals and other materials. You can see why working on a construction site may not be as safe as working in an office environment. Health and safety **legislation** has come into existence to improve safety and to reduce risk to health.

There are now many pieces of legislation that govern health and safety on site. The diagram below shows the main pieces of legislation that help to make the workplace safer.

Health and safety legislation

Some of the legislation is briefly described in the table opposite.

Risk assessments

The MHSW requires employers to carry out risk assessments, where the dangers of an activity are measured against the likelihood of an accident taking place. Making and updating risk assessments allows the identification of who is at risk, and means that appropriate control

Legislation

Legislation	
The Health and Safety At Work Act (HASAWA) 1974	This is the main piece of health and safety legislation. It requires employers to provide a safe place to work, provide and maintain safe machinery and equipment, provide safety training, have a written safety policy, provide personal protective equipment and ensure safe handling, transportation and storage of machinery equipment and materials. It also places duties upon employees: to take care at all times and ensure that they do not put themselves or others at risk; to cooperate with employers and use safeguards and equipment provided; and not to misuse or interfere with anything provided for their own or others' safety. A government agency known as the Health and Safety Executive (HSE) has the task of enforcing the rules of the HASAWA.
Construction Design and Management Regulations (CDM)	These affect not only the contractor but also the design team, as they now have an element of responsibility for designing projects that can be safely built. CDM also provides guidance for procedures for maintenance and demolition.
The Provision and Use of Work Equipment Regulations (PUWER)	These cover all working equipment such as tools and machinery. Employers should make sure that these are suitable for the job, properly serviced and repaired, and regularly inspected. The regulations also require employers to properly train and instruct employees so that they can safely use the equipment.
The Control of Substances Hazardous to Health Regulations (COSHH)	These control the use of hazardous substances on site. The employer is required to maintain, on-site, a file of information which includes correct storage, transportation and handling of the substances as well as advice on what to do in the case of spillage, **inhalation**, **absorption** or **ingestion**.
The Manual Handling Operations Regulations	These cover all activities where a person does the lifting instead of a machine. The recommended maximum weight a person should lift is 25kg.
The Reporting of Injuries, Diseases and Dangerous Occurrences Regulations (RIDDOR)	Under RIDDOR, employers are required to report accidents, diseases or dangerous occurrences. This information is used by the Health and Safety Executive to identify where and how risk arises, and to investigate serious accidents.

Activity 5.2

1 Consider a typical construction site: possibly a new housing site or even a extension to your school. How many potential hazards can you identify? Produce a poster that warns employees of all the potential hazards on a construction site.

2 Imagine that you are the health and safety manager for a construction company. Write a set of rules that could apply to all your construction sites.

Legislation – laws passed by central government

Inhalation – when a substance enters the body via breathing

Absorption – when a substance enters the body through the skin

Ingestion – when a substance enters the body through the mouth

Just checking

* Why do we need health and safety legislation?
* What is the difference between hazards and risks?
* What is a risk assessment?

WHAT MAKES A SITE VISIT SAFE?

You are about to make a site visit. What sorts of hazards might you come across, for which PPE might be needed?

Personal Learning and Thinking Skills

Remember! It is a your responsibility to maintain your equipment. Any problems with equipment should be reported immediately to your teacher, tutor or the person in charge.

5.3 Personal protective equipment (PPE)

Health and safety considerations are of paramount importance in the construction industry. It is vital that you learn about the purpose and use of personal protective equipment (PPE), not just for your own sake but for the sake of the people you work with and the general public.

Types of equipment

Personal protective equipment is anything that has been designed to be worn or held by someone to protect them from a risk. Employers are legally responsible for providing appropriate items of PPE and for making sure that they are being used correctly. Employers should also provide training in the correct use of PPE; employees should always make sure that they use PPE in the way they have been trained. If a piece of PPE is lost or damaged, this should be reported to the employer immediately.

	Name of PPE	Use	When it should be used
	Hard hat	A safety helmet to protect the head from falling debris	At all times on any site
	Safety boots	Usually steel toe-capped to protect feet from heavy objects	At all times on any site
	Safety glasses	To protect the eyes from flying debris	Task specific – e.g. cutting materials
	Safety gloves	To protect the hands from abrasive materials or chemicals	Task specific – e.g. stacking bricks
	Ear defenders	To protect the ears from excessive noise on-site	Task specific – e.g. when using woodworking machinery

	Barrier cream	To offer some protection to the hands from various chemicals	Task specific – e.g. concreting or brick laying
	Dust masks	To protect from breathing in dust	Task specific – preparing surfaces, painting and decorating
	High-visibility vests	So that individuals can be easily seen	At all times on any site
	Respirators	For use when fumes are toxic	Task specific – e.g. painting, decorating, spray painting

There are nine PPE mistakes in this picture.
Can you spot them all?

Activity 5.3

1 Who is responsible for keeping PPE in good condition?

2 Why is it important to wear barrier cream when concreting or laying bricks?

3 Create a leaflet highlighting what safety equipment should be used on-site. You should show essential items, which should be worn at all times, and other items of PPE for specific tasks. You could use images to make your leaflet stand out and make your point clear.

Case Study

Joel has just reported to site on the first day of a new job. The person in charge gives him a hard hat, high visibility jacket and safety glasses to wear on site. He starts to put on the equipment and becomes aware of a crack in the hard hat. What should he do? Can the helmet still be worn? Can Joel start working on site with this?

Just checking

* When should PPE be worn?
* What PPE should you always wear on site?
* Whose responsibility is it to maintain PPE?

5.4 Access equipment

The work of the decorator often requires the use of ladders, stepladders, **hop-ups** and other items of access equipment. Usually, it is only low-level access equipment that is needed, for example to reach the top of a wall or a ceiling. However, some buildings, particularly older ones, have rooms that are much higher than in most modern houses.

Types of access equipment

Access equipment is a general term that applies to equipment used to gain access to work areas that cannot be reached from the ground. These could be ceilings, the tops of walls, the tops of doorframes and architraves, high-level windows or any other internal feature that is near the top of a room. It could also be guttering, windows, fascias and soffits on the outside of a building. Normally, internal features can be reached with low-level access equipment such as hop-ups or stepladders, but sometimes trestles and lightweight staging may be required.

When working externally, the decorator may need to use ladders, extension ladders or even scaffolding to access work areas. A ladder should be used at an angle of approximately 75° and should always be secured at the top or bottom to prevent it from moving during use.

Safety checks

When using access equipment, health and safety is paramount. All equipment should be checked for defects or damage before use and should never be used if it is defective. The table shows the most commonly used items of access equipment, and the safety checks that should be carried out for each.

Item of equipment	Safety checks
Ladders	Check for loose or damaged **rungs**, **stiles** and ropes (on some extension ladders). Damage could include splits or cracks in wooden ladders, or corrosion or other damage on aluminium ladders. Ladders should only be used at the correct angle and should always be secured.
Trestles	Check for loose, split or damaged cross members and stiles. Check that hinges are secure and operating smoothly. Check that trestles are fully open when in use, and that at least 1/3 of the trestle is above the working platform.
Stepladders	Check for loose or damaged treads, stiles, hinges and ropes. Never use unless fully opened, and do not stand on the top of a stepladder.
Hop-ups	Ensure that the hop-up is sturdy and well built. Working platform should be at least 500 mm × 500 mm.

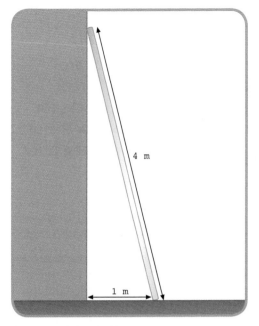

Correct angle for a ladder

Wooden stepladder correctly set up.

There are a few more crucial factors to remember when working with ladders:

* Never work sideways on a stepladder.
* Always face the work being undertaken.
* Never go above a height where there is no handhold at the top of a stepladder. This is usually the top three steps.

Case Study

A local decorator has been employed to carry out some internal and external decorating work at a large Victorian house. Using your knowledge of access equipment, plus further research, answer these questions.

1. What type of access equipment would be suitable when hanging lining paper to the large ceiling in the lounge?

2. What type of ladder should *not* be used to access the guttering at the front of the house, which has overhead power lines running very close? Explain why.

3. Why should wooden ladders and stepladders only be treated with clear varnish and not painted?

4. While carrying out safety checks on a wooden extension ladder, a decorator discovers that some of the rungs are loose. What should they do?

Hop-ups – a small item of access equipment, usually handmade of wood, consisting of a single step and a working platform approximately 500 mm by 500 mm in size

Rungs – the part of a ladder that your feet go on

Stiles – the sides of a ladder

Just checking

* What are the main factors to consider when choosing access equipment?
* What angle should you use a ladder at?
* How should you check if a trestle is safe?

BRICK OR BLOCK?

What is the difference between a brick and a block? Describe the differences to a partner.

5.5 Brickwork 1: Bricks and blocks

One of the main materials used for building are bricks and blocks. These come in many different styles and sizes. Using the right bricks or blocks for the job is crucial – and you will need to know the set formulae for working out the length of either a brick wall or a block wall.

Bricks

A standard brick is the following size – 215 mm × 102.5 mm × 65 mm.

Walls are always designed to brick sizes, so you need to know that the modular size of bricks, when laid with a 10 mm joint, is 225 mm × 75 mm. You can work out the length of a brick wall by multiplying the number of bricks by 225 mm and subtracting 10 mm. For example, a wall 10 bricks long will be 2240 mm in length. Look at how this has been worked out:

Number of bricks × 225 mm – 10 mm = length of wall

10 × 225 mm – 10 mm = 2250 mm – 10 mm = 2240 mm

Facing – the part of the brick that can be seen

Aesthetically pleasing – looking good!

Header – a brick that passes through a one brick wall from the inner to the outer face at 90° to the face of the wall

Arris – the edge of a brick formed by the meeting of two faces, e.g. header face and stretcher face

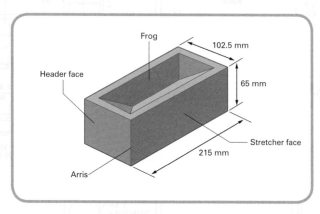

Standard brick

Types of brick

There are three different types of brick:

* **solid** which have no cavities or depressions
* **perforated** which have holes in them, up to 25% of the gross volume
* **frogged** where the brick has a depression in it; the depression can be in one or more than one of the faces of the brick, but it cannot exceed 20% of the gross volume of the brick.

There are three main categories of brick according to how they are used.

1 **Facing bricks** are bricks that can be seen. They are free from any surface damage and are designed to be **aesthetically pleasing**.

2 **Common bricks** are bricks that are not meant to be seen. Many are for use underground or in a place where they will be covered by something (for example, plaster or render of some kind).

3 **Engineering bricks** can also be used as facing bricks. However, they have a very high strength and a high resistance to water penetration. There are two classes of engineering brick: class A, which are blue in colour and have the highest strength and resistance to water (these are often used as damp-proof course); and class B, which are red in colour, have a smooth face and are perforated.

There are also some special types of brick that are specifically designed
for internal and external angles other than 90°.

Special bricks

Blocks

A block looks like the photograph opposite. It doesn't look very exciting, does it?

Blocks are made of concrete. They can be dense and suitable for structural walls and below ground level use. They can be lightweight and are therefore suitable for non-load-bearing partitions. There are different types of blocks, including solid, insulated, aerated and keyed.

Blocks come in a standard size of 440 mm × 215 mm, giving a modular size of 450 mm x 225 mm. As with bricks, you can easily work out the size of a wall made of blocks, this time by multiplying the number of blocks by 450 mm and then subtracting 10 mm. So a wall 10 blocks long will be 4490 mm.

Number of blocks × 450 mm – 10 mm = length

10 × 450 mm – 10 mm= 4500 mm – 10 mm = 4490 mm

A block

Activity 5.5

1 Work out the length of a brick wall that is: **a** 15 bricks long, **b** 26 bricks long, **c** 42 bricks long, **d** 20 bricks long.

2 Work out the length of a block wall that is: **a** 5 blocks long **b** 25 blocks long **c** 45 blocks long **d** 15 blocks long.

3 Think about your house, school, or college. Which parts are made of bricks, and which of blocks? Write a list of where each is used, doing some research if you need to.

Just checking

✱ What is the difference between a brick and a block?

✱ What different types of brick are available?

✱ What standard sizes do blocks come in?

5.6 Brickwork 2: Sundry materials

When building, there are a number of other materials and components you will need to use to ensure a quality build. These things help to ensure that the building stays waterproofed and safe. Without them, damage could be done which would have significant costs, in terms of both time and money.

Damp-proof course (DPC)

A damp-proof course is required in any building by regulation and is put in place to keep out moisture. You will have seen the damage that can be done to houses by floodwater in the news but the damage that damp can cause can be just as bad. The damp-proof course stops the moisture from rain that soaks into the ground – or groundwater itself – from getting into the structure of the building.

A damp-proof course is a layer of moisture resistant material, the same width as the brickwork or blockwork wall, positioned at 150 mm above ground level. There are various materials used for DPCs including PVC, polythene, Class B Engineering bricks, bitumen and slate.

Wall ties

Wall ties allow the inner and outer skins of a wall to be held together. They can be made from a variety of strip-like materials, including stainless steel, galvanised steel and plastic strip or wire. Each wall tie is constructed with a twist or bend near the centre to stop water passing between the two skins of the wall. Wall ties are built into the brickwork as it progresses, at set distances. There are many different types of wall tie available including butterfly, fishtail and double triangular.

Mortars

Mortar can be either a mixture of sand and lime, or a mixture of sand and cement, with or without lime. The lime is added to make the mortar more workable. In reality, on a building site mortar will always contain cement. Common mixes are at a ratio of 1:3 (cement:building sand) or 1:1:6 (cement:lime:building sand). It is important that mortar stays workable long enough for bricks to be laid, but it should really be used within two hours of mixing. Batches of mortar mixed should be relatively small, as any mortar that starts to set before use has to be thrown away.

Mortar has a very important part to play in the construction of buildings, as it is the mortar that transfers the stresses uniformly through the brickwork. If the mortar is not as strong as the bricks, cracks can appear along the joints of the brickwork. If the mortar is stronger than the bricks, cracks form and shrinkage can appear – not only along the joints, but through the bricks as well. This could weaken the whole structure of the building. Mortar should always be slightly weaker than the bricks or blocks it is used with.

Fish tail

Today, many sites use pre-mixed mortar that is delivered in plastic tubs and 'retarded' with a chemical retarding agent, so that it can be used over a period of 48 hours.

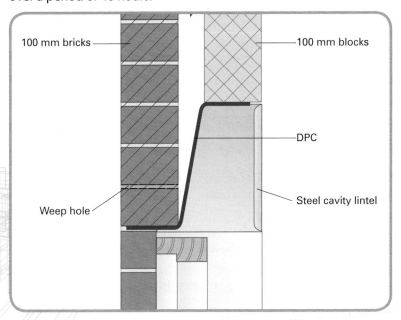

Lintel in a wall

Lintels

Lintels are the beams over a door or window head. They are designed to carry the weight of brickwork over an opening, and are made in a variety of different materials and forms. In domestic construction, they are mainly pre-cast concrete, pressed steel or concrete boot.

Cavity wall insulation

At construction stage, **cavity wall** insulation can be fixed to the outer face of the inner skin of a cavity wall. The insulation usually consists of sheets of expanded polystyrene, which help to insulate the building in an economical way. It is important to remember, however, that this material requires careful installation to avoid rain or groundwater penetration. It is important that no cavity bridges are present as this becomes an issue for water penetration. The insulation used can be a full fill or partial fill.

Cavity wall – two layers or 'skins' of wall held together by wall ties, usually made from brickwork (external skin) and blockwork (internal skin)

Activity 5.6

1 Why is the final strength of mortar dependent on the temperature at the time of laying the bricks?

2 Why should bricks not be laid in freezing conditions?

3 Why should newly laid brickwork be covered with hessian or other material, or a waterproof material if frost or rain are forecast?

For your project

When undertaking practical work at school or college, a sand and lime mortar is used. This will not permanently set the bricks or blocks you have laid. This is a good idea for the school or college, as you would have a particularly difficult job taking down a wall each time you build it!

Just checking

✱ What material are DPCs made from?

✱ What are the common mixtures of mortar?

✱ What different types of wall tie are there?

5.7 Brickwork 3: Tools

A wide variety of tools are used in bricklaying. Great care should be taken when using tools, and they should always be properly cleaned after use. Good quality tools and use of the right tool for the job assist in the production of quality work.

GET PRACTICAL!

Your tutor will show you how to use tools correctly – remember that you should never use a tool that you have not been trained to use, you should always use the correct tool for the job and you should never play with or mess around with a tool. You should always wear the correct personal protective equipment (PPE). Write down the tools and PPE that you think you will need to complete your practical assessment.

Perps – short for perpendicular joint, the vertical joint between two adjoining bricks

Modular size – the size of a brick including a bed joint and perpend joint: 225 mm long by 75 mm high

Plumb – vertical or upright

Profiles – wooden 'stop ends' used as a temporary vertical abutment and to support the corner blocks once the line has been correctly set up to gauge

Face plane deviation – a bump or hollow in the work, usually checked by holding a straight edge diagonally across the work and checking for gaps

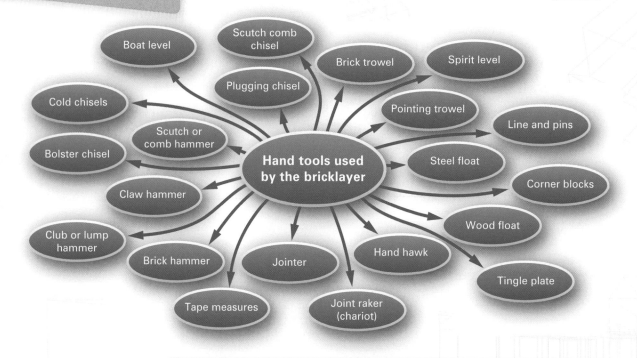

Activity 5.7

1 Some tools are listed in the diagram that are not included in the table of tools needed for your own activity – see if you can find out what type of task these are used for.

2 Select three tools from the table and identify any risks associated with their use.

3 Produce a safety leaflet that promotes the message, 'The right tool for the right job'.

Tools you will need to complete your practical task

	Brick trowel	The main tool used by the bricklayer. Also known as a walling trowel. Used to roll and spread mortar to form a uniform bed joint and to apply mortar to cross joints or 'perps' – this is sometimes known as 'buttering' the bricks. It has a hardened edge, so an experienced bricklayer can use it to cut bricks.
	Jointer	Used to form a tooled joint – often known as a 'bucket handle' joint. Also known as a jointing iron.
	Hawk	Used to hold a small quantity of stiff mortar when filling joints and jointing. In new work where joints only need joint finish applying, the bricklayer may use the flat blade to hold mortar for occasional joints needing filling.
	Bolster chisel	Used for cutting bricks accurately to required size. Made from hardened tempered steel with a blade 64–100 mm wide. Some come with plastic safety grips with hand protection.
	Club or lump hammer	Heavy hammer used with bolster chisel to cut bricks. Also used with other chisels for removing bricks, knocking out holes through walls and removing joints (with a plugging chisel).
	Tape measure	Used for setting out the length of your work and checking for dimensional accuracy upon completion.
	Gauge rod	Used for setting out work to correct height or gauge. Has markings at 75 mm centres to suit **modular size** of bricks.
	Spirit level	Used for setting out, to check that work is level and **plumb**. In your practical task you will use it to set up your **profiles**, and complete quality control checks upon completion. Use its straight edge to check for **face plane deviation**.
	Line and pins	Used once corners have been erected to ensure that bricks are laid in straight lines. The pins act as storage for the line, which is wound onto the pins when not in use. Required length of line can then be easily unwound.
	Corner blocks	Used as an alternative way of holding the line in place, fitted over the corners of the brickwork. Tension in the line holds the blocks in place. Line easy to raise as each course is completed.

For your project

You are allowed to have pre-cut bricks supplied for your use. If you do cut any bricks, you should use a bolster chisel and lump hammer at a safe cutting station, and you will be required to wear eye protection. Remember that this is a 'taster' course, and the use of trowels and brick hammers for cutting bricks should be left to more experienced bricklayers.

Just checking

* What different sorts of chisel might a bricklayer use?
* What tools will you need to complete your assessed practical task?
* What are the correct tools to use when accurately cutting bricks?

5.8 Brickwork 4: Bonding

Bonding is the name given to the different patterns of the bricks in a wall; it's produced by the way you lap one brick over another. Brickwork is bonded for strength – to distribute heavy loads and to help resist lateral forces. Most brickwork is built in half brick walling, which is a single skin of brickwork typically found in cavity wall construction. A one brick wall comprises two skins of brickwork tied together by the use of wall ties or **headers**.

Why bond?

As a small child you probably stacked bricks as a tower. Can you remember how easy it was to knock the tower over? If a wall is unbonded, each brick would be placed directly on top of the brick below, effectively producing a series of side-by-side towers. This will not lead to stable brickwork!

Stretcher bond

This is a half bond where the bricks overlap by half a brick. Stretcher bond is used mainly as a half brick skin of a cavity wall, although it can be used as a one brick wall (in this case, wall ties have to be used to bond the two skins together, because of the absence of headers in this bond). Loads are spread effectively because a load applied to a brick is spread to two bricks in the course below and three bricks in the course below that and so on – providing a triangular spread of the load.

Stretcher bond or half bond brickwork in a cavity wall

LET'S GET LAYING BRICKS!

Look at nearby buildings. In your own words, explain why the brickwork is more stable than a pile of building blocks.

Activity 5.8

1 Think about what would happen if brickwork was not bonded and explain the main reasons for bonding brickwork.

2 Produce a sketch of either an English bond or a Flemish bond wall, and label the headers, stretchers and queen closers.

3 Find out what English garden wall and Flemish garden wall bonds look like. How do they differ from English bond and Flemish bond?

Coping – a capping used to finish off and protect the top of a brick wall

For your project

When working on your project you'll have to identify the type and quantity of materials that you will require – remember that in a half brick wall you need 60 bricks for every square metre of brickwork.

English bond

English bond is essentially alternate courses of headers and stretchers. It is a quarter bond and requires a 'queen closer' to start off the bond – this is a header split along its length. Can you spot the queen closers in the header courses below?

English bond brickwork

Flemish bond

Like English bond, this is a quarter bond requiring a queen closer to start the bond. However, with Flemish bond, the headers and stretchers alternate within each course. Many people feel this is the most attractive and aesthetically pleasing bond, especially if the headers used are in an alternative-coloured brick.

Brick-on-edge coping

One brick walls used externally as a boundary or garden wall require a **coping**, to provide an attractive finish and to protect the top of the wall from the elements. A brick-on-edge provides an attractive alternative to a pre-cast concrete coping.

Flemish bond brickwork

Just checking

* What are the three main types of brickwork bond?
* Which bonds use headers to tie the two skins of brickwork together?
* How does bonding help to spread the load of a structure?

MIND THE GAP

Why do you think a brickwork joint is 10 mm wide? Write down some reasons this might be an important factor in laying bricks.

Functional Skills

Produce a flow chart that outlines the processes used in producing quality brickwork.

Bed joint – the horizontal layer of mortar on which a masonry unit are laid

Activity 5.9

1 Using your understanding of the methods used to produce well blended brickwork, produce a step-by-step guide to remind students of the correct methods when completing their own practical work.

2 Investigate brick sizes with the materials you are using. You could measure and survey individual bricks or lay out rows of bricks placed end to end (say 20 bricks long), and see if there are any differences in the row lengths.

5.9 Brickwork 5: Laying bricks to line

Good quality brickwork is built level, plumb and straight, with a finish that provides a pleasing appearance, with well blended bricks that are clear of mortar splashes or smears. Here you will discover some simple procedures that will help you to achieve this.

Let's get laying!

Bricks are not all exactly the same size or shape. The mortar joints in brickwork accommodate slight differences in size and allow the brickwork to look neat and tidy by keeping the top arris flat and level. The diagram below shows how, by using a line on the top front edge of each course, the **bed joint** then accommodates any differences in the size of bricks.

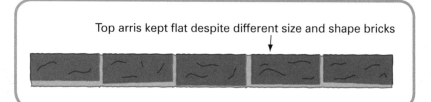

Top arris kept flat despite different size and shape bricks

Irregular shaped bricks laid to line

The bricklaying process

When building any wall, the corners first have to be built in the correct positions (unless profiles are being used). The bricklayer will then use a line that is attached, level to the course height, to either the profile or the pre-erected corners, using corner blocks or line pins. The line must be pulled tight to prevent any 'sag', which would lead to inaccurate work. Bricks can then be laid to line, which involves pressing or tapping the bricks down until the top arris is level with the line. When you look down onto the top of the brick course, there should be a slight gap (the thickness of a trowel) between the line and the face of the brick. The line should not touch the brickwork at any time as this could cause the line to be pushed outwards, resulting in the wall becoming curved. The diagram opposite shows the position of a line on a correctly laid brick.

When working to line over very long courses of brickwork, a tingle plate is used to support the line at the mid-point and prevent sag. A tingle plate is a flat plate with three prongs; the line passes under the two outer prongs and over the central prong. It is set up at mid-course as shown opposite (the diagram also shows the use of line pins and corner blocks – the same method would normally be used at both ends of the wall).

Selection of bricks

Bricks come in slightly different shades and sizes owing to the variation in the firing process when the bricks are manufactured. When in the kiln, bricks closer to the heat source tend to end up slightly smaller and darker than bricks further from the heat source. However, when the bricks are stacked and shrink-wrapped in packs, the bricks in each pack tend to come from the same section of the kiln and so are all similar in size and colour. If bricklayers used bricks from one pack at a time, this would lead to brickwork that had an unsightly, patchwork appearance. Bricklayers therefore always mix up bricks from at least three different packs, so that the brickwork has an even blend of colour.

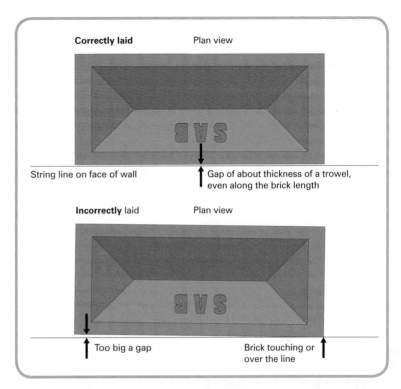

Correctly laid   Plan view

String line on face of wall   Gap of about thickness of a trowel, even along the brick length

Incorrectly laid   Plan view

Too big a gap   Brick touching or over the line

A brick correctly laid to line

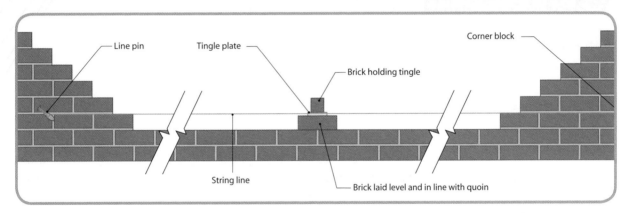

Line pin   Tingle plate   Corner block

Brick holding tingle

String line   Brick laid level and in line with quoin

Setting up a line with a tingle plate

For your project

Remember that, in your project, your will have to identify site procedures that lead to quality brickwork. The areas covered in this topic will guide you in the identification of some of these appropriate procedures.

Just checking

* What is the major function of the brickwork bed joint?
* How should a line be set up and used?
* Why do bricklayers work from three different packs of bricks?

LET'S GET IT RIGHT!

Think about the buildings you know and use – your school or college, your home, buildings in your locality, etc. Have you ever closely examined the brickwork? Do some of the brick-built buildings look better than others? Why? Write down your thoughts.

In order to produce high quality brickwork, it is important to have effective quality control. On-site, the bricklaying foreman or site manager will normally undertake the necessary quality control checks. However, the architect may also employ a clerk of works, based on-site, to check that the project is constructed in line with the specification for materials and workmanship.

Brick joints

Jointing ensures that joints are completely filled with mortar, provide weather resistance and improve the aesthetic appearance of the brickwork.

	Tooled (bucket handle) joint	The most common brickwork joint and the quickest and easiest to complete using a jointing iron. Sheds water easily, so suitable for outdoor work.
	Recessed joint	Suitable for indoor use only as the horizontal 'ledge' formed by the joint would hold water and saturate the brick. This could cause 'freeze thaw' problems in frosty weather, where water in the pores of the brick freezes and expands – if repeated, this results in damage to the face of the brick. Joints are raked out using a 'chariot'.
	Flush joint	Completed using hardwood timber or plastic block to smooth and compact the mortar surface into place. Requires regular size bricks as deviations are easily seen. Provides a rustic look, but not the best weather resistance, so better suited to **sheltered** locations or indoor work.
	Weathered or struck joint	Produced using a pointing trowel. Joint slopes slightly allowing water to run off the surface of the joint and down the face of the brick easily. Suitable for **exposed** conditions.

Sheltered – not exposed to the worst of the elements; usually protected from the wind and associated driving rain

Exposed – opposite of sheltered, subject to the worst weather conditions

For your project

In your project, your will have to identify site procedures that lead to quality brickwork. The areas covered in this topic will guide you in the identification of some of these appropriate procedures. You will need to produce quality control records similar to the records above, together with dimensional checks of length, height, plumb, level and face plane deviation.

Quality control

Example of a quality control record for a brickwork panel, to diploma specifications.

	Comment	Pass/Fail
Brick selection and blend	Bricks exhibited slight variations in colour and size, and carbon deposits (firing burn marks) were present on some bricks but most packs had similar qualities. I have blended them in the finished wall to provide an aesthetically pleasing outcome.	Pass
Mortar batching and workability	The mortar was mixed by the technician at the central batching plant. I re-worked the mortar at the spot board so that it could be rolled and spread with good workability and consistency.	Pass
Pointing and jointing	I used a jointer to produce a bucket handle joint and this was completed in the correct order: perps first followed by the bed joint.	Pass
Correct brick orientation	All bricks were laid in correct orientation with the correct face side, and frogs uppermost.	Pass
General cleanliness	Some drying out still required at the time of taking the photograph but brickwork is generally clean and well presented. There are no smears or splashes of mortar present on the face of the brickwork.	Pass
Vertical joint line	Joints on alternate courses were in line when checked with edge of spirit level.	Pass
General aesthetics	Well presented attractive brickwork.	Pass
Dimensional tolerance	All dimensions within tolerance of 3 mm.	Pass

Activity 5.10

1 Produce a poster that explains the advantages and disadvantages of the different jointing methods.

2 Describe the features or attributes of high quality brickwork.

Personal Learning and Thinking Skills

Using appropriate headings from the quality control table above, complete a subjective analysis of a section of existing brickwork.

Protecting newly laid brickwork

On-site, after the completion of each day's work, the brickwork should be covered with a plastic sheet to protect against rain washing cement out of the mortar joints and forming streaks down the face of the brickwork. The scaffold board closest to the wall should be turned to a vertical position to prevent splashes caused by rain falling onto the horizontal scaffold platform. If an overnight frost is expected, the brickwork should also be covered with hessian sacking to protect it. Bricklaying should be stopped when the temperature is falling at 3°C, and can be started when the temperature is rising at 1°C.

Just checking

* What are the different brickwork joints called?
* What should you record for your project work quality control checks?
* Why does newly laid brickwork have to be protected?

Carpenters and joiners use a wide range of **hand tools** and **portable power tools**. Safety procedures must be followed when working with tools and equipment to ensure the safety of all on-site personnel. Carpenters and joiners are highly trained professionals who follow industry guidelines to ensure that their work adheres to the correct standards.

Tri-square

Sliding bevel

Combination square

Marking gauge

Mortice gauge

Crosscut saw

Panel saw

Coping saw

Smoothing plane

Hand drill

Mitre square

Screwdriver

Mallet

Claw hammer

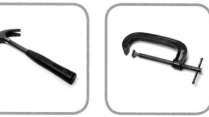
G clamp

Hand tools and equipment

Each tool that a carpenter or joiner uses is individually designed to complete the task as quickly and accurately as possible. Carpenters and joiners need to be able to use many hands tools to a high degree of skill, to ensure the build meets required standards. Above is a selection of hand tools regularly used by carpenters and joiners.

Portable power tools

Portable power tools can also be used to complete many jobs quickly and accurately. Carpenters and joiners can use these but need to be aware of all the safety aspects surrounding the equipment.

Hand tools – tools that are hand held rather than freestanding or major pieces of machinery

Portable power tools – tools, mainly powered by electricity, which are small enough to carry

110v hammer drill

110v powered plane

110v heavy-duty plunge router

110v portable circular saw

110v chop saw

110v jig saw

110v belt sander

110v orbital sander

240v cordless drill

110v cordless screwdriver

Activity 5.11

1 Identify a range of hand tools within your workshop that are used by carpenters and joiners. Try to draw as many as possible. Put a name to each on your diagram. Create a table giving the advantages and disadvantages of each tool and any potential Health and Safety hazards that could be involved during use.

2 Mark out, or cut out using the correct technique, a dovetail joint on a piece of timber.

Protective clothing must be worn at all times, and regular maintenance of all power tools is a must. A double insulation sign and the BS kitemark should be on all the power tools that are used – but this does not always mean they are in correct working order. Portable power tools should be cleaned daily if used daily, as a build-up of dust can cause a detrimental effect on the motor.

Health and safety

Carpenters and joiners are required to follow health and safety procedures on site. This can be from wearing the right PPE to making sure that the carpenter or joiner is trained sufficiently in using a particular tool or piece of equipment. Many other forms of health and safety awareness are really a matter of common sense: not wearing loose clothing or jewellery, regular maintenance of tools and equipment, securing work at workstations before use, and ensuring that all places of work are kept clean and tidy. If a portable power tool is connected directly into a mains power supply (240 V), there is a risk that any electric shock might be fatal. Only tools that use a reduced 110v power supply through the aid of a transformer can be used on a construction site. Many pieces of equipment have age restrictions on use and risk assessed under the Provision and Use of Working Equipment Regulations (PUWER) 1998.

Personal Learning and Thinking Skills

Imagine you are about to use a portable circular saw on site. In groups create a safety document detailing:

* the safety checks you would carry out before use

* what safety procedures you would need to follow during use

* what you would do after the tool has been used.

Functional Skills

Look at the tools in the pictures above. Revise their names for three minutes. When the time is up, close the book and write down as many as you can remember.

Just checking

* What are the different hand tools used by a carpenter?

* What are the advantages of using power tools?

* Why is health and safety especially important with power tools?

5.12 Carpentry and joinery 2: Softwoods and hardwoods

A wide range of softwoods and hardwoods are regularly used in the construction industry. They vary in size, appearance and cost, and some are easier to work with than others. Softwoods are used mainly in areas that are unseen such as trussed rafters and joists; hardwoods have a more desirable appearance but are more expensive and so are mainly used as veneers.

SOFT OPTION?

Give three advantages of using softwoods over hardwoods and hardwoods over softwoods when building a house.

Softwoods

Softwoods are usually used in areas that will remain unseen or unfinished. Most softwoods that are seen have to be painted, varnished or stained. As a general rule, softwoods are more cost-effective than hardwoods.

Softwood	Description
Cedar, Western red	Reddish-brown **wood grain**, good resistance to rot and insects; popular for outdoor use; colour does fade with time; nails can work loose and surface dents easily.
Fir, Douglas	Pinkish-brown wood grain; popular in house building – very strong and quite cheap; knot-free wood sometimes sold as British Columbian pine; can crack easily outdoors and does not paint well.
Hemlock	General purpose softwood used for doors, floors, joists, etc.; strong and easily worked but not good for outdoor use or for being painted. It can also be used for structural timber.
Parana pine	Fine-textured wood, attractive cream or brown, often knot-free; very strong but can warp easily; splits outdoors and has a poor surface for painting.
Redwood	Most popular for the home carpenter – inexpensive, reliable and easy to work with; good for painting; also known as Scots pine, Baltic pine and red deal.
Whitewood	Like redwood but softer, with a finer texture; cream wood does not darken with age or absorb preservatives, so not used outdoors.
Yew	Orange to brown in colour; very heavy and close grained; often used by cabinetmakers.

Hardwoods

Hardwoods are much more visually appealing than softwoods but can be very costly. They finish well and are used on items that are to be seen. Hardwoods are often used as veneers to improve the appearance of cheap framed items, while keeping costs down, e.g. bedroom furniture or kitchen units. Using veneers also contributes to sustainability by saving on valuable resources.

Sustainability

Timber is frequently used in the construction industry, so it is important to recycle and design with re-use in mind. Wood has a

Functional Skills

Explain five differences between hardwoods and softwoods.

tendency to warp, bend, split or cup if not seasoned correctly, and this usually prevents it from being used.

Hardwoods are a scarce commodity and can be very expensive and are therefore often used as veneers. A lot of softwoods are now regularly recycled in order to produce manufactured boards. These are then used within the construction industry and play a key role in the design of most new buildings. Managed forests have also been developed in order to replenish diminishing levels of timber.

> **Wood grain** – the direction of growth and natural fibres in the wood

Hardwood	Description
Ash	Pale colour; many uses – panelling, flooring, etc.; often used for tool handles.
Beech	Pale brown, straight grain; often used for furniture to create a frame for veneering; not used much outdoors.
Cherry	Orange sheen and wavy grain; used as a veneer more than a solid; often chosen by cabinetmakers and craftsmen.
Chestnut	Similar to ash but not as expensive; can substitute for oak.
Elm	Brown, rough grain; very durable; now scarce owing to Dutch Elm disease.
Iroko	Rich red, brown grain; hardwearing; can be used indoors and outdoors; a cheap substitute for teak.
Jelutong	Pale colour, smooth surface; good for carving as it has a soft grain.
Mahogany	Fantastic appearance; often used as a veneer but also as solid wood, though expensive; several types available, each with different appearance.
Meranti	Usually used as a substitute for mahogany; cheaper, easier to work with and good appearance.
Oak	British oak is durable and very tough; expensive and can be difficult to work with or glue; liable to split when nailed.
Sapele	Looks like mahogany but cheaper; tendency to warp; normally acquired as veneer because staining can be patchy.
Teak	Rich brown colour, often used as veneer; resistant to rot, water and fire – ideal for use outdoors.
Walnut	Mid-brown grain, often with a swirling pattern; associated with antique furniture; often used as veneer.

Activity 5.12

1 Try to find out what sort of countries produce softwoods and hardwoods. How do you think this might affect the woods' different properties? Further the investigation by creating a table that includes a description of their appearance and the cost of a particulaar wood.

2 Why are there so many different types of hardwoods?

Just checking

✱ What are the main differences between softwoods and hardwoods?

✱ Which woods are best suited to outdoor use?

✱ What factors come into choosing wood, apart from the purpose?

5.13 Carpentry and joinery 3: Manufactured boards

Manufactured boards are widely used in the construction industry and are specified for a variety of jobs. Recycled materials can be used to produce manufactured boards, saving on natural resources. There are many other advantages of using manufactured boards, as you will find out.

Manufactured boards

Manufactured boards can be relatively inexpensive when compared to softwoods and hardwoods – a great advantage when large quantities are needed. They are also available in large sheets, so can cover vast areas quickly: for example, flooring or roofing. The appearance is usually poor, so they need either to be finished or to be used where they will not be visible.

Manufactured boards are hard to join and chisel, but can be cut easily. The fact that they are manufactured means that they are in regular supply. They do not have a natural grain, and contain resins and glues, so they can be hard to work with, although they are durable and hardwearing. Manufactured boards that are used to cover large areas need supporting, as sheets may bend if they are being used to bridge a gap.

Manufactured board	Description
Plywood	Made up from an odd number of layers each usually 1.5 mm thick; the grain of each layer is at right angles to the layer either side of it; can range from 3 to 18 mm in thickness; different grades: INT for indoor use, WBP weather and boil proof, EXT for exterior use.
Blockboard	Inner part made from strips of softwood glued together; core sandwiched between two layers of wood; usually 12 to 25 mm thick; not suitable for outdoor use.
Chipboard	Small pieces of wood glued together to form board; cheaper than plywood and blockboard; often used as base for kitchen units and bedroom furniture; poor appearance; not suitable for outdoor use.
Medium Density Fibreboard (MDF)	Smooth finish, available in a range of sizes and thicknesses; can be used for panel boards or wall lining; not suitable for outdoor use; often used as base of veneered furniture.
Hardboard	Usually available in 3 to 6 mm in thicknesses; often used for covering floors, doors and drawer bottoms; smooth finish, easily decorated.

Advantages and disadvantages

Advantages	Disadvantages
Available in large flat sheets, e.g. plywood.	Thin sheets do not stay flat unless supported.
Do not warp as much as natural timbers owing to good dimensional stability.	Sharp tools required when cutting; tools easily blunted.
Can be finished/decorated in different ways.	Can be difficult to join with traditional joining methods.
MDF and plywood sheets now more flexible – can bend round shape and formers.	Cutting and sanding can generate hazardous dust.
Not natural resources so they save on valuable resources.	Need decorating to improve appearance.
Waste material can be recycled and used to manufacture new boards.	Have to be treated to ensure that they become waterproof and suitable for outdoor use.
Relatively inexpensive compared to hardwoods.	

Plywood and blockboard are the most expensive manufactured boards, with hardboard being the cheapest. Manufactured boards have to be treated in order to withstand outdoor conditions, and are generally used for flooring or covering large areas quickly. There are no natural defects in manufactured boards, so buying can be done without the need to examine them for the best quality. Veneers can be used to improve the appearance and they can also have a melamine coating to protect them and to change the style or colour.

Sustainability

Manufactured boards are frequently used in the construction industry. As they are man-made, they dramatically reduce the amount of natural resources used. They are often made from recycled materials, which again reduces wastage. These materials are also hard wearing and will last a long time and so will not need to be replaced regularly.

Activity 5.13

1 Architraves, mouldings and skirting boards are now often made from manufactured boards such as MDF. Explain why this is.

2 Many softwoods and hardwoods can vary in quality. Explain why manufactured boards are more consistent and how this can be an advantage? Investigate how they are manufactured and how this in turn saves expense for the consumer.

Just checking

* What are the main types of manufactured board?
* Why is manufactured board popular in the modern construction industry?
* How does using manufactured board promote sustainability?

5.14 Carpentry and joinery 4: Miscellaneous materials

There are many different miscellaneous materials used throughout the construction industry. Some are visible, others are hidden, but all are needed to allow jobs and tasks to be achieved successfully. These materials range from **adhesives** to sliding door gear, and our buildings just couldn't be buildings without them!

All sorts of different materials and items are used to construct and finish off buildings. **Door ironmongery** is just one example. Items such as locks, bolts, letter plates, knockers and handles are all frequently used in construction but as 'trimmings' they fall under the miscellaneous umbrella. There are many different types of locks, bolts, letterplates, knockers and handles available, all of which are commonly used in manufacturing interior and exterior doors.

MISCELLANY MIND MAP

List as many items as you can that are classed as miscellaneous within your classroom. Remember – do not include standard materials such as timber, glass or brickwork.

Rising butt hinger

Tee hinge

Mortise dead lock

Band bolt

Just some of the miscellaneous materials used in the manufacture of doors

Adhesives

Adhesives are substances used to bond surfaces together. Because of their chemical nature, there are a number of potentially serious risks connected with adhesives so they must be stored, used and handled correctly.

The most common adhesive used in schools is waterbased PVA, which is relatively cheap and takes little time to apply. Casein is also used in schools; it is more expensive and takes longer to apply, but is waterproof and therefore can be used outdoors. Other types of adhesive can be seen in the picture opposite.

Activity 5.14

1. Why are the items named in this topic classed as miscellaneous materials?

2. Take a tour of your classroom. List as many miscellaneous materials as you can that are used in second fixing. Write down what type of miscellaneous materials they are and what job they are performing.

3. Why are these materials so important when constructing a building? Make a list of your reasons.

A range of adhesives

Fixings

There are lots of different types of fixings that are regularly used to help with the construction of buildings. Anything from a corner wall plate to a plastic plug can be classed as a miscellaneous material. These items will be used for many jobs all over the building, and many can help decrease the time taken during the construction process. They can also make construction a lot easier, as they are designed to help complete specific jobs.

The 'fixings' category includes items such as nails, screws, pins, bolts, washers, rivets and plugs. Each type of fixing is carefully designed to fit a specific purpose.

> **Adhesive** – glue
>
> **Door ironmongery** – any metal items that are associated or used with doors

Fixing	Types
Screws	head type, countersunk, raised or rounded head, minor screw head, pan head, flange head, mirror
Plates	hanger, wall, corner, stretcher
Cramps	galvanised steel frame
Hangers	timber-to-timber joist, TW-type, TWR-type, hooked joist
Anchors	Framing, nylon, plastic, collapsible, metal collapsible, rubber sleeve
Toggles	gravity, spring
Plugs	plastic, moulded plastic, proprietary, hammer
Hinges	standard crank butt, cast butt, rising butt, loose pin butt, helical or double action
Nails	lost head, oval wire, annular, ring, round wire, star-shaped, masonry, anchor bolts
Others	star dowels, pull handles, gear, tooth washers, tooth plate connectors, restraint straps, zinc plated screw ties, frame fixings

Carpentry fixings

The image opposite shows the different methods for attaching joists. Where the old method is used, you can see the effect that damp walls can have on timber. Using the TW-type hanger is much quicker, and the fixing is much stronger.

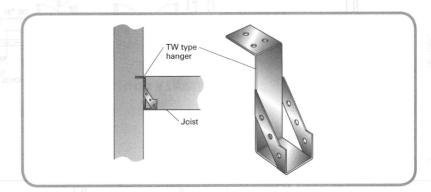

TW-type hanger

Just checking

* What does miscellaneous mean?
* What broad categories of materials come under the 'miscellaneous' umbrella?
* How can miscellaneous materials make a job quicker or better?

5.15 Carpentry and joinery 5: Quality control

Quality control is an important factor when considering building materials. Materials that are selected for a job need to be tested for quality. Tests may come in the form of recording tolerances or just performing a visual check. Many different factors affect the quality of materials.

Conversion and seasoning

Once trees have been felled, they need to be cut into usable planks. This can be done by a number of methods, including: through and through, tangential, quarter, boxed heart.

The way that the wood is converted can have an effect on the quality of the wood itself. For example, through and through sawing can make the wood prone to large amounts of shrinkage or distortion. The tangential sawn timber is often used for floor joists and beams, as it provides the strongest timber. Quarter-sawn timber is the most expensive as it takes the longest to produce and creates the most waste, but it is the best quality of all the **conversion** techniques used. Boxed heart sawn timber is normally used when the heart of the tree is ruined. The wood that is cut is often used for boards, because boards made from this style of wood will not distort easily.

Timber has a natural content of moisture. This is gathered during tree growth and stored in the timber even after the tree has been felled. The moisture must be removed to ensure that there are minimal defects after use.

There are two main ways of drying out the wood: air **seasoning** and kiln seasoning. Air seasoning is much cheaper, but is a longer process. These treatments need to be done to ensure that the wood is of good quality for use.

Quality control

The testing of materials is very important when constructing structures. A material's tolerance needs to be taken into consideration by the architects, so that they can pick the most suitable material for the intended job. Quality control can also come in the form of selecting materials through a visual test, e.g. whether the material is aesthetically pleasing, or that it does not contain defects to surfaces. Other quality control tests may be done on site, such as checking for glue runs, or examining dry assembling joints to ensure that they fit together successfully and accurately before any adhesives are added.

Quality control could be simply measuring and checking throughout the construction process, making sure that materials are stored correctly when not in use, and working to any accepted guidelines and standards during construction.

QUALITY COUNTS

Can you imagine what would happen in the construction industry if there were no controls on quality? Who would suffer? What might happen? Discuss your thoughts with a partner before reading on.

Conversion – the process of cutting trunks into usable planks of wood

Seasoning – the removal of moisture from timber after conversion has taken place

Activity 5.15

1 Name three different visual checks that could be carried out on a piece of timber.

2 Why is experience an advantage when employing a carpenter or joiner? Think from the viewpoint of an employer and of a future owner of the project that they will be working on. List the advantages and disadvantages of using an experienced joiner.

3 Carpenters and joiners often 'dry assemble' joints. What does this involve and why is it used? Write a brief report.

Timber seasoning defects	Timber natural defects
Bowing – bad stacking during seasoning (drying out of timber) causes the wood to bow; can ruin the wood or means that it can only be used as short lengths.	Heart shakes – caused mainly by disease; the inner trunk shrinks while the outer stays its original shape.
Springing – during seasoning, inner stresses cause the boards to curve towards the edges.	Cup or ring shakes – separation of the annual rings, normally due to bad weather such as wind.
Winding or twist – caused by either poor stacking or seasoning. The wood is almost ruined and can only be used as short lengths.	Star shakes – cracks around outside of the log, caused by the inside staying its original size while the outer shrinks.
Cupping – caused through shrinkage during drying – most common in flat sawn boards.	Knots, mark the start of branch growth; can be 'dead' which are often loose and fall out; but live knots are not a real problem although, if large, are weak structurally.
Shaking – the board is dried too quickly, causing it to crack, usually along the grain.	
Collapse – rarely occurs but is caused by drying out too quickly, so that the cells collapse.	
Case hardening – caused by drying out too quickly – the outer cells become hard, sealing off the inner moisture.	

Bowing

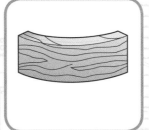
Springing

Winding (or twist)

Cupping

Shaking

Collapse

case hardening

Just checking

* What is the purpose of quality control?
* How can conversion and seasoning affect the way wood reacts to its environment?
* What tests can be done to determine whether the material is best for a job?

The efficient transportation, storage and use of resources is very important within the construction industry. If natural resources are treated correctly during construction, there is only minimal wastage. The cost of buildings can be reduced when materials are used efficiently, because little will need to be scrapped or recycled. Both planks and sheet materials can easily be ruined if not transported and stored correctly or used efficiently.

Storing sheet material

All sheet materials should be stored in a warm, dry place, ideally stacked flat on timber **cross-bearers**, spaced close enough together to prevent sagging. Alternatively, where space is limited, sheet material can be stored on edge in a **purpose-made rack**, which allows the sheets to rest against the backboard in a true plane. Leaning sheets against walls on edge or on end is not recommended, as they will take to on a bow that is difficult to reverse. Sheet material needs to be stored correctly to ensure that the cost of materials is kept to a minimum.

Timber that is supplied in shrink-wrapped plastic packs should be stored in them until required for use. Care must be taken not to damage the plastic. Veneered or other finished surfaced sheets should be stored good face to good face, to minimise the risk of surface scratching.

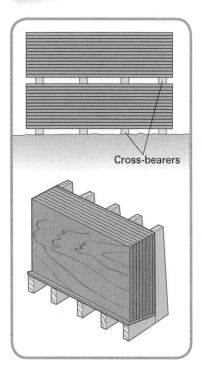

Cross-bearers

Materials should be stored like this in order to prevent unnecessary damage or sagging

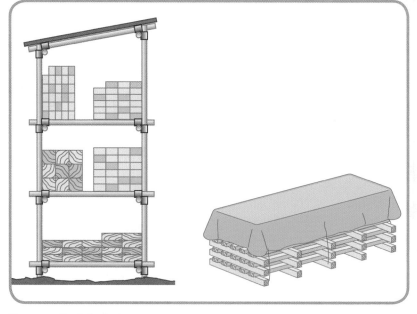

Storage methods for timber

Using sheet material

Sheet material should not be used wastefully. Material should be marked out and cut in such a way that it maximises the amount of timber used and minimises the waste, whether cutting regular or irregular shapes. When ordering materials, time should be taken to make sure that there is minimal wastage: for instance, floor joists ordered for a particular room should be planned and calculated to give as little wastage as possible.

Storing adhesives and other hazardous substances

Adhesives, finishes and other hazardous substances would have to be stored in a secure metal cabinet and the requirements of the COSHH regulations must be fully met. The contractor would be required to keep on-site a file of info detailing how to correctly handle, store and use the material together with the actions necessary in the event of spillage, contact with skin, contact with eyes, swallowing etc.

Sustainability

A lot of natural resources are used throughout construction, so it is important that any work carried out should be completed efficiently. Materials can become damaged and wasted during transportation and storage, so this needs to be planned and carried out effectively, with the aid of storage racks and cross-bearers. Materials should be picked for the job, so that they achieve their maximum lifespan and do not need to be replaced too often.

How a typical floor with stairwell would be constructed and how the floor joists would need to be arranged to minimise wastage

Activity 5.16

1 Explain why flat storage is recommended for doors, frames and sheet materials. What would happen if sheet material was not stored correctly?

2 What is the purpose of covering stored building materials? Why is it done and what advantages does it bring to both the contractor and the future owner?

3 Imagine that you are in charge of a materials store, and have to train some new recruits. Write out the key bullet points, in order of importance, that you would want them to remember at the end of their training.

Cross-bearers – timber used to help stack materials correctly

Purpose-made rack – an item manufactured to allow materials to be stored without getting damaged

Just checking

✱ Why do materials need to be transported and stored correctly?

✱ What impact does correct use of materials have on waste?

✱ What other benefits come from the efficient use of resources?

5.17 Carpentry and joinery 7: Wood joints

JOINING THINGS TOGETHER!

Think about why there are so many wood joints that can be used in construction. What are they for? Why have different kinds? Write down some of your thoughts.

A wood joint is a way of joining two or more pieces of wood together securely. Wood joints are used extensively within the construction industry by carpenters and joiners. Many parts of the building have to be **fabricated** using wood joints, which vary in type and size. Hand tools are normally used to produce wood joints, but power tools are also used. Here you will find out the main types of wood joint used and how they are prepared.

Wood joints

This diagram shows the materials and wood joints that would be required for just one item, a typical garden planter.

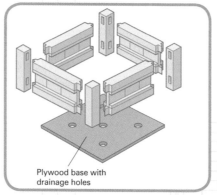

Plywood base with drainage holes

Materials and joints needed for a typical garden planter

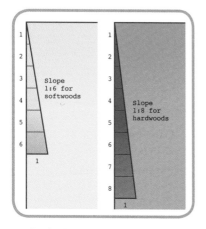

Angle of a dovetail joint

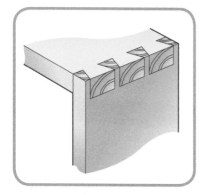

Example of a dovetail joint

Many different types of wood joints are used within the construction industry. When a wood joint is required, a skilled carpenter or joiner would use a range of tools and equipment to manufacture the most suitable one for the job. The wood must be marked out accurately and then the material removed using the correct tools. A trained carpenter or joiner would be able to create a wood joint with ease and this would be produced very quickly and very accurately. Joints are used throughout the building and are of different types such as: mitre joint, bridle joint, mortice and tenon joints.

Wood joints can also be produced using power tools, and this can have the advantage of all the joints being manufactured exactly the same and very quickly. A typical example of this would be a biscuit router, which allows large planks of wood to be joined together in strips to protect them from defects such as bowing. When wood joints are used, they enable the item to be manufactured securely as they provide a large surface area to apply the adhesive to, as you can see in the diagram. Wood joints are commonly used on windows and doors but can be included in features throughout the building, e.g. architraves, skirting boards. They are also an essential part of flat pack assembly units, used in the bathroom, bedroom and kitchen.

Wood joint

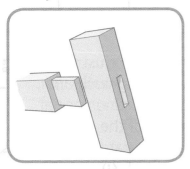

Through mortice and tenon

This joint can be used on windows and doors. Material is removed to allow room for part of another piece of wood to be placed tightly into position.

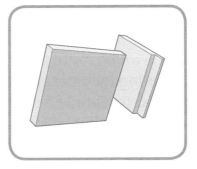

Lap joint

The correct amount of material is cut away from one piece of wood to allow another piece of wood to fit into place.

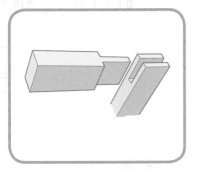

Corner bridle joint

Often used in making gates or doors. This joint provides strength to the item and is suitable for corners.

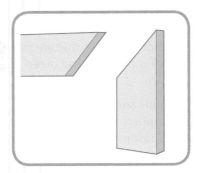

Mitre joint

One end of each of two pieces of wood is cut at 45°, so that when placed and glued together they form a 90° angle.

Fabricated – to put together, make from parts or create

Health and Safety

There are several health and safety issues you should consider when preparing wood joints. PPE (see pages 116–117) should also be worn.

* Tools should be kept sharp and stored appropriately when not in place.
* Never use a tool for a job for which it was not intended.
* Tools should not be forced – let the tool do the work.
* Work areas should be kept clean.
* Work pieces should be secured before any work is done.
* Hands should be kept away from sharp tools and teeth or blades.

Just checking

* What is the purpose of wood joints?
* What are the main types of wood joint?
* What health and safety considerations are there when preparing wood joints?

5.18 Painting and decorating 1: Decoration

There is much more to decorating than just painting. Decorating includes painting, hanging wallpaper, applying textured finishes and producing special finishes and effects. After the work of the decorator is completed, rooms are further decorated with furnishings, curtains, pictures and ornaments. The way a room is decorated can change the way it feels and can have a psychological effect on its users.

SETTING THE MOOD

Think about a room in your own home – perhaps your bedroom. Write down some ideas about how you could decorate it to make it more comfortable. Remember – furniture, fixtures and fittings can all have an effect on how the room will make you feel.

Tints – colours with white added

Shades – colours with black added

Colour

Colour is one of the most important factors in creating the right atmosphere in a room. Some colours are used to make a room feel warm or cool; others are used because of the way in which the room is used. Colour schemes that are mainly red, orange or yellow can make a room feel warm; blue and green colour schemes make a room feel cooler.

Restaurants are often decorated in very bold warm colours. This creates an atmosphere that is initially welcoming but, after time, can make you feel a bit restless. This effect helps to ensure that once they have eaten customers will leave the restaurant and make space for the next customer.

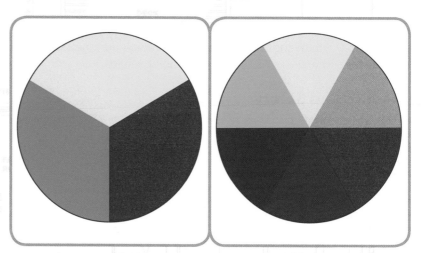

Three-part colour wheel   *Six-part colour wheel*

In basic colour theory there are three primary colours: red, yellow and blue. These cannot be made by mixing any other colours together. Secondary colours are produced by mixing two primary colours together: red and yellow mixed together make orange, red and blue make purple, and blue and yellow make green.

A colour scheme that uses two colours that are opposite each other on the colour wheel is called a complementary colour scheme. A colour scheme that is based on **tints** and **shades** of a single colour is known as a monochromatic colour scheme.

Texture

Texture can be used to create the right feel in a room in many ways. It is often seen as the concern of the interior designer, who may recommend the use of rugs, curtains, cushions or other soft furnishings to introduce texture to a room. However, there are also a number of ways in which the decorator can use texture. For example, materials such as Artex™ are often used on ceilings to produce various effects or patterns. Such materials can also be applied to walls and, used effectively, can give a room a rustic feel or make it seem informal or relaxed.

Another way in which the decorator can use texture is by hanging wallpapers with a textured finish or an embossed pattern. One such wallpaper is Lincrusta Walton™, a putty-like material that is rolled onto a heavy paper backing with patterned rollers to produce a range of effects. Other wallpapers, such as blown vinyl or Anaglypta™ are much cheaper and simpler to hang; they come in a wider range of patterns, and can be used to similar effect in adding texture to a room.

Lincrusta Walton wallpaper

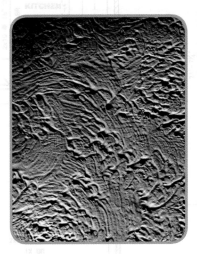

A broken leather effect produced with Artex™

Case Study

Harriet has a decorating business, and employs seven decorators. She has been asked to submit a tender for a contract with a locally owned food chain to carry out the redecoration and refurbishment of several restaurants. Using your knowledge of decoration, and through further research, try to answer the following questions:

1 One of the restaurants has an area that attracts a lot of direct sunlight and becomes very warm, particularly during the summer months. What colours or colour schemes could Harriet recommend to help make this area feel cooler?

2 In one of the restaurants the walls, ceilings, doors and other surfaces are all smooth, and the seating areas feel clinical. What sort of materials could be used to give the restaurant a more welcoming feel?

3 In one of the restaurants, the owner has suggested a colour scheme based on pastel colours. What does that mean?

Just checking

✳ What are tertiary colours?

✳ Which colours could be used to create a feeling of warmth in a room?

✳ What is a complementary colour scheme?

5.19 Painting and decorating 2: Tools and equipment

TOOLS FOR THE JOB!

Painters and decorators put the finishing touches to any building or structure. Take a few moments to write down as many reasons as you can think of for applying paint. There are more than you might at first think!

As with any craftsperson or professional working in the construction industry, painters and decorators need a range of specialist tools and equipment to enable them to do their job. Some of the tools are used for preparing surfaces, some for applying paints, stains, varnishes and glazes, some for applying textured finishes and some for hanging wallpaper.

Tools

Some of a painter and decorator's tools will be for routine everyday work and others for much more specialised work. The photographs below and oppposite show the tools required to build a basic toolkit for routine work as well as some specialist equipment.

Stripping knife/scraper

Filling knife

Shave hooks

Basic toolbox

The best quality scrapers and filling knives have a one-piece blade and **tang** that runs the full length of the knife.

This helps to make the knife strong enough to perform heavy-duty work.

Dusting brush

Paper hanging brush

Plumb bob and line

Flat brushes

Tang – the metal piece that goes into the handle of a scraper or knife

Woodwork – all of the elements of a room that are made of wood, e.g. skirting, doors

Cross-lining – hanging lining paper horizontally on a wall

LPG – liquid petroleum gas

Broken colour – multi-coloured effects

Case Study

Alex is an apprentice painter and decorator working for a small domestic decorating company. He has been given the task of stripping the wallpaper in a large dining room, painting the ceiling and **woodwork**, and **cross-lining** and papering the walls. Using your knowledge of tools and equipment, carry out the following tasks:

* List all of the tools and equipment that Alex will need.
* Write a brief description of what Alex will use each tool for.
* List the three shapes that shavehooks are available in.
* Write a brief explanation of the difference between a filling knife and a scraper.

LPG torch/gun

Hot air gun/stripper

Steam strippers

Overgrainer

Extension pole

Roller tray

Scuttle

Mottler

Drag brush

Pencil overgrainer

Stippling brush

Flogger

Equipment

There is also a wide range of equipment that is needed to carry out painting and decorating work. Again, some equipment is needed for everyday work and some is needed for much more specialist work. Some of the basic equipment needed for routine work is shown above and opposite.

Specialist tools

These tools are used for specialist work, such as applying textured finishes and creating special effects such as graining, marbling, stencilling and **broken colour** work.

Softeners can be made using either badger hair or pure bristle and are used to 'soften' a finish by removing any harsh edges in a specialist effect. Badger hair is softer than pure bristle and can be used with both oil-based and water-based materials, while bristle softeners are best used only with oil-based materials.

Health and Safety

To reduce the risk of fire when using **LPG** torches you should always stop burning off at least 30 minutes before the end of the working day. You can then check that no areas are still smouldering before leaving.

Just checking

* What type of finish would you need a stippling brush for?
* What piece of equipment would a decorator use to help remove old wallpaper?
* What shows how good a scraper or filling knife is?

5.20 Painting and decorating 3: Materials

Painters and decorators use a wide range of materials in the work that they do. Some of the materials are used to help clean and prepare surfaces, and some are to provide finishes. The range of materials used includes paints, stains, varnishes, glazes and wallpapers.

Acrylic – a resin that is used in some water-based paints

Tub paste – a ready-mixed wallpaper adhesive that is often used for heavier wallpapers and vinyls

Embossed – a pattern that is raised from the surface of the paper

Surface preparation materials

Before applying paints and other finishes it is important to make sure that all surfaces are clean, smooth and free from dust or grease.

Sugar soap	Cleaning material – looks a bit like sugar when in powder form; mix with water to use.
Liquid paint remover	Solvent- or water-based – it is painted onto old paint films so they blister and can then be scraped off.
Shellac knotting	Methylated spirit-based – applied over knots in timber to stop resin seeping out and damaging paint film.
Fillers and stoppers	Powder-based or ready-mixed – used to fill cracks, holes or other surface defects before painting.

Paints, stains, varnishes and glazes

These are either solvent- or water-based. Traditionally, painters and decorators opted for solvent-based materials, which are thinned with white spirit, methylated spirit or some other solvent, depending on the material being used. However, because of improvements in manufacturing, quality of finish and the increasing need to protect the environment, water-based paints are now more widely used.

Case Study

Phil works for a local decorator and has been asked to talk to a customer and make some recommendations about what finishes to use for some decorating that they want doing. Using what you have learnt about decorating materials, try to complete the following:

1 Recommend a material that can be used on new timber to prevent the resin from seeping out of the knots.

2 Recommend a suitable adhesive for use with the vinyl wallpaper that the customer has chosen for the lounge.

3 Suggest three types of wallpaper that could be painted over for use in the hallway.

4 Suggest a material that could be used on the pine floorboards to create an oak colour.

Primer	First coat applied to surface; different primers used for different surfaces such as wood, metal, plaster, plastic, etc.
Acrylic primer/ undercoat	Water-based wood primer, also used as undercoat before water-based gloss; dries very quickly.
Undercoat	Applied after primers but before finishes; helps to cover what is underneath build firm thickness and give to good surface for finish.
Alkyd gloss	Solvent-based finish; hardwearing and easy to clean.
Water-based gloss	Sometimes called **acrylic** gloss, not such a high-gloss finish as solvent-based, but dries quickly; brushes can be cleaned with water.
Emulsion	Available in matt, soft sheen or silk finish, water-based; mainly for internal walls and ceilings.
Eggshell	Water- or solvent-based finish; dries to low sheen.
Masonry paint	Water-based finish, smooth or textured, for external walls.
Varnish	Clear finish in matt, satin or gloss, solvent- or water-based.
Wood stain	Used to change colour of timber, does not usually protect surface; varnish can be applied over top of stain to protect it.
Scumble glaze	Solvent- or water-based clear glaze mixed with coloured stain to make semi-transparent glaze; used for broken colour work or special effects .

Wallpapers and pastes

There are several different types of wallpaper, and a range of different pastes are used to hang them. Preparatory wallpapers are those that need to be painted or papered over, including lining paper, wood ingrain, blown vinyl and Anaglypta™. Finish wallpapers are those that require no further treatment once they have been hung, including standard, washable and **embossed**. There is also a range of more specialist wallpapers available, including contract width vinyl, Lincrusta, hessian and flock.

Which paste for which paper?	
Lining paper	Cellulose or starch paste
Wood ingrain	Cellulose or starch paste
Blown vinyl	**Tub paste**
Vinyl	Cellulose or tub paste
Lincrusta	Lincrusta glue
Contract width vinyl	Tub paste (N.B. the wall should be pasted, not the paper)

Just checking

* What is the key difference between a preparatory wallpaper and a finish wallpaper?
* What is shellac knotting used for?
* Why are water-based paints used more often these days?

5.21 Painting and decorating 4: Painting

WHAT FOUR?

Look at the four reasons for painting listed here. Write down what each of them means and, for each of them, give an example of where paint is used in this way.

As far back as anyone can remember, people have been decorating their homes, including using paint. Painting is about much more than just making a room look nice. There are actually four reasons for painting: decoration, identification, protection and **sanitation**. Whenever paint is applied to a surface, it is for one of those four reasons.

The work of the painter and decorator involves much more than just painting. First, surfaces have to be properly prepared by removing dirt, dust, grease and old paint finishes that are cracked or flaking. Old wallpapers also need to be removed, and the surface needs to be washed to make sure that all of the old paste has been removed. If surfaces are not clean, any new paint or wallpaper will not be able to stick properly.

Surface preparation

A sound surface is one that has been previously painted but is in generally good condition. There may be some small areas where the coating has broken down and there is flaking, cracking, blistering or peeling. Areas like this will need to be scraped off, and primer must be applied to the bare surface underneath. Removing small areas of paint and applying primer to the bare surface underneath is called **spot priming**. Unsound surfaces are those on which the coating has broken down over the majority of the surface area. These surfaces must be completely stripped, cleaned and primed before applying further finishes.

Examples of a sound and an unsound surface

Case Study

Harriet is a painter and decorator who has been asked to decorate the rooms in a new house. Using your knowledge of painting, answer these questions.

1 What would be a suitable water-based paint system for the softwood skirting and doorframes in the lounge?

2 What technique will Harriet use to ensure that brush marks are kept to a minimum?

3 What would be the most suitable method of paint application for the walls?

4 Recommend one possible paint system for the hardwood floor in the hallway.

Application techniques

Sanitation – when referring to paint, it means providing a surface or finish that is easy to keep clean

Spot priming – applying primer to small areas that have been stripped to the bare surface

Laying off – using the tips of the brush to ensure that the paint you have applied is even. Laying off also reduces brush marks

Paint systems

Most surfaces that are painted require more than one coat of paint. Moreover, there is usually more than one type of paint involved. Taken together, all of the coats that are used, from the first coat – the primer – to the finish coat, are called a paint system. This table shows some examples of common paint systems used on different surfaces.

Application methods

Paint and other surface finishes can be applied in a number of different ways. Most domestic painting is carried out using either a brush or a roller. However, other methods include spray, paint pad, paint mitten or dipping. When using a brush, there are three basic actions: brushing the paint on, cutting in and **laying off**.

Surface	Paint system	Number of coats	Solvent-based?	Water-based?
Softwood	Shellac knotting	2	Yes	No
	Wood primer	1		Yes
	Undercoat	2 or 3		Yes
	Finish – e.g.			Yes
	● Gloss	1		
	● pt Eggshell	2		
Plaster	Emulsion	2 or 3	No	Yes
	● pt Matt			
	● Soft sheen			
	● Silk			
Plastic	Usually thinned gloss	2	Yes	No
Hardwood	Clear or coloured varnish	2 or 3	Yes	Yes
	Clear or coloured wax	2 or 3		

Just checking

✱ What are the four reasons for painting?

✱ What is an unsound surface?

✱ What methods of application are there?

5.22 Painting and decorating 5: Wallpapering

After painting, the hanging of wallpaper is probably the most common way of providing a decorative finish. There are many different types of wallpaper including preparatory papers, relief papers, vinyl papers, washable papers, simplex papers, duplex papers and ready-pasted papers. As well as providing a finish for a surface, wallpapers serve other purposes, as you will discover.

Types of wallpaper

Preparatory wallpapers are those that do not provide the final finish to a surface. For example, lining paper is often used to cross-line walls before the finish paper is hung. Cross-lining helps to provide a smooth surface with an even **porosity**, to assist the adhesion of the paper that is hung on top of it. This table shows some common wallpapers, their uses and the best type of adhesive to use.

Wallpaper name	Type	Common uses	Adhesive
Lining paper	Preparatory	Cross-lining walls and ceilings, sometimes hung and painted over	Starch paste Cellulose paste
Vinyl	Finish	Often used in 'high traffic' areas because it can be wiped clean	Cellulose Tub paste
Anaglypta™	Preparatory	Used on walls and ceilings to provide a surface that can easily be repainted, to change colour or simply to freshen up the existing colour scheme	Starch paste Cellulose paste
Blown vinyl	Preparatory	Similar to Anaglypta™ in its use, but easier to strip as it is a peelable duplex paper	Tub paste
Simplex patterned paper	Finish	Cheap finish paper for general use on walls	Cellulose paste

Lining paper is available in a range of different grades from 400 which is very thin to 1000 which is a thick, heavy paper. It is also available in single, double, triple or quadruple roll lengths.

Wallpaper symbols

When producing wallpapers, manufacturers provide pasting and hanging instructions that give the decorator essential information to ensure that the wallpaper is prepared and hung correctly. As well as instructions about pasting and soaking time, wallpaper labels tell the decorator which batch the individual roll is from. It is important to ensure that, when a wallpapering job is carried out, only rolls from the same batch are used. This will help to ensure that there is no difference in the shade or colour between rolls. Most manufacturers use a set of international symbols to provide key information about their wallpapers, some of which you can see in this table.

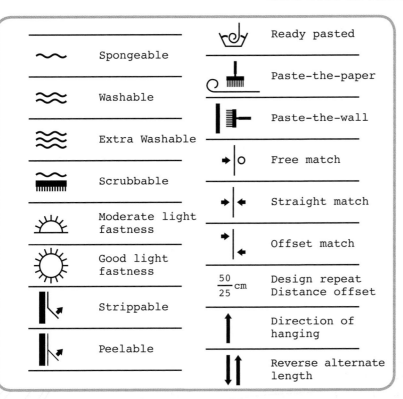

∼	Spongeable		Ready pasted
≋	Washable		Paste-the-paper
≋	Extra Washable		Paste-the-wall
≈	Scrubbable	→|o	Free match
☀	Moderate light fastness	→|←	Straight match
☀	Good light fastness	→|←	Offset match
	Strippable	$\frac{50}{25}$ cm	Design repeat Distance offset
	Peelable	↑	Direction of hanging
		↓↑	Reverse alternate length

International wallpaper symbols

Case Study

Some domestic customers have asked their decorator to make some recommendations about what wallpapers would best meet their needs when redecorating their lounge, bedroom and hall, stairs and landing. Using your knowledge of wallpapers and pastes, and by carrying out further research, answer these questions.

1 One wall in the lounge is subject to a lot of direct sunlight. What wallpaper property would help to minimise fading? What international wallpaper symbol would you find on the label?

2 In the hallway, the customers would like a wallpaper with a raised pattern, that could be left on even if they want to change the colour scheme in the future. Name two wallpapers they could use.

3 On the label of a wallpaper that the customer has chosen, $\frac{50}{25}$ cm' is shown. What does it mean?

4 The customer would like to use a wallpaper for the bedroom that will be easy to remove next time they decorate. What wallpaper could be recommended?

Porosity – the extent to which a surface will absorb moisture; a porous surface will absorb more moisture than a non-porous surface

Just checking

✳ What wall covering has a raised pattern produced by embossing a putty-like material onto heavy paper?

✳ Why does wallpaper sometimes blister?

✳ What types of material are classed as specialist wall coverings?

5.23 Painting and decorating 6: Quality control and common defects

PAINT AND PAPER

There are three main types of defect in decorating: surface defects (painting), paint film defects and defects of surface coverings (wallpapering). Try to list as many paint film defects and defects of surface coverings as you can think of.

A wide range of defects can occur when carrying out decorating work. Some are surface defects, some are defects in the paint finish and some are defects of surface coverings. For example, if gloss paint is applied and has runs in it, it is a paint film defect; if there are bubbles in wallpaper when it dries, it is a defect with a surface covering; and a wall that is painted but has holes on it has surface defects.

Surface defects

Surface defects refer to problems with the surface that is to be decorated, ranging from scratches, dents and holes to mould and fungus growth, dry rot and **efflorescence**. Usually any surface defects would be corrected before decoration and, if treated properly, should not cause any further problems.

Causes and treatments

Defect	Cause	Treatment
Dry rot – a fungus which attacks timber	Timber with a moisture content over 20% in a humid environment with poor ventilation	Stop cause of dampness and/or increase ventilation, remove all affected areas, and treat surrounding areas with wood preservative
Holes, scratches, cracks	Cracks – often caused by surface shrinkage and holes and dents, usually through some kind of rough treatment	**Rake out** cracks to remove loose material before filling and rubbing down to smooth finish; fill and rub down holes and scratches; large holes may need filling more than once
Staining	Water, smoke, dust or old surface coatings	Most can be sealed with shellac knotting or pigmented shellac
Efflorescence	Moisture penetrates cement-based surface and causes water-soluble salts to rise to the surface; as moisture dries out, salts crystallise and stay on surface	Dry brush salts away; do not wash because salts dissolve and then reappear as surface dries

Efflorescence – the appearance of white salt crystals on the face of cement-based surfaces such as brick, block or render

Rake out – use a scraper or other tool to scrape along the middle of a crack to remove loose material before filling

Paint film defects

Some paint film defects are caused by incorrect or poor application, some by the surface that is being painted and others are due to the weather or some form of chemical breakdown.

Defects of surface coverings

Many things can go wrong when hanging wallpaper, some due to the surface and others due to the pasting or hanging of the wallpaper.

Causes and treatments	Defect	Prevention
Runs, sags, tears or curtains	Poor application	Apply paint evenly to surface and lay off properly
Bleeding – when the surface or something on the surface causes discolouration of paint film	Usually by applying paint onto surface painted with or stained by bitumen, nicotine or smoke, but also by painting over untreated knots	Seal surfaces by coating with aluminium sealer or shellac
Cissing – when paint cannot form a continuous film on the surface that it is applied to	Usually by painting onto greasy or shiny surface	Clean surfaces properly and abrade for good key for the surface coating
Blooming – when a gloss finish lacks shine	Usually by painting in damp or humid conditions, but also by applying gloss finish to insufficiently sealed absorbent surfaces	Ensure surfaces are properly sealed before painting; apply in appropriate conditions

Defect	Cause
Overlapping	Poor hanging leads to an overlap in the joint between two pieces of paper
Paste staining	Paste gets onto the face of the paper and causes stains on the surface
Creasing	Usually caused by poor hanging, over brushing or trying to manipulate the paper into an awkward position
Peeling	Usually due to poor pasting technique leading to areas being missed, paste being too thin or the incorrect paste being used
Loss of embossing	Usually caused by over brushing or applying too much pressure when hanging a relief patterned paper

Defects in paper hanging

Case Study

Mike has just taken on a contract to renovate an old manor house that has been vacant for the past 35 years. Some of the windows have been broken and the building is very cold and damp. Mike will have to overcome a number of defects to restore the property to a liveable standard. Using your knowledge of decorating defects and by carrying out further research, try to answer the following questions:

1 What action should Mike take to treat the areas that show efflorescence?

2 There has been a small fire in one bedroom. How can Mike make sure the smoke stains do not bleed through the new finishes?

3 There is a lot of dry rot. How should it be dealt with?

4 Many of the walls show extensive mould growth. How should this be treated?

Efflorescence

Key fact

Pigmented shellac usually contains aluminium for a silver colour or titanium for a white colour.

Just checking

✱ What is the most common cause of wallpaper peeling?

✱ What defect can occur if gloss paint is applied over a surface coated with bitumen?

✱ How can you prevent blooming?

5.24 Building services 1: Tools and equipment

WHAT'S IN YOUR TOOLBOX?

Look at the tools in this section and discuss with a partner the ones you are familiar with already. Quiz your partner about each tool: what is it used for, how is it used, and what safety precautions are needed when using it?

In general, 'services' means water, gas, electricity, air conditioning, heating, communications and drainage. Building services can be grouped into two categories: mechanical and electrical installations, and plumbing installations. Plumbers and electricians use a lot of basic equipment every day. You need to be able to identify the basic equipment and know what it is used for.

Tools and equipment

Tool name	Use
Spirit level	Used to check whether a component or pipe run is vertical or horizontal
Screwdriver	Many types of screwdriver are used by plumbers and electricians including cross head (Phillips and Pozidriv), slotted or normal
Hammer	A variety of hammers for different jobs: ball-pein, cross-pein, claw and lump hammers do jobs such as driving in a fixing such as a nail, levering out nails, or are used with other tools such as a cold chisel or a punch
Wrench	For gripping pipes, holding them in position, or tightening or loosening nuts and bolts
Spanner	Spanners come in four main types: ring, box, open-ended and adjustable
Pliers	Many different types of pliers for a variety of different jobs (electricians' pliers should always be insulated)
Hacksaws	For cutting metal and plastics, tube or sheet – the correct blade should be used for a given job
Tube cutters	For cutting pipes and tube – some for copper and stainless steel, others for plastic pipes
Side snips	For cutting electric wires
Electrical test meters	For measuring voltage, current and resistance
Cable strippers	For stripping the insulation from wires
Blowlamp	For heating copper pipe when soldering a joint in pipework
Files	For finishing the surface of materials such as metal or plastic – different shapes and sizes for different jobs: flat, round, half round, square etc.
Tape measure	To measure lengths of pipe etc. and for correctly positioning equipment and components
Drills	Three main types: pillar or bench drill, hand drill and power drill
Saws	Different saws for different jobs – power saws can be used for cutting floor boards to access wiring or pipework

Below are some images of common tools used by electricians and plumbers.

Spirit level

Screwdriver

Hammer

Wrench

Pliers

Hacksaw

Spanner

Side cutters

Tube cutter

Insulation stripper

Electrical test meter

Blowlamp

Files

Tape measure

Power drill

Flooring saw

Activity 5.24

1 Create a safety leaflet for the safe use of power tools. Include information on any PPE that may need to be worn when using the piece of equipment.

2 Pick three of the tools in the table that are unfamiliar to you. Investigate them further. Demonstrate to another pupil, or teacher, how this tool is to be used safely.

3 Using the Internet or a catalogue, find all of the tools in the table and write down their costs. Work out the cost of a full toolbox.

Case Study

John is an electrician who is doing some work in a house and needs to lift some floorboards to gain access to the wiring. What tools might he need to use? What safety aspects will he need to consider before starting this work? Will he have to wear any PPE? Can you write a sequence for this task in the form of a flow chart? You must include the tools and equipment used.

Health and Safety

When using any tool, it is important to use the correct tool for the job. Always use the tool in the correct way. Keep all tools clean and sharp, and do not use them if they are damaged.

Just checking

✱ What tool would you need to use for stripping insulation from wires?

✱ Why might you need to use different saws for different jobs?

✱ What health and safety check would you carry out on a power tool?

5.25 Building services 2: Materials (plumbing)

Plumbing is an ancient skill dating back to Roman times; in fact the word plumbing comes from the Latin for lead, which is what water pipes used to be made of! Many different materials are used in everyday plumbing work. It is important that you can identify the types and properties of materials used in this area in order to select the correct material for the job.

Properties of materials

Materials react in different ways to different situations. For example, some conduct electricity or heat, others don't; some are flexible, others are rigid; some are strong, others pliable.

Pipework materials

There are many factors that affect the choice of material for the installation of pipework. These include cost, appearance, pressure and water type. The two most common materials used for pipework are metal and plastics.

Metal

Copper tube is used in the plumbing industry on a large scale. It is a malleable material and is used in different forms for above-ground plumbing and for underground plumbing for supplying water. There are different grades of copper tube, which are outlined in the table opposite.

Two types of steel are used in pipework:

* low carbon steel is commonly used and comes in three different grades of weight – light (used for **conduit**), medium and heavy (used for water supply)

* stainless steel is very shiny and aesthetically pleasing, which is why it is frequently used for where pipework can be seen: for example, when plumbing in a towel radiator in a bathroom.

Lead is mainly only used for protecting buildings from the weather. However, in the past, lead was used for pipework. These days, plastic materials are used to avoid lead poisoning.

Plastics

Many types of plastic are used in the plumbing industry:

* Low-density polyethylene (LDPE) – a flexible material used for chemical waste

* High-density polyethylene (HDPE) – a more rigid version of polyethylene used for the same purpose

* Polyvinyl chloride (PVC) – fairly flexible, used for drainage pipework

Conduit – a channel used to protect cables and wiring

* Unplasticised polyvinyl chloride (uPVC) – a more rigid form of PVC, usually for cold water supply

* Acrylonitrile butadiene styrene (ABS) – used for waste, overflow and in small diameters; used for work that requires a higher resistance to heat than PVC

* Polypropylene – used for pipework for high temperature water.

It is important to note that plumbing fittings and components are manufactured in standard sizes. What a difficult job it would be if fittings were manufactured with slightly different internal diameters or external diameters!

Grades of copper tube

Grade	Classification	Diameters	Lengths	Characteristics
Grade X	R250 half hard straight lengths	12–54 mm	1 m, 2 m, 3 m, 6 m	Used for domestic installations. Not to be used underground. Available in chromium plated for when pipework is seen and an aesthetically pleasing finish is needed.
Grade Z	R290 hard straight lengths	12–54 mm	1–3 m and 6 m	Unbendable. Stronger than grade X, and hardened during manufacturing. Available in chromium plate finish.
Grade Y	R250/220 soft coils	15 and 22 mm	25 m coils	Bending equipment is not required as it is very soft and easy to bend as it is fully annealed. Available plastic-coated, in blue for water service or in yellow for gas. Pipe with a wall thickness of 1 mm is suitable for underground installation.
Grade W	R220 soft coils	4, 5, 6, 8, 10 and 12 mm	10–30 m	Used for pipework runs in solid floors, can be bent easily, and available plastic-coated, in white for heating or yellow for gas.

Health and Safety

There are a number of regulations and standards that outline the quality of materials to be used in different types of plumbing work. It is important that these regulations are adhered to, as it can be dangerous or expensive to replace poor quality fittings or to repair the damage caused by these fittings or materials.

Just checking

* What influences the choice of material?
* Why are standard sizes used?
* Why has the use of lead changed?

5.26 Building services 3: Materials (electrical)

Electricians work closely with many other members of the construction industry to enable building to happen. Many different materials are used in an electrician's work. It is important that you can identify the types of materials used in this area in order to select the correct material for any job.

Cable types

The type of cable selected depends on a number of factors: the environment it is to be installed in, the size of conductor, the insulation and the material that the conductor is made of. For domestic electrical installations, PVC-insulated cables are generally used. This is the most economical way of installing power and lighting circuits. The material that the conductor is made from is really a choice between aluminium and copper. Copper is the material generally chosen, due to its better conductivity, although it is more expensive than aluminium.

Components

Consumer unit

This is where the electricity is divided up for distribution around the property. It contains (MCBs) miniature circuit breakers to protect lighting, heating and cooker circuits, and (RCDs) residual current devices to protect any socket outlets. The consumer unit also houses the main switch to isolate the property's power supply. You will need to use this component in your practical work.

Socket outlets

These are common devices used for plugging in electrical equipment such as hairdryers, vacuum cleaners, televisions and computers. Sockets can be mounted flush to the wall – a metal back box is used and inset into the wall – or mounted on the surface of the wall into a plastic pattress.

One-way switched lights

These are light switches that can be turned on and off in one place only, like the ones found in most rooms in your house.

Activity 5.26

1 Collect samples of different types of cable – safely! Label the different parts and state what they are made from.

2 Sketch a design for the wiring from a consumer unit to include a ring main that feeds five socket outlets. Label all components and wiring.

3 Find images of all the different components, and familiarise yourself with them. Make a list of the ones you can see in your home, school or college.

For your project

As part of Unit 5 in the Diploma, you have to complete a piece of practical work. In choosing building services, you have to mount wiring and components onto a board. You will need to know what type of cable to select for the different components – and, indeed, what the components are. See the diagram to learn about the different types of cable you may need to use.

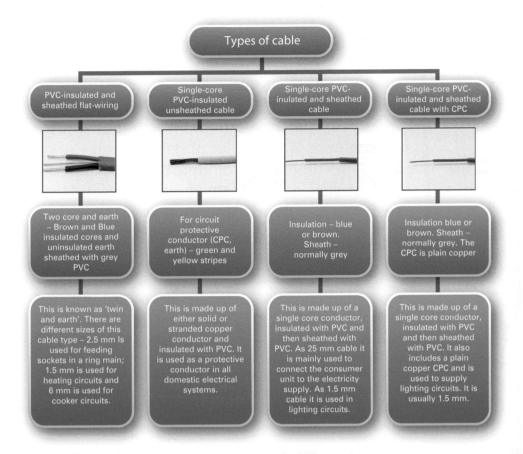

Types of cable

PVC-insulated and sheathed flat-wiring	Single-core PVC-insulated unsheathed cable	Single-core PVC-inulated and sheathed cable	Single-core PVC-inulated and sheathed cable with CPC
Two core and earth – Brown and Blue insulated cores and uninsulated earth sheathed with grey PVC	For circuit protective conductor (CPC, earth) – green and yellow stripes	Insulation – blue or brown. Sheath – normally grey	Insulation blue or brown. Sheath – normally grey. The CPC is plain copper
This is known as 'twin and earth'. There are different sizes of this cable type – 2.5 mm Is used for feeding sockets in a ring main; 1.5 mm is used for heating circuits and 6 mm is used for cooker circuits.	This is made up of either solid or stranded copper conductor and insulated with PVC. It is used as a protective conductor in all domestic electrical systems.	This is made up of a single core conductor, insulated with PVC and then sheathed with PVC. As 25 mm cable it is mainly used to connect the consumer unit to the electricity supply. As 1.5 mm cable it is used in lighting circuits.	This is made up of a single core conductor, insulated with PVC and then sheathed with PVC. It also includes a plain copper CPC and is used to supply lighting circuits. It is usually 1.5 mm.

Two-way switched lights

These are lights that can be turned on and off in two places. For example, the top of stair light can be turned on at the bottom of the stair and off at the top, or vice versa.

Spurred sockets

These are the same as socket outlets but are not part of the ring main. They can either be spurred off an existing socket on the ring main or joined by a junction box or switched fused spur.

Switched fused spur

This is a fused switch to supply a socket or appliance.

Junction box

This is a component that allows a lighting or power circuit to be extended. However, joints and connections in electrical circuits should be avoided if at all possible (see jointing methods).

Junction box

Cable clips

These are designed to fix cable to surfaces. They are made of plastic and have a small nail to hold the clip in position. There is a maximum spacing for these clips which is different for the different types and sizes of cable.

Just checking

* Why are there different types of cable?
* What is a consumer unit?
* What type of cable is used for supplying electricity to outlet sockets?

5.27 Building services 4: Jointing methods

For both plumbers and electricians, jointing is an everyday part of the job. In each case, there are a variety of different methods and components to choose from. It takes a lot of skill to be able to carry out these methods of jointing. It is important that care is taken, as the safety of the worker and the customer is of utmost importance.

Plumbing

Joining copper tube

Compression joints, soldered capillary joints and push-fit joints are the three main methods of joining copper tube.

Compression joints can be either non-manipulative (known as type A) or manipulative (known as type B). The non-manipulative joint is more common than the manipulative. The main difference between the two is that the type A joint uses a compression ring to create a watertight seal. The type B joint involves the pipe being flared, so that an adaptor can be fitted.

Soldered capillary joints are normally soft soldered. This is done in one of two ways:

* integral solder ring – where the solder is already in the fitting

* end-feed – where the solder is end-fed from some separate solder.

Push-fit joints are available in metal, but are most commonly plastic. They involve simply pushing the fitting onto either plastic or copper pipe, where a grab ring is used to hold the fitting in place and an O-ring is used to make a watertight joint.

Electrical work

Cable joints and connections should be avoided. In domestic installations, joints are not generally used because most installation is behind plasterboard walls and therefore inaccessible. Joints in electrical circuits are also a weakness, which can cause overheating and, in extreme cases, fire. Where a joint or connection is unavoidable, a suitable type must be selected. Joints and connections include:

* plastic connectors

* porcelain connectors

* compression joints

* uninsulated connectors

* junction boxes

* soldered joints.

HOW MANY JOINTS?

The water and electricity in your house have to travel. Think about where they have to go from and to. Estimate how many joints are involved in (a) the plumbing system and (b) the electrical circuit.

Activity 5.27

1 Find images of the following brass fittings: straight adaptors, straight couplers, tap connectors, stop ends, tees, elbows, wall-plate elbows, bent and straight tank connectors. Make a file of what you find.

2 Find a manufacturer's list of push-fit and capillary fittings. Compare them in terms of cost, what the manufacturer says about them and how they look.

3 Find two different sockets or light switches. Inspect them and describe how you would terminate a cable in each accessory.

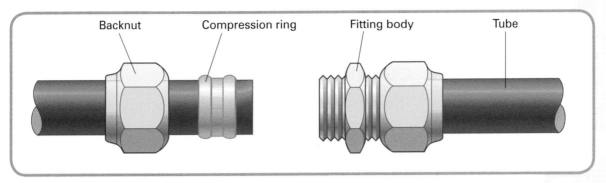

Non-manipulative compression joints

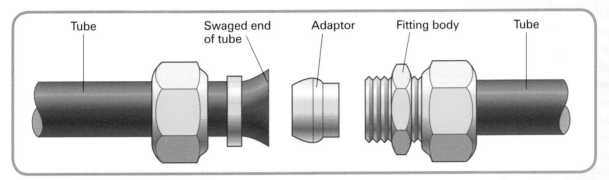

Manipulative compression joints

For your project

For Unit 5 of the Diploma, learners are required to carry out two pieces of practical work. These involve mounting and wiring electrical components, and mounting pipes and components. Use what you have learnt in this section about jointing methods to complete your work.

Terminating cables

When a cable is joined to a socket, consumer unit, switches or any other accessory, it is known as a termination. There are different types or termination including claw washers, strip connectors and solderless lugs, but two types are most commonly used.

Pillar terminals – a brass pillar with a hole in the side where the conductor (cable) is pushed through and held in place by a small screw.

Screw head, nut and washer terminals – the conductor (cable) is formed into a small loop or eye and placed around the shaft of the screw or nut. The rotation of the screw or nut will close the joint and hold it in place.

Just checking

* What is the difference between a type A and a type B compression joint?
* What are the two ways of soldering a capillary joint?
* Why should jointing in electrical circuits be avoided?

5.28 Building services 5: Quality control and common defects

The construction industry is responsible for providing us with places in which we can live, work, relax and have fun. We all rely on the industry, including building services, to provide quality environments for us to partake in these activities. Quality control plays an important part: it is the mechanism which ensures our enjoyment and safety in these environments.

Plumbing

Quality control

Quality control in plumbing is of utmost importance. Water can cause major damage to belongings and property if there are leaks or burst pipes. Pipework is usually hidden under floors or behind walls; if the necessary quality checks are not performed and a leak is present, it can take hours, days, months or even years for a leak to be discovered, resulting in major damage to hidden areas. There are various performance checks that can be carried out to plumbing work.

Check every joint for leaks – use a visual check and feel around the joint for water.

Check the performance of the component – check that it works correctly; for example, with a ball valve, make sure it is not leaking and that it fills to the correct level.

Check aesthetics – use visual checks and a spirit level to ensure that the pipework, fittings and components are level and square.

Common defects

* Substandard installations – poor quality workmanship.

* Defective materials and components – poorly manufactured materials and components.

* Leaking joints – where a joint is not watertight.

* Blockages – debris in pipework or fittings.

Activity 5.28

1 Look at exemplars of plumbing and electrical work. Investigate the different procedures involved in carrying out this work.

2 Craig is a plumber. He has just installed a radiator and pipework. After leaving it for a while, he has noticed the carpet around the base of the pipework is wet. What should he be checking now?

3 Work in a pair. Practice the process of connecting a conductor to a termination. Get your partner to check the quality of your work.

4 Work in a pair. Practice the process of making a compression joint. Get your partner to check the quality of your work.

Electrical

Quality control

There are two main areas of quality control in electrical work: checking for performance and checking the aesthetic appearance. Every new installation or maintenance procedure that involves the power being disconnected must be tested and certified after completion. This is a quality control procedure that ensures the safety and performance of the system.

When checking performance, there are two main types of test: non-live tests which are carried out on the electrical work before the electricity supply is connected, and live tests which are carried out with the supply connected.

When checking aesthetic appearance, it is important to ensure a quality finish. All accessories should be straight or square, and wiring should be neat and in straight lines, unless a change of direction is needed, in which case care should be taken when forming the bend to avoid damage to the cable or conductors. Clips should be used at various intervals to secure the cable.

Order	Test	Regulation
1	Continuity of protective conductors including main and supplementary bonding.	713-02
2	Continuity of ring final circuit conductors.	713-03
3	Insulation resistance.	713-04
4	Site applied insulation.	713-05
5	Protection by separation of circuits.	713-06
6	Protection against direct contact by a barrier or enclosure provided during erection (generally determined by visual inspection).	713-07
7	Insulation of non-conducting floors and walls.	713-08
8	Polarity.	713-09
9	Earth electrode resistance (where the electrode is part of the installation).	713-10
10	Re-check polarity, where necessary.	713-09
11	Earth fault loop impedance.	713-11
12	Prospective fault current.	713-12
13	Functional testing of residual current devices (independent of test facility in device).	713-13-01
14	Functional testing of switchgear and controlgear assemblies, drives, controls and interlocks.	713-13-02

Common defects

* Loose connections or bad connections – conductors not terminated securely.

* Manufacturing defects – poor quality accessories which do not function properly.

* Wrong selection of equipment – using equipment that is not fit for purpose.

Just checking

* What quality checks would you carry out in a new plumbing installation?
* Which tests are to be carried out first in electrical work?
* Why is it important to make sure the work is aesthetically pleasing?

Introduction

In this unit you will look at the affect of the built environment on the communities within it. This includes the benefits of sustainability to the built environment and the use and practices that can be employed on construction projects to contribute to a sustainable community. Property is a valid asset that contributes to the community and the economy as a whole. You will learn about this in detail, looking at property markets and their contribution to wealth and a sustainable environment. You will be able to explore the many factors that affect the local property market through local research.

Many run down areas are often improved through several factors, government intervention being just one. You will understand what the benefits of regeneration are and the impact of improvement on an area to the wider community as a whole. Improvements involve the maintenance of the built environment. This involves several different job roles beyond those used to construct the built environment, and you will learn about these job roles and the professional organizations behind them.

How you will be assessed

This unit has three tasks to complete. The first requires a report into sustainable practices from the perspective of a consultant called in to advise on a supermarket development. The second task asks you to act as a journalist working for a newspaper and comment on the local property market. The third task is based around recruitment in the maintenance sector and the roles and careers within it.

On completion of this unit, you should:

LO.6.1 Know how sustainability affects the built environment

LO.6.2 Be able to evaluate the contribution of the built environment to society and communities

LO.6.3 Understand how the built environment can be improved to benefit individuals and communities

LO.6.4 Understand the job roles, progression routes, occupational structures and the importance of teamwork relating to building maintenance and facilities management.

THINKING POINTS

Decisions made at the design stage of a project can have far reaching consequences in terms of sustainable practices. Many large organisations need to take this on board when preparing business strategy. For example, ensuring their building projects all contain a strong green sustainable theme. A long term approach must be made to save energy, raw materials and wastage of manufactured products. Any clear direction by one major organisation will be followed by others. Government policy and funding also has a major impact on sustainability.

The UK property market has seen major price increases especially around our capital cities. Many factors account for this, from wages to location and school catchment areas. Property is important and getting on the first 'rung' of the ladder can be an important decision to make for the first time buyer.

When building projects are finally handed over to the client the maintenance of the built environment begins. This keeps the building serviceable. This means keeping the building in a safe working condition with all systems, such as fire detection, operating correctly. It is essential to organise and manage this maintenance so the value of the property is maintained and the local environment standard is not run down and neglected. Otherwise this would quickly bring many social and economic problems into the area.

The materials we use in modern buildings have to make a sustainable contribution to the environment. Materials may be replenished, have an element of recycling within them or be reusable after the life of the building. This helps maintain and extend the life of the earth's resources.

Natural products

Timber

Timber is the ultimate natural product: it can be grown over and over again, and it absorbs carbon, while giving off oxygen. It has a reasonable life span if treated, and can be engineered into many timber products for use in a house, from the roof to walls, floors and external cladding. Timber-framed housing is one of the most thermally efficient forms available today. Cedar external boarding is low-maintenance, long lasting and pleasing to look at.

Green roofs

This new concept uses specially grown plants and alpines planted onto a roof. These absorb water and sunlight, the roof grows slowly, and a natural, eco-friendly roof covering results.

Natural insulation

Sheep's wool can be processed into wool batts, which can be used to insulate lofts and wall cavities. Wool is totally renewable, eco-friendly, naturally breaths moisture and is exceptionally warm. Hemp is another grown product that can be processed into an insulation product with similar properties. Straw technology (the waste from producing grain) is now taking shape, with treated bails used to form walls with high insulation properties. Another option is earth-sheltered construction, where part of a building is surrounded by earth or built into the ground for excellent insulation.

Recycled products

Demolition waste

Crushed concrete and brickwork from demolition can be used to level up land and for hardcore. The reuse of demolition waste on site must be built into a program of works, with a crusher provided to produce the product.

A green roof incorporating a waterproof layer, on a sustainable building in Northumberland!

Glass

The use of recycled glass is being widely tested. Ground glass can increase tarmac's non-slip properties, and can be added to concrete to provide an alternative aggregate. Glass is often recycled into flat panes at the factory.

Steel

Steel has an element of recycling in its manufacture. Cold rolled steel channels have now been successfully used as a modular form of prefabricated construction, cladded with plasterboard to form internal walls, and with an external brick skin to form an external wall.

Timber

Timber can be recycled into a range of products. Chipboard and MDF are both formed from waste from primary timber products.

The benefits

Here are just some of the benefits of using sustainable materials in new developments. These materials:

∗ save on finite oil resources

∗ can be replaced time and time again

∗ reduce energy costs

∗ do not harm the environment

∗ reduce the carbon footprint.

Sustainable site practice and processes

Buy locally

If you use local resources, you cut down on transport, reducing the carbon footprint on the building by reducing the CO_2 emissions.

Reduce wastage

Ordering correctly and ensuring the correct use of materials reduces wastage, which harms the environment by landfill, and saves the energy used to manufacture the material.

Prefabrication

With this system, larger panels can be factory constructed more efficiently than on-site, saving time and energy.

Breeam certification

This is a certification scheme looking at the total energy costs associated with the construction and running of a project. Stringent key details have to be met to get certification for a building.

A natural insulation product

Activity 6.1

1 Ask the sales representative from a local timber supplier to give a talk on timber products. Ask them:

What products can be manufactured from the waste from saw mills?

Does the glue in chipboard harm the environment?

Is the timber used in timber-framed houses treated with any chemicals?

2 Produce a marketing poster for a sustainable building material. In less than 10 words, write this slogan for the centre of the poster.

3 Can newspaper be recycled into an insulation material? Do some research to find out. and produce an A5 leaflet that explains this as a product to use in houses.

Just checking

∗ How can sheep's wool be used in a construction project?

∗ Why is chipboard linked to sustainability?

∗ What would be a good sustainable site practice?

6.2 Sustainable maintenance

The life of a building can be extended by specifying the use of better, maintenance free materials from the outset. These may cost more, but using them will reduce the long-term spend on maintaining our homes and properties, and will save on valuable resources.

Essentials

Good design

Good design is essential to the life of a building. If the designer has taken into account the Working at Height Regulations and the Construction Design and Management Regulations, it will be safe for the maintenance team to undertake future repairs. Good design in the way water is directed off a structure is also a valuable inclusion, preventing many potential problems.

Access

Access is essential to reach the parts that need attention. For example, using pivot windows in high-rise structures enables them to be serviced and cleaned from the inside floor level, safely and securely. Access points, ducts and chambers must be designed with safety in mind.

Environmental friendliness

The cost of a material must be balanced against its future or whole life cost. Is it worth buying a cheap material that will cost a lot more in 10 years time to replace and maintain? Does the maintenance require the use of chemicals, such as timber stain containing chemical toxins? Does the replacement material come from a sustainable local source? These are all factors that you must consider carefully.

Poor maintenance has resulted in weeds growing out of this pavement

WHY MAINTAIN?

Keeping a property in good condition provides several things: a sense of living in a good community, reduction in crime figures and a greater lifespan for our heritage in the UK. What would happen if we just left buildings to deteriorate and decline? Write down some thoughts.

Maintenance schedule – a program or plan of what will need maintaining, what needs to be done and when

Personal Learning and Thinking Skills

Conduct an independent enquiry into maintenance issues in design. What considerations need to be taken into account at an early stage?

Lifecycle costing

The initial cost of the design and construction of a building is not the only cost to consider. You must look at the future running and maintaining of the building and its services. Including certain systems now will reduce maintenance costs in the future, saving energy, time and carbon emissions of the project over its lifecycle.

Benefits

There are many benefits to sustainable maintenance.

* It saves valuable resources.

* The additional cost of using an oil-based element, such as guttering, outweighs the long-term maintenance costs of an element such as timber, which needs painting.

* Sustainable maintenance is safe.

* It reduces the use of chemicals that could damage the environment.

* It encourages designers to prioritise sustainability.

* It is helps create a lower lifecycle costing.

Sustainable maintenance practices

Regular service intervals

Never try to save money by missing a service interval on a piece of equipment, plant or construction item. This may create more damage than anticipated, and will cost more to the environment in the long run: for example, failing to renew tap washers wastes water.

Planning

Ensure that a **maintenance schedule** is planned, financed and resourced. This should include the green areas of the external landscaping of a building, which are often neglected but add to its sustainable role in the community.

Lifespan

Use maintenance products that will extend the life of the material or building. Use current technology that will last longer, giving additional life to the building or structure. For example, you can condition the air to a bridge deck, which saves on painting and prevents rust, as the moisture is removed from the air.

Activity 6.2

1 Take a close look at the building that you are in now. Identify three areas of its structure that could be upgraded with sustainable maintenance-free materials. For example, this could be existing timber fascia that could be replaced with uPVC. Take two photographs of these and place them in a Word document. Write next to each photo why you think these areas would benefit.

2 Look at the way in which rainwater is dealt with in your building. How is it directed to the drainage system? What maintenance do these systems require? Write up your findings in a short A5 leaflet.

3 Take a photograph of an older building in your area and print it off.

Identify areas on the external envelope of the building that would benefit from renewal using sustainable materials. For example something that is flat on a roof?

4 Find suitable materials on manufacturers' websites, for example a green roof system. Print off pictures of these and stick each next to the existing item on your photo.

Just checking

* How can we ensure that building maintenance is sustainable?
* What is a maintenance schedule?
* Why is lifecycle costing important in maintenance?

6.3 Sustainable communities

More and more people are trying to find ways to look after the world's precious resources and reduce the negative human impact on the environment. One way to do this is by forming a sustainable community – a grouping of people with a shared belief in living a sustainable life in homes, using services and transport that are all as sustainable as possible.

Activity 6.3

1 Take a look at the BedZED development case study opposite. Does this way of living have any problems? What are the benefits of living in such a way?

2 Why do you think education comes first in the table of benefits above? Write your reasons down. What do you think should come first? Explain why you hold that view.

3 Visit the government website http://www.communities. gov.uk/communities/ sustainablecommunities/ whatis. What are the components of a sustainable community? What does environmentally sensitive mean? Why should sustainable communities be fair for everyone?

Note the materials used to construct the buildings in this sustainable community project

The BedZED sustainable community

The Beddington Zero Energy Development, or BedZED as it is known, is the UK's largest eco-village – situated in a busy part of south London. This is a fantastic example of a sustainable community of people living and interacting together. Started in March 2002, BedZED now comprises 100 homes, community facilities and workspace for 100 people.

This example illustrates how eco and green construction can work together to develop a lifestyle that can be easy, accessible and affordable, and provide a good quality of life. For example, the heating requirements of BedZED homes are around 10% that of a typical home. This provides massive savings for the occupants and for the developer.

Why live in a sustainable community?

The idea of people pulling together to form a sustainable community is fast developing into the way forward and is supported by the UK government's policies on this aspect. Living in a sustainable community has many benefits, not only for its occupiers but also for the rest of the world.

Benefits of living in a sustainable community

Education	Many sustainable communities use their development as a 'showcase', to spread ideas around the rest of the population and raise finances to expand their projects.
Energy	Many of these projects use wind turbines and solar power to provide electricity for the homes, which cuts the reliance on the UK's National Grid system and reduces carbon emissions.
Resources	Eco homes are developed from recyclable or renewable materials – things that can be grown or reused. Timber is the material of choice, as it absorbs CO_2 and gives out oxygen while growing.
Recycling	Rainwater may be collected in lakes and used to flush toilets; dry toilets can provide compost for use in growing food; reed-bed sewage systems provide a clean, alternative way of processing waste.
Research	The whole community project provides an ideal avenue for research and further development, with new ideas tried out before implementation.
Social	A sustainable community can be an important point for interaction with other cultures and beliefs, promoting friendliness, low crime, tolerance and respect.

The voice of the sustainable community

Living in sustainable communities allows a voice to grow and be heard by the people who make major decisions about the way we live. Sustainable communities can offer this 'voice of experience' on a number of issues.

What is it like to live in such a community?

To live in a sustainable community is unique; you must share certain ideals, which may include:

* a keen recycling culture
* a desire to help others
* a desire to protect the environment
* 'go green' status
* religious beliefs.

These are all ideal qualities to invest in living in such an environment. Much of everyday life would be fairly similar to that in an ordinary community, but a green 'thread' would run through every aspect of it, from schooling to transport, leisure to work. To keep the ideals focused, and to keep developing, the community would need good structures, leadership and mechanisms for people to be involved.

> **Functional Skills**
>
> What issues around sustainability exist in your local area? Use the Internet and local newspapers, as well as interviews, to find out more.

> **Personal Learning and Thinking Skills**
>
> In pairs, discuss your research into living in a sustainable community. Would you like to live there? If not, why not? Contribute to this lively debate.

> **Just checking**
>
> * What are the benefits of living in a sustainable community?
> * Why does the Government promote sustainable communities?
> * What impact can a sustainable community have on the wider world?

6.4 Construction and the economy

We all need buildings to live, work and play in: they are an essential item in everyday living. The UK construction industry is therefore an essential part of the UK economy. Employing over 2 million people in over 250,000 companies, the UK construction industry has the second largest of any EU member state, and contributes nearly 9% of the UK's **GVA**.

A booming economy means booming construction

Construction's national contribution

The construction industry contributes in several ways, not just to the economy, but also to society in general. The UK housing market is currently in a boom period, with a shortage of new homes for our growing population. Construction produces many beautiful buildings that enrich our living environment: for example, the Wembley Stadium, the Swiss Re Building and the Canary Wharf Complex. It has also given us a substantial heritage of old buildings and monuments, such as the historic architecture of Bath. Construction provides buildings that we can be proud of, and plays a key role in creating and maintaining our unique British culture.

Contributing to the local economy

The construction industry also has an important impact on local economies. It supports:

* employment for operatives and craftspeople – construction projects employ local labour

* local material suppliers – through quarries, builders' merchants and others

* the development of a large range of specialist subcontractors – electricians, plumbers, etc.

* training schemes and apprenticeships – this is a vital part of the industry sector

* the continuation of traditional techniques such as slate, limestone and timber processes.

Traditional roofing helps the slate industry and gives work to the subcontract roofer who fixes the slates in place

GVA – Gross Value Added, an indication of how much each sector contributes to the UK economy

Blue-collar worker – a member of the working class who performs manual labour and earns an hourly wage

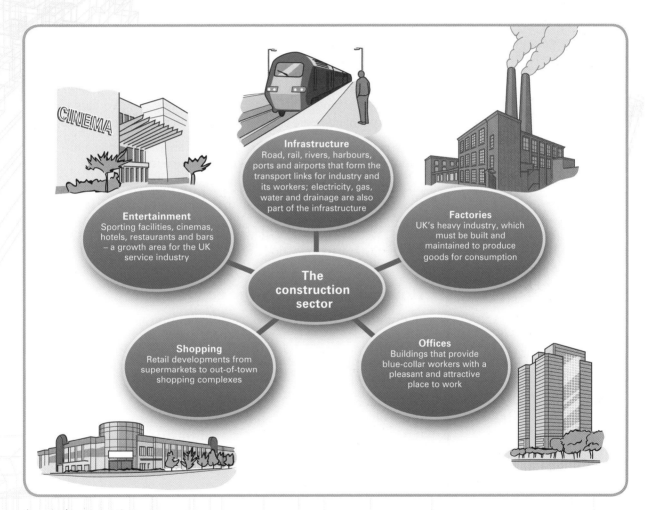

Infrastructure
Road, rail, rivers, harbours, ports and airports that form the transport links for industry and its workers; electricity, gas, water and drainage are also part of the infrastructure

Entertainment
Sporting facilities, cinemas, hotels, restaurants and bars – a growth area for the UK service industry

Factories
UK's heavy industry, which must be built and maintained to produce goods for consumption

The construction sector

Shopping
Retail developments from supermarkets to out-of-town shopping complexes

Offices
Buildings that provide blue-collar workers with a pleasant and attractive place to work

Areas in the construction sector

Just checking

✳ What key areas does the construction sector cover?

✳ How does construction contribute to the national economy?

✳ How does it contribute to local economies?

6.5 Housing and the economy

It is important to recognise that housing has an effect on the economy – and vice versa. The state of the economy can affect the demand for housing overall, or what sorts of housing are in demand. At the same time, strong demand for housing can give the economy a real boost. Here we look at how housing and the economy link together.

Access and affordability

If people cannot afford to buy or rent properties privately, this impacts on the provision of social housing and other schemes provided by the government, which in turn affects the economy. Local authorities have in place schemes and policies to assist with access and affordability of housing as part of a national government strategy. Alongside banks or mortgage companies, there are housing associations, public sector providers and schemes to assist first-time buyers, key workers and local authority tenants. Here are some of the schemes currently available.

Slow-start mortgages – where the terms are more gentle and affordable at the start, then rates go up after a few years.

Shared ownership – where first-time buyers/key workers can buy a share in a property, to help them to get onto the property ladder.

Affordable housing – a proportion of housing reserved for those who cannot compete in the local housing market, those with specific needs, or essential workers.

How housing affects the economy

Here are just some of the ways in which housing affects the economy.

House prices – If house prices rise, people can increase spending. This is because they can remortgage or take a bigger loan out against the value of their property. Higher spending can then contribute to economic growth.

Rates of interest – Lower interest rates allow the consumer to spend less on paying interest and thus allow them to spend more on goods and services, including houses. Higher interest rates means people must spend more on paying off interest, so they are more cautious on spending on goods and services.

Location of housing in relation to workplaces – Where people work, spend and have leisure time partly depends on where their housing is. If they do not live close to their workplaces, they may spend elsewhere, which affects the local economy.

Cheaper housing on city outskirts – Many people buy properties on the margins of cities, but the attractiveness of this depends on the availability of transport.

Location of housing in relation to transport links – If the housing is close to effective transport links, people can commute to work, even if they cannot afford to live near to work.

Accommodation for essential workers – Essential workers are needed in all areas of the economy, and often schemes are put in place to help.

Activity 6.5

1 Create a guide to buying a house for a first-time buyer. The guide should feature information on what schemes are available to help them buy their first home.

2 Imagine you are a nurse.

'Hi, I'm Olivia. I need to find a property to live in close to work, or at least near to effective transport links. I am finding it difficult, as my salary is only £17,000 per year. All the houses near to the hospital seem to be around £150,000! I can't afford that on my own.'

Make a list of the advantages and disadvantages of owning a property near to the hospital in the middle of a city, and owning one on the outskirts where you travel in to work. Which would you choose?

Personal Learning and Thinking Skills

Investigate the availability of affordable housing in your area. Try looking on your local council's website or, if there is a large new development in your area, try looking up affordable housing on the developer's website.

Land prices

The price of land affects the selling value of houses, what people can afford and where people can afford to buy housing. The cost of land is a major factor affecting our economy. Here are some suggestions as to what causes land prices to rise.

Lack of urban decay (rundown) • Location in relation to good quality jobs • Good transport links • **What makes land expensive** • High employment • Good healthcare • Pleasant surroundings • Good schools • Low crime

Just checking

* What schemes are available to support people who could not otherwise afford homes?
* How do house prices affect the economy?
* What causes land to be expensive?

6.6 Housing in the UK

There are many different types of housing in the UK – various styles, shapes, sizes, prices and also different types of ownership. In this topic, we will discuss the various types of property available and general issues which affect the property market in the UK.

WHO LIVES IN A HOUSE LIKE THIS?

Discuss with a partner why there need to be different types of housing – why people might choose a bungalow rather than a house, or a flat rather than a detached house, for example. Feed your findings back to the group.

Activity 6.6

1 Using the legs from the 'housing' diagram opposite, and the Internet, copy and complete this table to define all types of housing.

Type of housing	Image	Description

2 Look up 'community regeneration' followed by your county on the Internet (e.g. 'community regeneration Yorkshire') and find out what type of regeneration is going on in your local area.

3 Look around your local area, in estate agents, in newspapers or on the Internet. See if you can find buildings that are being used as houses or flats but have had a prior use. Try to list as many different previous uses as you can. Do these types of housing share any characteristics? What sort of people would buy them? Make notes on what you find.

Types of housing

Type of housing	Characteristics
Local authority	More commonly known as council housing. Tenants live in this type of housing and pay rent to the local authority. The building is maintained by the tenant, but any major refurbishment is done by the local authority. An emergency system is in place for tenants to report things such as water leaks or loss of power; if they report a problem, a representative will come and fix it.
Private	Available in all parts of the UK. Individuals, partners or groups can buy properties and own them, using cash or mortgages.
Sheltered accommodation	Provided in many parts of the UK, usually for older members of the public. Sheltered accommodation usually takes the form of flats or bungalows that people rent, but which are maintained by an organisation or the local authority. People who live in this type of accommodation also have access to a residential warden if they require assistance, but do not require full residential care.
Affordable housing	This is where a proportion of housing is set aside for people who are unable to compete in the housing market, or who have special housing requirements. Government planning legislation ensures that any large new build has to provide a proportion of affordable housing.
Shared ownership schemes	These are available to some first-time buyers, key workers and social tenants. This scheme enables some people to buy a share of a home, to enable them to get a first step on the property ladder. There are strict rules on who can buy in this way and how to do so.

Regeneration

In many parts of the country, regeneration is underway. Areas that have been in decline are being rejuvenated and given lasting improvements, on a social, environmental and economic level. Homes are being refurbished; affordable housing, housing partnerships and social housing are being developed in a drive to provide sustainable communities in pleasant surroundings. Keepmoat is one company specialising in the regeneration of communities in the Midlands and the north of England. They are responsible for the refurbishment of over 34,000 homes a year, and play a leading role in regeneration. You can check out their website and have a look at their project at: www.keepmoat.com

Styles of housing

This diagram shows a number of styles of housing, some of which you will be familiar with.

Reuse

In an increasing number of developments, we are seeing the redevelopment or change of use of existing structures into housing. This could be for aesthetic reasons, or could be a way of utilising existing structures in an area where there is little or no land on which to build. Some of the most popular and notable changes of use involve redeveloping old, distinctive buildings such as churches, windmills, waterworks or industrial buildings.

Just checking

* What different types of housing are there?
* What does regeneration mean?
* What type of buildings may be reused for housing and why?

6.7 The property market

The property market concerns the supply of homes for sale, where new homes are built and come onto the market, and the demand for homes from the people who wish to buy them. Demand and supply are closely linked. When the supply of property is scarce or limited but demand is high, the price of property can rise; if the supply is plentiful or demand is low, the price can fall.

Is this housing affordable?

The property market in the UK covers domestic homes and commercial buildings, whether privately owned or rented. The face value of a home is not just the bricks and mortar: it is the price that someone is willing to pay for the property that sets the rate you can sell it at. People place a high value on property as it has been a substantial and good investment for a number of years.

Public or private?

In the UK, property is in either the public or the private domain.

Public

This is owned by the state. Property such as hospitals, schools and local authority housing all fall into this category. These assets have been provided through taxation of the population, producing funds which have been reinvested into public buildings for the benefit of local communities. Public housing includes housing provided by the local authorities to rent out to individuals and families who cannot afford to purchase a private property outright.

Private

This is property that is owned by individuals or companies, and not by the state. Private property covers many different types of properties, and includes clients such as property developers. Private housing can be owned by individuals or by companies such as housing associations, who offer rental properties to individuals who cannot get onto the property ladder or require social supported housing.

Types of property

In the UK, many different types of properties have been developed in both the public and the private sectors. Examples include:

* residential housing – detached, semi and terraced

* retail properties – shopping units and malls

* commercial properties – offices and shops

* industrial properties – factories and units

* infrastructure – such as airports, hospitals, schools and universities.

Housing associations exist to support people on low incomes who cannot enter the private housing market due to a range of factors explored on page 184. These associations are often non-profit making: rather than creating profit for anyone, the funds raised are put back into the association's work and invested in new projects as time goes on. Housing associations also provide warden controlled accommodation for individuals who may need help coping with ordinary living.

Functional Skills

What are the different types of property in your local area, and what are the current market issues for each type of property?

The first-time buyer

With the boom in UK house prices over the last 10 years has come the inevitable shortfall in people's wages and income. The result is that now many people cannot afford to get onto the property ladder and are unable to take the first step to owning a new home. People may now have to rent, as this is cheaper, but renting does not produce any assets for the individual. This situation has generated a sizable property market of 'buy to let'. 'Buy to let' is where private individuals or companies purchase properties and renovate them, then rent them out to tenants. The value of their investment increases with property values, and an income is generated via the rent.

Social housing is provided as part of the planning regulations, where private housing developments have to provide some affordable homes as part of any development.

Affordable homes have limited designs

Just checking

* What is a private house?
* What types of buildings would be public?
* What is a first time buyer, and what problems may they face?

6.8 Influences on the property market

There are many influences on the UK property market, from the growth of the UK economy, to employment security, to the time of the year – no one is interested in buying a house just after paying for Christmas! First-time buyers are now finding it extremely hard to get on that first rung of the property ladder and may have to save several more years for the initial deposit.

The market

'Everyone should have the opportunity to rent or buy a decent home at a price they can afford, in a place where they want to live and work.' (www.communities.gov.uk/housing/about/)

The government are developing plans to build over three million new homes by 2020, which will include more affordable housing and rentable properties.

The development of property enables an individual or company asset to be formed. From this asset, the individual or company can raise finance to develop more properties in the UK economy, creating a continuing flow of development. This process can be a business which is very lucrative: there are now several property millionaires in the UK.

The impact of this sort of development on the economy does not stop once the houses are built. Each of the houses requires servicing and maintaining, which generates further income to the economy. A strong property market enables the UK economy to grow.

Influences

A number of factors influence the shape, size, strength and buoyancy of the property market. These include:

* the cost of borrowing – cheaper loans mean people can afford to buy

* fashion – for example, currently renting is seen as 'dead money': you do not add any value to the property as you do not own it

* UK and global economies – for example, when people from the London Counties invest in properties in the North, house prices there increase substantially

* the amount of housing been built – if supply is limited, prices are high; if supply is plentiful, prices fall

* population growth – as more people need housing, demand grows, inflating property prices

* demographics– for example, if there are more old people, there will be a greater need for single-storey homes, so builders will want to build bungalows.

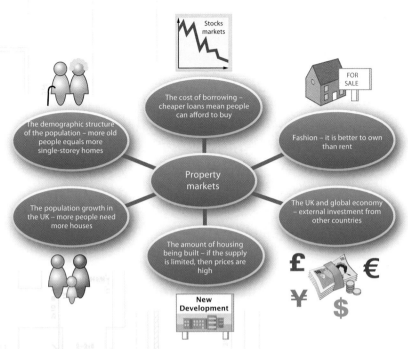

The economy and the market

The UK property market has been in the ascendant for the last decade. Strong growth has been matched by growth in investment in property, which is currently seen as a reliable and stable economic factor. Inner cities are the areas that have benefited most from this type of investment with Leeds City Centre now being the next 'capital' of the North. The property market has increased so much that many buyers not only look in the UK, but also for an investment abroad, where prices are cheaper.

However, the value of property can go down in times of recession: when wages are low and supply exceeds demand, people selling property may have to lower their asking price.

Government intervention

The government has many policies that can affect the property market one of these is the HIP. This is the Home Information Pack, which is part of a new procedure that the government has brought in to try to make selling and buying property easier. The Energy Performance Certificate, part of the HIP survey, gives in effect an energy rating to the property for sale such that a potential buyer is aware of where it lies on a scale. The HIP rating for the property can be displayed on the 'for sale' board – it is rather like buying a washing machine which can be a grade A to F.

The second intervention is in the base rate of lending. This is the amount of interest that the Bank of England charges the lenders to borrow money. This is then passed down to buyers who take out a mortgage on a property. The lower the rate the better the property economy is.

FEEL GOOD FACTOR

The built environment can help to give you a feeling of well being. How does your local area do this? Think about what makes you feel secure or comfortable, and where you can work rest and play. Write down some notes about ways in which your local environment works well for you.

6.9 Improving the built environment

There are many ways to improve the built environment, particularly when areas have gone into decline. You may have noticed the number of home improvement programmes that are on the television. In fact, there are whole channels on digital television dedicated to it! It is seen as fashionable to improve your own home and people often do. Often, however, people may not notice improvements that are going on in the wider community around them.

Enhancing the built environment

The built environment can be improved in many ways in order to enhance the physical, spiritual and emotional well being of the individuals and communities who use it.

How can we enhance the built environment? Here are some suggestions.

* Refurbishment
* Modification
* Change of use to meet perceived needs
* Bringing it up to current and future standards
* Making it more desirable
* Improving efficiency
* Having better insulation
* Making it more eco-friendly

Often these improvements are made by people other than homeowners. Other stakeholders in the community are responsible for maintaining and improving the built environment; they include: councils, local authorities, developers, retailers, police or schools.

How does this help?

Safety – run-down buildings and boarded-up houses are associated with crime; the enhancement of these areas promotes the feeling of safety.

Health – poor quality housing which is damp and cold, infected with insects, fungal growth or vermin does not create a healthy environment and can lead to disease and health problems; a warm, dry environment with good heating and ventilation systems leads to good indoor air quality and more hygienic conditions, and therefore good health.

A modern enhanced interior

Modern housing

Housing in need of refurbishment

Security – modern or refurbished homes have five-point locking systems on doors, three-point locking systems on windows, house alarms and sometimes CCTV. All these measures help to provide a feeling of security and well being.

Layout – in the past, layouts of the built environment included walkways and ginnels, which could sometimes create a means of quick escape for criminals in the community. These days, better layouts are planned in new builds to minimise the security risk and encourage a stronger community feel.

Clean – modern, easy-to-clean surfaces promote good hygiene standards. Also, landscaping, tree planting and street furniture, such as benches and bins, all assist in making an area look clean and comfortable to live in.

All the above factors help make individuals proud of their communities and encourage them to take responsibility for it and to look after their surroundings.

Economic prosperity

High quality, clean, secure and comfortable surroundings can indicate a strong economy in a community. This can lead to the location or relocation of quality employers to an area, enhancing the economic cycle. For example, if a company was thinking of locating to a particular area, they would be looking for signs of a strong economy, to show that the community has money to spend in the business. They will probably be looking for an area that is clean, secure and well looked after by its community because this creates the impression that the economy in the area is healthy.

Just checking

* Why should we try to improve the built environment?
* How does improving the built environment contribute to our well being?
* How can improving the built environment aid economic prosperity?

REFURBISH OR DEMOLISH?

You live in a historic part of the country with many old and established traditional buildings. A supermarket has purchased the bank's old office building and is preparing to demolish it! What arguments could you put forward to prevent this?

6.10 Refurbishment and conservation

When our useful buildings exceed their life span, many need to be revitalised. This process is known as refurbishment and allows a building's life and usefulness to be extended by many years. Similarly, historic or architecturally unique buildings can be conserved, to protect them against age and wear. This retains the building's unique character and environment.

Refurbishment

This allows the useful life of an older building to be extended. Old technologies can be removed and replaced with up-to-date systems and materials, bringing a new lease of life to a **dilapidated** old building. Refurbishment also creates an opportunity to safely remove any harmful materials, such as asbestos. Refurbishing a building can be a long-term, sustainable option instead of demolishing a structure and having to start again from the foundations.

Dilapidated – run down and of no use

Listed buildings – buildings graded by English Heritage to preserve them for the future

Functional Skills

Choose a historic building that you admire. Paste an image of this building into a Word document and add some short sentences explaining why it should be conserved.

Conservation

This conserves the existing structure in its original historic entirety. Conservation mainly applies to historic buildings and structures classified as **listed buildings**. Any work undertaken on such buildings has to be in keeping with the original. In some cases, exact replicas must be used: for example, to match original wallpapers. Conservation enables our heritage to be saved for our future generations to enjoy and appreciate.

This brickwork cannot be touched and must be conserved as built

The process of refurbishment

When a building is reaching the end of its serviceable life, it can become an increasing financial burden on the owner. The building will generate high annual maintenance costs, just to keep it running, as parts of its systems will have worn out and need replacing as they break down.

A typical refurbishment would follow this sequence.

* The building goes through a design stage, where the existing structure is surveyed, and the new design is agreed with the client (this is often classed as a change of use, so must comply with current legislation).

* The building is stripped of all the elements that are going to be upgraded.

* Any harmful elements, such as asbestos, are removed.

* The new design is constructed, and the services are installed over the existing structure.

* The building is commissioned and handed over.

The process of conservation

This process differs from refurbishment in that only elements that require conserving may be removed. If a building is listed, these elements may have to be replicated like for like, to maintain the historical integrity of the structure. For example, this may involve manufacturing paints to match the existing ones in texture, colour and chemical composition.

Conservation employs many specialist subcontractors, who undertake some of the skilled work. Some skills are becoming increasingly rare – thatching or creating plaster mouldings, for example. Some of these old skills have been lost completely, and modern techniques have to be adapted to replace the old ones and to enhance the existing building.

We also have to remember that our modern buildings must be designed with conservation in mind. Money invested in better quality materials in the first place will make this job easier in the future.

This Tudor building has to be conserved

Activity 6.10

1 Take a look at a map of the region in which you live. Identify some historic towns or other areas within this region. Identify some historic buildings and structures that you would consider worthy of saving for the future.

2 Enter 'refurbished building' into a search engine. Look through the images that this brings up, then for three of these images answer these questions:

* What is the new use of this building?

* How old is the building?

* What benefit has this building brought to the community?

Just checking

* What does refurbishing a building involve?
* Does conservation matter to a structure?
* What is a listed building or structure?

6.11 The role of the surveyor

For thousands of years, people have relied on surveyors to accurately measure and position buildings, from the Egyptian Pyramids to the Channel Tunnel. The surveyor uses their skills and a range of instruments to study and examine land and buildings, often producing detailed drawings and reports for the people who employ them.

The Great Pyramid extends over a vast area!

Types of surveyor

There are many different types of surveyors working today. The following table illustrates the different classifications and what role each takes.

The roles of different surveyors

Land surveyor	This role deals with the surveying of land, and may involve the work of the **Ordnance Survey** using electronic equipment and ICT.
Site surveyor or setting-out engineer	This role deals with the accurate setting out of the building project to the details provided by the designer such that it is in the right place.
Building surveyor	This role deals with building defects, the surveying of property for valuations and advice on refurbishments, conservation surveys, energy efficiency and condition surveys.

* *Answer: They used vertical poles in lines to create a straight line by using eyesight, and ropes to measure the diagonals.*

A skilful job

Surveyors are required to have a number of professional qualifications – the work is difficult, and the responsibilities are huge – but they also need excellent communication skills. This is because they often have to pass over important information accurately to another person. For example:

* a land surveyor produces a drawing of the dimensions of a plot of land that is to be sold: if this is wrong, there could be serious legal problems

* a building surveyor produces a written report on the valuation of a house and its current value: accurate information is needed when thousands of pounds are involved

* a site surveyor marks the ground where the excavator driver has to dig the drainage trench: without the right information, the trench could go in the wrong place, jeopardising the whole job.

Which type of surveyor is this?

Surveying equipment

This table illustrates the sort of equipment that the different types of surveyors use in their jobs.

Surveyor	Equipment used in surveying
Land surveyor	* level * theodolite * computer * 50 m steel tape * electronic distance measurer * GPS
Site surveyor or setting-out engineer	* steel tape measure * steel road pins * wooden pegs * theodolite * GPS
Building surveyor	* digital camera * damp meter * folding ladders * notebook * 5 m steel tape

> **Ordnance Survey** – an organisation that has mapped the whole of the UK to a grid reference system and produces detailed maps of the UK

Just checking

* What different types of surveyor are there?
* What makes a good surveyor?
* Is there any special equipment you need for surveying?

6.12 The responsibility of maintaining the built environment

After the construction stage comes the maintenance phase. Many different roles and responsibilities are involved in keeping the building in a fit condition for users – from maintenance engineers right through to the professional facilities manager roles. Many more personnel are involved in maintaining the built environment, from the skilled trades maintenance personnel to the managers who supervise the work as it proceeds. Together they form the maintenance team.

General classification of roles

People who maintain the built environment can be divided into several categories.

Operatives and craft persons in the maintenance team	The operative and craft person will undertake any repair work to the building to correct any defects that a supervisor or manager has identified as needing to be corrected. In older structures, this can often be specialised work: for example, a thatched roof repair on a listed building.
Maintenance supervision	The supervision will be carried out by the maintenance engineer or manager who will schedule, cost and organise the resources required to undertake repairs.
Professional estates and facilities managers	This covers the roles of estate agents who look after the conveyancing of property, valuers who value property for tax and selling, building surveyors who look at surveying buildings and facilities managers who look after the whole life costs of a building .

Maintenance operative and craft roles

These roles cover the work that will be required to maintain a building. These people will have to have a detailed knowledge and understanding of the systems and services contained within the building, so that they can react fast to any failed system. These roles would cover work such as:

* replacing electrical fittings such as complex lighting tubes
* maintaining fire alarm systems
* undertaking repairs to damaged doors
* landscaping maintenance.

Maintenance supervision

These roles cover the supervision on the maintenance crew who will undertake the work on site. They include the following responsibilities:

* ensuring electrical work is isolated during servicing
* regular testing of fire alarm and smoke detection systems
* scheduling of a maintenance program
* ensuring that sufficient resources are directed onto the work.

Professional estates and facilities roles

The estate agent

This role deals with the buying and selling of the built environment, including:

* letting property and its maintenance in the rental market
* selling property
* dealing with leases on property.

The facilities manager

This role is at the higher managerial level. Facilities managers deal with a variety of aspects of the building including:

* cleaning and waste removal from the building
* organisation of contractors to maintain the building
* the energy efficiency of the building
* development of cost reduction systems.

The building surveyor

This person deals with the survey and valuation of properties. Typically this would cover:

* detailed survey of a property for a buyer
* survey of the structure
* damp and timber survey
* valuation of a property for a mortgage.

Professional associations

The facilities manager would be a member of the IFM. The Building Surveyor would belong to the Royal Institute of Chartered Surveyors (RICS).

Key users of the built environment

We must not forget the people who will live and work within the built environment, for they are the end users who must feel safe and comfortable in it. Their views must be carefully considered and acted on, and their views must be included in the planning of any adaptation or refurbishment of their working environment.

These operatives are laying services into the ground for gas and water

This operative finishing work on some carpentry

> **Just checking**
>
> * What does a facilities manager do the built environment
> * Is supervision required during maintenance?
> * What sorts of organisations might professionals belong to?

Introduction

We need to protect our built environment not only against the elements of the weather and climate but also from the people who use, work and play within it. Wear and tear on a building does occur and should be taken into account in the design stage when specifying materials. More money spent on durable finishes will mean less maintenance costs in the future. Life cycle costing is now becoming a leading method in comparing one design against another, not just the construction cost but the whole life cost of the project.

Maintenance has to be organised, managed and delivered. In the second learning outcome the learner examines the processes, roles and services that can be delivered under the facilities management umbrella. The impact of undertaking maintenance in this way is explored on the life span of a structure. There are many benefits, both social and economic, to the local community in maintaining the environment.

How you will be assessed

This unit can be assessed around an activity. Your tutor will identify a local organisation that is involved in facilities management to act as a real life scenario to answer the tasks. You will then act in the role of a managing director who requires a report on its facilities management provision. This report will be tasked against the three learning outcomes.

On completion of this unit you should:

LO.7.1 Know about maintenance of the built environment

LO.7.2 Understand how services are provided

LO.7.3 Be able to analyse facilities management provision.

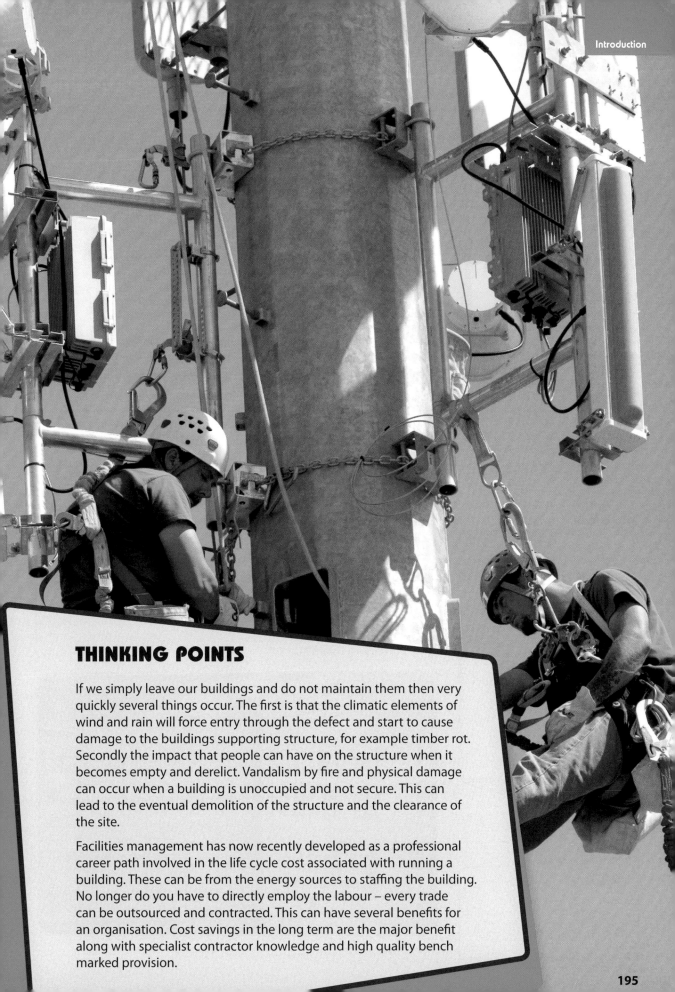

THINKING POINTS

If we simply leave our buildings and do not maintain them then very quickly several things occur. The first is that the climatic elements of wind and rain will force entry through the defect and start to cause damage to the buildings supporting structure, for example timber rot. Secondly the impact that people can have on the structure when it becomes empty and derelict. Vandalism by fire and physical damage can occur when a building is unoccupied and not secure. This can lead to the eventual demolition of the structure and the clearance of the site.

Facilities management has now recently developed as a professional career path involved in the life cycle cost associated with running a building. These can be from the energy sources to staffing the building. No longer do you have to directly employ the labour – every trade can be outsourced and contracted. This can have several benefits for an organisation. Cost savings in the long term are the major benefit along with specialist contractor knowledge and high quality bench marked provision.

7.1 Facilities management provision

Facilities management provision can include many aspects of housing and property services. It can cover both the public and private sectors, from local authority housing to the estate agents who can look after your rental property portfolio. In essence, you are employing the skills of an expert to manage your built environment.

WHAT FACILITIES DO YOU HAVE TO MANAGE?

A building does not just consist of walls, a floor and a roof. What other elements are there to a building? What about the people who live in the community? Write down your thoughts on what and who is involved.

Facilities Manager

Being a facilities manager is very challenging: you have to wear several different hats, from estate manager to services engineer. The facilities manager is concerned with the day-to-day running of a building occupied by a business or organisation. For example, here are just some of the facilities you would find in an **NHS** hospital, all of which would need to be managed efficiently. Much can be gained from looking at the whole-life of a building in these terms.

Facility	What needs managing?
Incineration	Clinical disposal of biological waste in a controlled manner.
Waste disposal	Removal of waste from bins and kitchens.
Heating	Provision of heating boiler services, controls and maintenance.
Emergency power supplies	Servicing of the emergency power for operating theatres and high-dependency units.
Ward cleaning	Managing of the cleaning services.

Personal Learning and Thinking Skills

Other services come under the responsibilities of the Facilities Manager, such as maintaining lighting. Can you name a few? Work with a partner, and try to think beyond the normal maintenance manager role.

Tender – the process of bidding for providing a service to a specification

NHS – National Health Service

A modern hospital requires many facilities which you cannot see as this plant room shows

206

Who does the facility works?

The facilities manager controls the facilities budget for the building. He or she has two choices for how to obtain services for the building. He or she can:

* employ operatives directly on a contract to undertake the work
* compile **tenders** where specialist contractors bid for the work over a certain time.

It is the facilities manager's responsibility to ensure that the service gives value for money, and that it is financially efficient to work in this way.

Monitoring and performance

Facilities contracts have to be monitored by the manager, to make sure that the agreed targets are met. For example, the manager might regularly check the level of cleanliness on the hospital wards, or might keep track of the number of times grass is cut on a school sportsfield during the summer.

Monitoring can be done through performance indicators – standards set so that you can measure how the contractor is performing against them. Performance of the systems can also be monitored for the amount of energy and resources used and the amount saved by energy reduction measures.

Client feedback

Facilities management does produce very useful statistics on the various systems in the building. This gives the client a valuable source of information, which can be used to drive down capital and running costs on future projects. The designer can then take these on board during the next feasibility design stage of a rolling program of buildings or structures. Feedback is also needed onbuilding materials components. Have these performed as well as expected, and are they fit for purpose?

Activity 7.1

1 Type 'facilities management' into a search engine and see if you can find any organisations for facilities managers in a professional role. List these as website addresses.

2 Open up one of the websites that you have found in question 1. Find out what this organisation does for its members. Does it have any aspects that you think are particularly good? Pick these out and explain why you think they are good.

3 Can a facilities manager join any other professional organisation, such as the RICS? Do some research to find out, and make notes on your findings.

Functional Skills

Interview the estates manager at your school or college, and discuss what services are provided for your organisation. Prepare relevant questions on this subject for your interview, and write up the interview in the form of a brief report.

Just checking

* What are does the term 'facilities' cover?
* What does a facilities manager do?
* How does a manager obtain the services a building needs?

7.2 Maintenance

Buildings need to be regularly maintained. This may be anything from painting exterior windows and doors to major structural work. Although the owner is normally responsible for this, the company that built the house can have an initial responsibility for problems that occur early in the life of the building.

The contract

Once a building has been designed, a contract is drawn up for the construction works, for example, the 'Standard Form of Building Contract' issued by the Joint Contracts Tribunal, such as JCT80 or IFC84. A contractual clause within these documents guarantees that any work that needs to be done because of poor build quality will be carried out and paid for by the contactors involved.

The **defect liability** period typically ranges from six to twelve months, during which time the contractor is responsible for making good any defects that arise. At the end of the defects liability period, the architect or supervising officer inspects the project and produces a list of defects that will require the contractor's attention. The contractor then 'makes good' the defects, and the architect or supervising officer then issues a 'certificate of making good the defects'.

The standard forms of contract provide for a 'retention' (typically 5%) to be held back on all payments made during the contract period. Half of this retention is paid to the contractor upon 'practical completion' (when the building is handed over to the client) and half is paid when the 'certificate of making good defects' is issued. This defects liability period is often known as the 'maintenance period' of a contract. The contract therefore provides financial incentives for the contractor to make good the defects. Although these may typically include minor repairs, major work must also be completed if needed. This allows the owner to have ease of mind during the defect liability period.

This agreement does not, however, allow for any problems that have occurred owing to the owner's actions or any exterior issues, e.g. weather. Floods and other damage created by the weather are not included in the contract.

Defect – a fault that has occurred that needs correcting

Liability – responsibility for any problems that have arisen

Defects

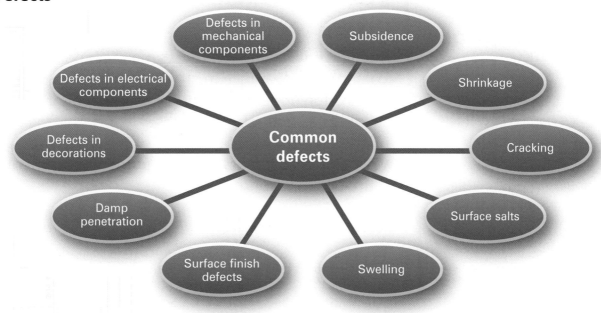

There are many defects that can occur within the first twelve months of a building being built, although defects this early are often uncommon. Defects that may occur include electrical problems such as lighting or problems with heating installations, defects in surface finishes, e.g. painted doors, poor build quality of kitchen, bedroom and bathroom units or exterior features such as paths and driveways. The most common defects are shown in the diagram above.

Guarantees

There are also wider guarantee periods that can last up to ten years. These are usually based around the structure of the building. The National House Building Council (NHBC) may offer a 10 year structural protection guarantee, which will cover any major structural issues.

Handover period

The defects liability period effectively provides a handover period, when the responsibility for maintenance passes from the contractor to the employer's maintenance team or the facilities manager. The facilities management team can also provide valuable feedback to the building designers by providing information on the performance and durability of the materials that they specified. Often, because of the need to build to a set cost plan, the architect does not have the opportunity to specify the highest quality materials and components. This leaves the client with higher maintenance costs. Well specified, higher initial cost solutions generally perform better and cost less to maintain; in the long-term, they may prove to be the most economic solution.

Activity 7.2

1 Explain the advantages to the contractor of having a defect liability period in a building contract.

2 Why are external conditions, such as weather, not included in this contract?

3 List a range of possible defects that could occur within a building, which may need to be repaired.

Just checking

* Why do properties need to be maintained regularly?
* What is a defect liability contract?
* What sorts of defects can occur within the first 12 months of a building being completed?

7.3 How facilities services are provided

The built environment requires maintaining in order to keep its appearance fresh, clean and up-to-date. This is often done by facilities management of the buildings, structures and external works. This makes a significant contribution to the economy, the social well being of residents and the future development of the built environment.

Economic contribution

The buildings we work, live and socialise in all require looking after – maintenance. Facilities management is the process of organising and supervising this work. The lifespan of a building can be 30 to 60 years, depending on the initial quality build. Some buildings are especially economically important. Large factories producing goods create revenue via local government taxes; banking and financial institutions serve this function too. All buildings need to be assessed for local council taxes, money which is put back into the local economy via services such as refuse collection.

The financial built environment makes a massive economic contribution

Social contribution

Buildings that are well designed make a significant social contribution to our heritage, from National Trust properties to museums and religious sites. A well maintained and safely designed environment makes its occupants feel good. Run down areas often have deeper social problems, from vandalism to youth disturbances. Green social community areas, with facilities for all, thrive socially and economically and contribute to the local needs and well being of all.

Types of service

Directly employed maintenance teams are slowly becoming a thing of the past: they are inefficient and expensive to run. Slowly, companies have moved over to facilities management, and contracting out services whenever needed.

Contracted services cover not just the physical built environment of a building but also its occupants. A complete hospital can be run through this function.

Lifespan

Facilities management and the attention paid to efficiency will extend the useful lifespan of any building, paying dividends in terms of avoiding costly refurbishments and alterations. Facilities management ideas can be incorporated into future developments too. Spending on long-term maintenance will have sustainable as well as economic benefits for the company.

Demolition and rebuilding should be avoided by spending a reasonable amount on specifications to extend the life of a building with little maintenance. This often comes through new technologies that can be applied to existing structures and buildings: for example, glass fibre roofing systems.

Activity 7.3

1 Find an aerial photograph of where you live. Look for a significant building within it: a church, a monument or a historic site that has been well maintained using facilities management. Identify what economic and social contribution these buildings make and produce a small poster with the photograph of the building and text to outline the benefits of this building.

2 Facilities management services are now often contracted out by a company. Establish one such service from within the building you are in now. Identify three advantages of contracting out this service.

Case Study

The Leaning Tower of Pisa in Italy has been closed to visitors due to its increased lean, which brought it dangerously close to self-destruction. Thanks to new technology, weights have been placed onto one side of the tower and a supporting band strapped around it. Directional drilling beneath the foundation has removed a tiny amount of soil at a time, allowing the foundation to settle back, bringing the tower's centre of gravity back past the point of no return. This monument contributes thousands of lira to the Italian economy every year.

Just checking

* What are the two ways facilities management services can be obtained?
* What sorts of economic contribution does facilities management make?
* How can the lifespan of the built environment be extended?

7.4 Facilities maintenance

The systems that are installed into a building or structure, whether they are human, electronic or material, require routine maintenance, to ensure that they run at their optimal performance. This means that the maximum efficiency is obtained from the amount of energy and cost that is put into the system. If you don't maintain the systems or maintain them poorly, the lifecycle costs of the building will rise!

The operation, management and protection of a building

Cleaning and housekeeping

This is often a facility that is contracted out to a subcontractor, who will undertake the cleaning work on an annual contract. Key performance indicators would be used to monitor the effectiveness of cleaning, especially in a hospital environment. Housekeeping would involve tasks such as the laundering of bed linen in a hotel, where specialist cleaners can use massive washing machines efficiently.

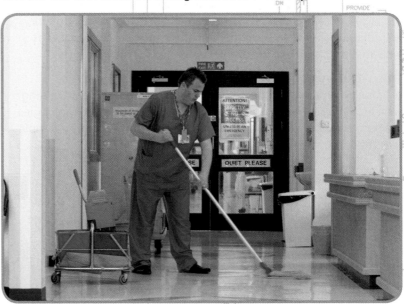

Hospital cleaning must meet stringent standards to reduce infection

Planned and routine maintenance

Term maintenance contracts often enable a contractor to maintain a building on rates per item. In this way, they are on call to undertake any scheduled or urgent repair work. Routine maintenance will be involved for systems such as fire alarm systems, where the detector heads require servicing and cleaning at regular intervals.

A CCTV service in operation

Security services

High specification buildings where the contents have a high value require security services. This may be external CCTV monitoring, or visiting or permanent staff. All security staff should be trained and suitably qualified. This security will often run for 24 hours a day, especially in financial institutions.

Lettings and general support services

Letting a building for a secondary use brings in valuable income to an organisation. For example, schools sports halls are often let out during the evening for sporting events. These lettings can be placed under a facilities management company, which will run and organise the timetable and bookings.

How are building maintenance and support services provided?

Many of the facilities services are provided through the process of tendering for the work. A specification is prepared by the client, who then sends the 'spec' out for prices. The contractor must be chosen carefully as it may be difficult to cancel a year's contract. The other option is to use directly employed labour, but with this option, there may be no control over quality or costs.

Health and Safety

Small organisations often cannot support a full-time health and safety officer. One solution to this problem is for a number of firms to pay for one staff member. Each of the firms will then benefit from the appropriate professional service, but at a fraction of the price.

Activity 7.4

1 Security services are an important feature of facilities management. There must be a relationship of trust with the company providing this service. Using the Internet, find out if there is a professional organisation for this service in the UK. Cut and paste their web page into a Word document and below it explain what the objectives of this organisation are.

2 Find the nearest sports hall to where you live: this could be in a school, or college, or a public building. Find out how many different types of organisations use the hall and for what purpose. Present this information in a table format that the facilities manager could use.

3 Facilities contractors must meet the term that the client has stated within the tender that they priced. What can a client do if the contractor does not perform? Make a list of possible items for an agenda that you could discuss with the subcontractor in a performance meeting.

Just checking

* What does the term 'facilities maintenance' cover?
* What is a letting?
* How does a manager obtain the services a building needs?

We can plan to maintain our homes, offices and other buildings. Setting aside part of the budget for repairs each year is a good investment. For large corporations, this can be a substantial amount of money. What might be the consequences if we didn't plan maintenance?

All of our buildings, whether historic or modern, will require some form of maintenance at some time. We have to undertake essential maintenance to keep them watertight, clean and in good condition. According to a BBC Survey in 2007, we spend an average of £6,000 per year on fixtures, fittings, repairs and maintenance on our ageing housing. That takes some planning!

Repairing a flat roof is specialist work

Activity 7.5

1 Walk down the street where you live, or look around the buildings where you are working now. Identify three items that need to be maintained. Why do you think this maintenance work has not been undertaken?

2 Look at the case study. Investigate the designer's duties under CDM using the Internet. Has the designer broken these regulations?

Case Study

There is now legislation under the Working at Height 2005 and Construction Design Management (CDM) Regulations 2007 that property maintenance needs to take into account – architects and designers must not produce a design that is dangerous to construct or to maintain.

You have been given the maintenance contract for a set of office units. They are only 10 years old and contain glass-roofed corridors that require the seals to be renewed every 10 years. This now presents some serious risks for the occupants.

* How will you undertake this task safely?
* How could this situation have been prevented?
* Would you expect a seal to fail after 10 years?
* What other design considerations could have been included?

Maintenance practice

Property maintenance involves many aspects. During the life of the building, these may include:

* cleaning guttering and downpipes

* renovation of flat roofs

* replacing windows

* upgrading the boiler

* renewing external and internal decorations.

The principle is first to repair the faulty element quickly before it causes more damage: for example, a leaking downpipe can cause internal damp and mould on the plaster finishes. The second element is to repair it well, using professional tradespeople who are qualified to undertake that repair. Money well spent here will benefit in the long run. The whole lifecycle of the building must be considered at the design stage, with careful thought put into the long-term consequences.

Reactive
This means reacting when an item breaks: for example, a cracked pane of glass is replaced the day after it is damaged. With this method, there is no forward planning, and so costs are unpredicted: you only know how much you have spent at the end of the year.

Cyclical
This involves undertaking annual or timed-interval maintenance on a property. For example, every four years you might repaint the external timber elements of a building to keep up the level of protection to the woodwork. This is therefore planned expenditure, requiring a specific budget to be set each year for maintenance items.

Preventative
This involves investing more in the property at the design and construction stage. The better materials, fixtures and fittings are specified, the less you will have to spend in the long-term on maintenance. Similarly, the design of the building can reduce the amount of long-term maintenance needed: for example, using self-cleaning glass walls.

Benefits of maintenance

There are many positive benefits of property maintenance:

* the social environment status is maintained and attracts other users

* the local financial economy is boosted – people want to live there

* other less well-maintained properties feel they have to catch up

* EU and government funding may be attracted to the area

* a clean and attractive environment is created for all.

Look at this building. What could happen to it?

Just checking

* What are the three principles of maintenance?
* What things can property maintenance involve?
* What benefits can property maintenance bring?

7.6 Sustainability: Lifecycle costing

When you think of a lifecycle, you usually think of living creatures – but buildings have their own lifecycles too. A building's 'life' starts with an idea and ends with demolition, and every stage it goes through has different costs. Looking at these costs from the very start of the process is called 'lifecycle costing' – an important part of producing sustainable buildings.

CAN A BUILDING HAVE A LIFECYCLE?

Buildings are not living things in the usual sense. How can they have a lifecycle? Write your ideas about the different stages in a building's life.

Lifecycles

The 'design to demolition' concept of whole lifecycle costing

Personal Learning and Thinking Skills

Find a new development near where you live. Try to find out who the designer was, or contact the estates manager from the development. Use your own initiative to contact the design office to ask about the sustainable lifecycle costs associated with this development.

Buildings may not be alive, but each goes through its own lifecycle, from conception through construction and improvement to deterioration and, eventually, demolition. Some buildings last for hundreds of years, others much less. All buildings outlive their usefulness and eventually wear out and are discarded.

For those involved in the construction industry, it is important to recognise that a building will not last forever, and to make sure that it is built in the very best, least wasteful way, for people and for the environment. How long will the building last? What will happen to the materials it is made of? What impact will it have on the environment during its lifetime? Will the land be easy to reuse? These are important questions to ask, and they need to be asked at the very start of any building project.

What is lifecycle costing?

Lifecycle costing is about balancing the initial costs of constructing a building against the longer-term costs that the building will create throughout its life. If you spend more on a quality design, you may be able to extend the life of the building, creating a sustainable product with the benefits of savings for the environment. Lifecycle costing compares the long-term costs at the design stage, so an informed decision can be made on what effect the development will have on the environment, with the financial implications of the development in full view.

Holistic – taking in the whole picture rather than looking at individual aspects

Lifecycle costing is also known as LifeCycle Assessment (LCA) or Whole Life Costs (WLCs).

The phases of lifecycle costing

Acquisition	The cost of the land, the construction of the building (both physical and financial costs) and the installation of any services.
Operation	The operating costs, the people who will maintain and run the building, the maintenance costs and the energy costs.
De-commissioning	The building's end-of-life costs – its eventual demolition, the reuse of the site and the recycling of materials.

Much can be gained from looking at the whole-life of a building in terms of sustainability. For example, energy-reducing fittings can cut the energy consumption of the project over a considerable number of years, creating a substantial financial saving and having a much-reduced impact on the environment.

The benefits

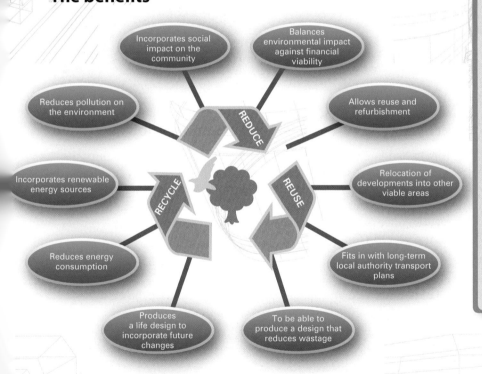

Incorporates social impact on the community

Balances environmental impact against financial viability

Reduces pollution on the environment

Allows reuse and refurbishment

Incorporates renewable energy sources

Relocation of developments into other viable areas

Reduces energy consumption

Fits in with long-term local authority transport plans

Produces a life design to incorporate future changes

To be able to produce a design that reduces wastage

REDUCE

RECYCLE

REUSE

Too often clients take the cheapest option, which provides a short-term solution but ignores the high maintenance costs that will be incurred during the life of the finished product. There are many benefits in taking a **holistic** approach to this aspect of sustainability.

7.7 Property services

Buildings are a valuable commodity and require continuous maintenance so that their value does not go down. For example, if you keep your home clean, maintained and well decorated, it can fetch a higher price then other homes in the same street. The property services sector is concerned with this sort of management of the building as an 'asset'.

WHO OWNS PROPERTY?

Property can be owned by the public sector. What do we mean by this? National monuments and government-funded buildings are owned and run by the state on behalf of the people. Does this mean that you can walk into a building and claim it? Write down your thoughts before reading on.

This public building has been paid for by people who pay local council tax

Property services and asset management

The management of building assets must often take into account the whole lifecycle costs of the building. This is because many buildings are owned as investments: for example, pension companies may own buildings, aiming to maximise the rent value and minimise the maintenance and running costs in order to create the greatest profits for the pension fund.

Elements of managing a property or asset

Public image, use and quality	Many retail outlets have a brand image that is conveyed through the design and signage on the exterior of their buildings. For example, McDonalds have 900 outlets in the UK, all clearly recognisable.
Risk	When property is bought for investment, the associated risk must be carefully considered. For example, purchasing a factory may have hidden costs in the form of asbestos removal.
Life expectancy	This concerns how long the building will be useful before major refurbishment work is required.
Legislation	Changes in the law may mean that upgrading is required. For example, disabled access or smoking facilities.
Local needs	The local market for any asset will vary. For example, office space in London attracts a higher rent due to its status the capital.

The social and economic benefits of property services

Social benefits

If we manage a building, maintain it to an excellent standard, upgrade it and continually improve its appearance and use, the social benefits for the local community can be enormous. The building may:

* provide a social focal point and meeting place
* provide extended services and access
* enhance the area economically
* provide a safe and secure place for the community.

Economic benefits

The economic benefits of managing property are considerable. A run-down area with little investment soon slips into dereliction and eventually has to be demolished and cleared. Here are just some of the primary economic benefits:

* providing opportunities for employment
* attracting further investment
* gaining higher status and added value for the area
* increased house and commercial values
* attracting European Union grants.

Regenerating an area with one project sells the concept to further developers, and hence the regeneration continues. Large parts of Glasgow near the river have now been upgraded with housing and office developments extending right along the old riverfront, providing a safe and secure social environment.

Glasgow's upgraded riverfront is now an attractive place to live and work

Activity 7.7

1 Take a look around the nearest major town or city to where you live and identify the publicly owned buildings. What are their uses? Do the buildings seem to be well managed and taken care of?

2 Identify an area of the UK that has undergone some financial asset investment. Look for some photographs of before and after. What specific benefits has this brought to the area?

3 Private investors are not the only people who can benefit an area. Where else might a local authority obtain investment for community assets and property services? Do some research and write up your findings.

Functional Skills

Use the Internet to investigate where funding can be obtained to develop property that is in the local community's interest. Tip: try 'Yorkshire Forward' as a starting point

Just checking

* What does the area of property services entail?
* What are the social and economic benefits of asset management?
* What are the differences between public and private investment?

Introduction

Welcome to one of the most important parts of the course – your own, unique project!

As you know, the Level 1 and Level 2 projects can be completed as a stand-alone qualification or as part of your Diploma. You can choose any topic that fits with the Diploma, and you will have 60 hours to complete it, with the support of your project tutor or assessor at every stage.

Why are you being asked to do a project? Because it gives you the opportunity to extend your learning in a topic or subject that you find particularly interesting or useful. You can explore your chosen subject or topic in depth, and produce a piece of work that is unlike anyone else's.

Your project will be assessed against the following criteria.

1 Manage your project – for this you will need to:

* complete a project proposal form

* explain why you have chosen your topic and describe the skills and knowledge that you want to improve

* identify project objectives

* plan your project activities and agree deadlines

* identify possible risks and how to overcome them

* keep records of all of your activities.

2 Use of resources – for this you will need to:

* research your topic using a range of different resources and different types of resource

* evaluate the reliability of your sources

* keep records of all relevant information that you find.

3 Develop and realise your project – for this you will need to:

* complete your project

* achieve your project objectives

* share your findings.

4 Review your project – for this you will need to:

* analyse your findings

* draw your own conclusions

* review your performance.

There are three different types of project outcome: ephemeral, artefact/
design or written. This table shows a few examples of the type of
evidence that could be presented for each.

Type of evidence	Example of evidence
Ephemeral	A performance, or one-off event, such as a role play or group activity. The outcome should be recorded, probably on video, and must show evidence of the stages you have gone through and how your ideas have been developed.
Artefact design	You will need to provide a description of the problem you wish to solve, sketches, diagrams or drawings of the design, and explanations of how your artefact works. You will also need to show evidence of improvements in your design through its development.
Written	A written report with findings and recommendations. As a minimum, your report will need to show what the project is about, what you have done and what your findings were.

To carry out your project successfully, you will need to do a number of
things including:

* choosing a project topic

* planning your project

* researching your project

* presenting your completed project

* evaluating your project and your own learning.

Here you will learn about planning, managing, presenting and reviewing
your project.

Before you start

Find yourself a notebook that you can use to write down
everything related to your project. This will become your project
notebook and will form valuable evidence of successful project
management and research activity.

Choosing your project topic

The first stage of your project is choosing a topic. Take some time to think
about the topics that you have studied as part of your course, or other
topics that you have heard about that interest you. It is a good idea to
list a few different topics as initial ideas, which you can discuss with your
project tutor before deciding which one to do.

These diagrams show the principal learning areas for your Diploma and may give you some ideas.

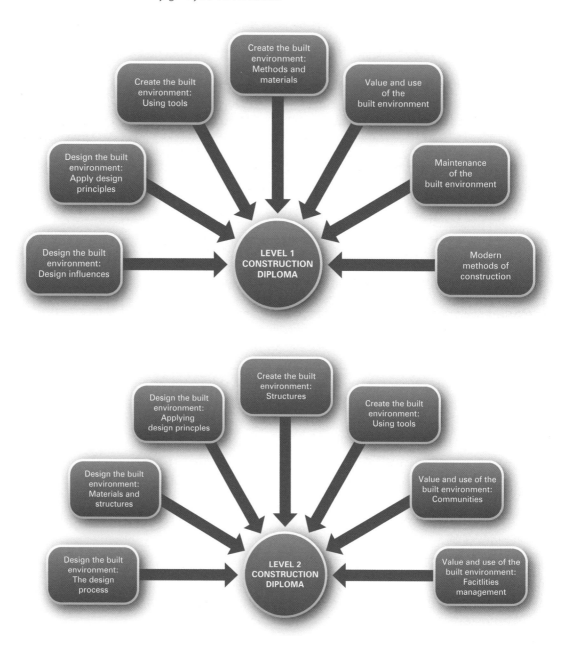

Some do's and don'ts for choosing your project

Do

✓ Make a list of several topics that interest you

✓ Talk to your project tutor about your possible topics – this will help you to make the right choice

✓ Choose a topic that you are really interested in

✓ Choose a topic that is related to your Diploma

Don'ts

✗ Choose a topic because you know somebody else is doing it

✗ Start your project without talking to your project tutor

✗ Choose a topic that is not related to your Diploma

Planning your project

Once you have identified your project topic, produce a project brief or a topic-specific question that identifies your **aims** and **objectives**. For example, if you choose to carry out your project on the topic of structures, your project brief should provide you with the opportunity to fully explore different types of structure and their possible uses. Look at the example below and think how you might produce your own project brief.

What are aims and objectives?

Case Study

Joshua is a project manager working for a local building contractor and has been asked to consider a proposal for the redevelopment of a site just outside the city centre, to include buildings for residential, commercial and leisure purposes. Joshua's aim is to provide the client with a range of construction options for the proposed redevelopment of the site. His objectives are:

1 Make a list of different types of structure, and state how they could be used on the site.

2 Recommend the most suitable method of construction for a new pub on the site.

3 List the advantages and disadvantages of a concrete-framed structure when compared to a steel-framed structure for the construction of a large multi-screen cinema on the site.

4 Describe the key factors that would influence the design team in choosing a suitable method of construction for the residential accommodation on the site.

The **aim** is to provide a range of construction options for the development of a site just outside the city centre that will include buildings for residential, commercial and leisure purposes. The **objectives** are the individual tasks or targets that the project manager will need to complete in order to achieve the aim.

Objectives must be **SMART**:

* **Specific** – an objective must contain specific detail about what needs to be done

* **Measurable** – you must be able to measure progress towards achievement and recognise completion

* **Achievable** – your objectives must be achievable within the constraints that you have

* **Realistic** – you must actually be able to achieve your objectives

* **Time-bound** – there must be a time limit for achieving your objectives.

Your project

REMEMBER

Not all projects are individual, and you may choose to do your project in a pair or a group. However, each individual must have their own project outcomes that they must meet.

213

Writing aims and objectives

Take some time to think about your own personal **aims** and the specific **objectives** that will help you to achieve your aims. For example, think about where you would like to be in five years' time and write it down in your project notebook. This is your aim. Next, think about the things that you will need to do, or achieve, in order to get there. These will be your objectives.

Remember to make sure that your objectives are SMART. If you are not sure if they are SMART or not, consider asking your project tutor to check them for you. The case study opposite may help you with this activity.

Tips for writing objectives

Remember to make sure your objectives are SMART:

✳ Keep your objectives as simple as possible – you need to know when each objective has been achieved.

✳ Try to order your objectives in some kind of logical sequence – it may help you to keep focused if you know that you cannot complete an objective until the one before is finished.

✳ Don't have too many objectives – you may end up feeling as if the project is never ending.

Project outcomes

Now that you have written your project outcomes, you can decide what evidence you will produce to show that you have met them.

How should you manage your time?

Once you have chosen your topic and written your project proposal form, you will need to start thinking about how long each part of the project is going to take. Think about how much time you have got to complete the project, and then set yourself some deadlines for completing various stages. This information must be included on your project proposal form, and you will have two **milestone** dates that must be agreed with your project tutor or assessor.

For example, if you have 12 weeks to complete your project, you might set yourself a time limit of one week to choose your topic and discuss it with your project tutor. Then your next time limit might be for deciding your aims and objectives.

You should map out the entire project with dates for achieving certain things. These could be your milestones. This will help you to manage your project effectively and ensure that you meet your overall deadline for completion.

Effective time management is vital if you are to complete your project on time. This means that, as well as setting yourself deadlines for completing the various stages or activities, you must also make sure that you identify the time itself. For example, you may decide to work on the project for three hours every week. If so, you will need to identify when those three hours will be and protect that time by making sure that nothing else takes priority. Perhaps you will plan to do an hour on Monday, an hour on Wednesday and an hour on Thursday. Alternatively, you may decide it is better to do three hours every Sunday afternoon. Whichever you decide,

Aims – a broad statement of intent: for example, 'in this project I aim to explore different types of structure and their different uses'

Objectives – what you are actually going to do: for example, 'list three different types of structure and state their most common uses'. It may help you to think of objectives as targets

Milestone – a point at which you will demonstrate progress towards your outcomes

Case Study: setting deadlines

Your Diploma teacher is planning a trip to a nearby construction site in four weeks' time. In order to make sure that the trip takes place without any problems, she will need to plan it in plenty of time. Here are some examples of the things that she will need to think about and do during the four weeks leading up to the visit.

* Contact the site manager to discuss the number of visitors, the arrival and departure times of the visit, the health and safety requirements and any other significant issues that need to be addressed before the visit can take place – by the end of week one

* Confirm the number that will be attending and book the transport – by the end of week two

* Make sure everybody is properly briefed about the visit and what they are looking for to enable them to complete the post-visit assignment that will be set – by the end of week three

* Discuss health and safety issues and remind everybody of the importance of following instructions whilst on site – by the end of week three

* Remind everybody of the meeting time and place to ensure a prompt departure – the day before the visit

it is important that you do not allow anything else to take that time. Tell the people that place other demands upon you, such as friends, family etc., that this time is already taken and that you cannot spend it with them.

What structure should your project have?

Having written your aims and objectives, you can start to think about how the project will take shape.

If you are writing a report, or for the written part of your project, a good way to ensure that you include everything that you need is to use a writing frame. This diagram shows a simple academic writing frame you could follow.

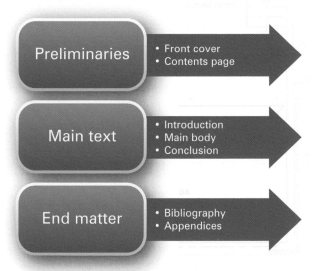

Preliminaries
- Front cover
- Contents page

Main text
- Introduction
- Main body
- Conclusion

End matter
- Bibliography
- Appendices

Preliminaries When completing a large piece of work, it is normal to include a front cover and a contents page. Your front cover will normally include information such as your name, the name of the person you are doing the work for, the title of the project, etc. You should check with your tutor what is required. The contents page will list everything that is included in your project, with page numbers for each section.

Main text The main text of your project will probably be split into three sections: introduction, main body and conclusion. The introduction should tell your reader what the piece of work is about and provide information on how you will tackle the questions, and will put it into context by providing some general information about the topic you are addressing. The main body of the project report is where you will answer the specific questions that formed the basis of your learning outcomes. Each paragraph should tackle a particular issue and each will lead into the next so that the report shows a logical development. The conclusion is where you will bring all of your ideas and findings together and explain how each of your learning outcomes has been met. The conclusion also provides an opportunity for you to make recommendations based upon your findings.

End matter After the conclusion, you should include a **bibliography** and any appendices. Make sure that you include all of the reference sources that you have used for researching your project in your bibliography.

Researching your project

When researching your project, you will need to think about where you can get the information that you need. There are thousands of books, journals and websites that you could access – but which ones will help you the most? And how will you find them? This table shows a range of different information sources that you can try.

Information source	Example
Books	Textbooks and dictionaries may prove very useful when completing your project. You could talk to your tutor about which books will help you most. Why not create a reading list in your project notebook?
Professional journals	Journals such as *Construction Management and Economics*, *Contract Journal* and *Professional Builder* – all linked specifically to the construction industry – may be helpful. There are many other construction journals that deal with specific areas of the industry, so look around to find the ones most closely linked with the subject of your project.
Audiovisual resources	DVDs, CDs and various software packages may be useful – but don't think you have to buy them. Visit your library and see what is available for you to borrow.

Top tip
Try setting yourself a rough word count for each section of the project. This will help make sure that you do not write too much on one part, or too little on another – and you'll be able to see the progress you are making!

Preliminaries – information that comes before the main part of a report

Bibliography – a list of magazines, books and newspapers that you have used in your research

The Internet	The Internet is a huge resource that is easily accessible and often much quicker than searching through books and journals. However, don't try to do everything on the Internet: using a variety of sources will give a much better, more rounded result – and the assessors will see it!

Books, journals and many audiovisual resources can be accessed at your local library or your school or college library. All of the resources at a library are catalogued and can be found quite quickly. Libraries usually have a librarian who can help you to understand the referencing system and enable you to find the resources you need as quickly as possible. The Internet, however, is not referenced in the same way, and you will need to use a search engine to find what you are looking for. When using a search engine you can enter keywords and it will find a huge range of sites where the keywords appear. However, not all of the sites will be relevant and you will need to work through them to find the ones that are most useful. Unlike published books or journal articles, much of the information on the Internet does not go through an editing process, and anybody can create their own site and put information on it. This means that not everything on the Internet is accurate or up to date. In some cases, information on the Internet that is presented as fact is not even true.

Another factor to consider when researching your project is how far back you wish to look and how many different sources of information you will use. If, for example, your project relates to something such as the Building Regulations, you need to find the most recent information possible because, over the years, regulations change and are updated. This means that information from five years ago could well be out of date as regulations could have been revised, updated or even replaced by new regulations. However, if you are looking, say, at types of building foundation, you may find that things have not changed very much for a long time and older information could still be valid.

Although books, journals and the Internet will all prove to be useful resources while researching your project, you may also wish to consider other research methods such as interviews or questionnaires. The opinions and views of people who have knowledge and experience in the area that you are researching can be very useful. For example, if you are researching health and safety in relation to the construction industry, you could interview safety officers on local construction sites or in local construction companies. If there are a lot of companies in your area that employ safety officers, you could consider sending out a questionnaire. This is a much more efficient way of contacting large numbers of people. However, you need to remember that not everybody will respond to a questionnaire, so think carefully before deciding to use one if you need responses from everybody.

Throughout the research stage of your project, remember to make use of your project notebook. Keep a record of all the information sources that you use. List book titles, authors, publishers, dates etc.,

REMEMBER

The Internet is only one source of information – and is not always reliable. Be sure to make use of books and journals too as you have to show that you have used different types of resources. Ask your tutor to recommend some useful reading material for your project.

Top tip

If you are interviewing people, ask to record the conversation using a dictaphone or digital voice recorder. You could use this to write up your notes later or simply include the recording in your evidence.

as this information will be needed for your bibliography. Don't forget to list web addresses and details of journal articles and people that you have interviewed or spoken to informally about your project. If you have interviewed individuals, or groups, keep a detailed record of what was said.

Presenting your completed project

Having completed the research for your project, you now need to think about how you will present your project, state your findings and make recommendations. You may be completing a written report, producing an artefact or preparing a role play or other activity. If you are presenting your project as a written report, without any kind of presentation, remember to plan your writing using a writing frame and set yourself some boundaries for how many words will be in each section.

Don't forget

A written report needs all of these!

* A front cover page
* A contents page
* An introduction
* A main body of text
* A conclusion
* A bibliography
* Appendices

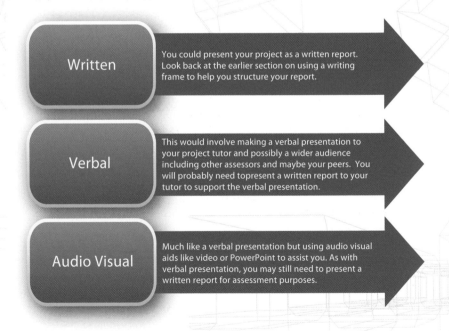

Written
You could present your project as a written report. Look back at the earlier section on using a writing frame to help you structure your report.

Verbal
This would involve making a verbal presentation to your project tutor and possibly a wider audience including other assessors and maybe your peers. You will probably need to present a written report to your tutor to support the verbal presentation.

Audio Visual
Much like a verbal presentation but using audio visual aids like video or PowerPoint to assist you. As with verbal presentation, you may still need to present a written report for assessment purposes.

The use of PowerPoint can greatly enhance a verbal presentation. PowerPoint is a presentation program within the Microsoft Office suite that can be used to prepare slideshows and presentations including visual effects, sound effects, charts, graphs, images and **hyperlinks** to help you get your point across.

Some PowerPoint do's and don'ts

Do

✓ Practise your presentation before you do it for real

✓ Make sure that you use a colour scheme or background that everyone can read

✓ Keep your presentation short and to the point

✓ Check that any hyperlinks in your presentation are still live

✓ Know what is on each slide and talk about it, without reading it word for word

Don't

✗ Put too much text on each slide

✗ Use more slides than you need to

✗ Make your presentation too long

✗ Read from your slides

> **Hyperlinks** – an active link in a document that takes you directly to a web address when you click on it

Evaluating your project

After all the hard work of choosing your project, planning your project, researching and presenting your project, you now need to review your project and evaluate your learning. Spend some time looking through your project notebook and reflecting on the various stages of your project. Think about what things you have learnt and what skills you have developed along the way. Maybe it is the first time that you have researched a topic on your own. Maybe it is the first time that you have interviewed people or written a questionnaire to help you collect information. Remember, your project assessor will be checking that you have effectively reviewed your project and evaluated your own performance. Think about what type of project evidence you are presenting and how you could most effectively show that you have evaluated the project. Don't forget that if you have done some kind of presentation, role play or other performance, feedback from those who observed it could provide useful evidence of how well you performed. Below are some examples of questions that you could ask yourself as part of the review process

Project evaluation

How many of your project outcomes did you meet?

✳ If any of your project outcomes were not met, why not?

✳ What conclusions have you drawn from your project?

✳ What problems did you encounter and how did you overcome them?

✳ What new skills have you gained from completing the project?

✳ Which of these new skills could be transferred to another area of work?

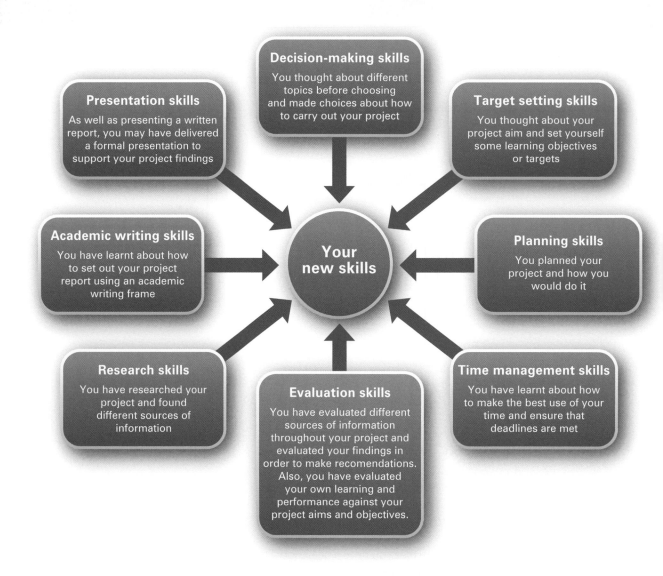

* If you were doing your project again, what things would you do differently?

Congratulations!

The Diploma Project is a major piece of work. If you have worked through this section of the book and completed your project, you have done really well. In doing your project, you will have learnt some very useful skills that could be of help to you in the future, even if you change your mind about your future career. Here's what successful completion of your project means for you.

All of these skills have great value in everyday life and will be of use to you whatever career you eventually choose. Well done!

GENERAL ASSESSMENT GUIDANCE

As well as the specific issues for each unit, there is some general guidance that will come in handy across all your units. They should also help you during your work experience and in your later life and career!

Time management

* Manage your time well. All the units have a number of different components that will have to be researched. Ensure that you keep your work safe and that any work in an electronic format has a secure and safe backup.

* Be well organised. This is your chance to show that you are an independent enquirer, a creative thinker, a reflective learner, a team worker and a self manager. Completion of the assessment tasks should allow you the opportunity to exhibit all these skills. Therefore it will contribute towards achievement of your Personal Learning and Thinking Skills.

* Prepare relevant questions. Be prepared with a list of relevant questions that you could ask if your teacher arranges either a visiting speaker or a site or office visit.

* Plan ahead. When preparing for your work experience make a list of things that you need to find out or observe. Remember to gain maximum benefit from the experience.

* Attention to detail. When completing your practical assessment work in unit 5 do so methodically and pay attention to detail.

Useful links

* Make good use of your work experience to find out as much as possible about issues that are relevant to your coursework. You may have the opportunity to work and meet with people in the design, construction, facilities management or property sectors, who will be able to answer your questions.

* A visit to building exhibitions such as Interbuild will allow you to gather technical information and build your own small product library.

* There is a wide range of manufacturer's websites that will help you develop a specification or practical project. Remember to search UK sites only so that you can specify materials that are suitable for UK climatic conditions or are sustainable.

Things you might need

* Your work needs to be in the form of an A4 word processed report. Your tutor should give you access to the required software to enable the correct presentation.

* You will need access to either traditional drawing methods which requires a parallel motion drawing board and drawing instruments or an architectural CAD system such as 'AutoCAD' or 'Autodesk Revit'.

* For unit 5 you will need good quality photographs of your practical work both 'in progress' and fully completed. Remember to include photographs that provide evidence of your marking out and that all photographs should include your identification i.e. name, candidate number and centre number.

* Remember that you can use modelling techniques to produce architectural models that can evidence your design. Remember that you will have to incorporate digital photographs into your report and e-portfolio.

* Access to a professional within the design sector of the construction industry. Remember you will probably have to interview people or ask questions in order to complete some of the assessment focuses.

* Obtain copies of service layout drawings so that you examine and investigate appropriate layouts.

* Access to a 'product library' such as the Barbour Index would help you develop your specification. You may be able to view a product library at a local architect or even at the local authority's architects department.

* When carrying out practical work remember to wear the correct Personal Protective Equipment (PPE) at all times and follow health and safety procedures outlined by your tutor.

Revision guidance for Unit 4

In this unit you will have to sit an external examination. This will be a traditional paper based multiple choice type examination. Your teacher will be able to show you an example question paper so that you can become familiar with the format and layout of questions. You will have to identify and use a range of technical information that is commonly used in the construction of the built environment. You will be tested on a range of methods, techniques, plant and tools used in the construction of groundworks, substructure, superstructure and external works.

* Produce a revision plan or timetable and try to stick to it.

* Make sure that you have a place where you can get on with revision without distractions.

* Reward yourself with treats; such as watching a DVD, when you have completed each section of planned revision.

* Use the revision checklist on pages 229–231 to make sure you have covered everything you need to revise.

Unit 1 assessment guidance

In this unit you will investigate factors that influence the design of buildings including infrastructure, community and environmental issues, sustainability and legislation. You will also gain an insight into the scaling and distribution of services at a local and site level. In addition you will gain an understanding of how to use and apply technical information.

Remember to maintain a focus on sustainability and impact on the community and the environment throughout the project.

How you will be assessed		
What you must show that you know	**Guidance**	**To gain higher marks**
Know about the factors that influence the design process	✴ Try to identify the needs and concerns of the local community in order to determine the social impact of the project ✴ Look at the provision and planned provision of infrastructure and infrastructure capacity in the locality of your project. Consider road and rail links and availability ✴ You will need to find out about local planning issues and how projects often have to be modified before approval is obtained	✴ You need to clearly describe a wide range of local factors that influence the design process ✴ You will clearly describe how legislation will influence the design of the project ✴ You must clearly describe and justify a wide range of sustainable design features
Understand how the nature and availability of utilities affect the design process	✴ On site visits, or during your work experience, look at drawings that show the layout of external services ✴ Contact architects, other building design professionals or visiting speakers to get their views on how the availability of services impacts upon design	✴ You must clearly describe the environmental impacts caused by utilities distribution ✴ You must describe and justify all the key features of service distribution within the project
Be able to understand and apply technical information	✴ Look at examples of specifications for building projects in your area ✴ Investigate product libraries or trade literature ✴ Collect climatic data such as maximum and minimum temperatures, wind speeds, rainfall and snowfall ✴ Interview local builders, architects or building control officers to find out if special construction details are needed in the area ✴ Find out what details and practices are considered to be 'robust'	✴ You must be able to select and evaluate technical information ✴ You must produce a specification that clearly describes and justifies all the requirements of the external building envelope ✴ You must provide evidence that your specification is suitable for local climatic conditions. Your research into local detailing and robust practice will help here

Unit 2 assessment guidance

In this unit you will carry out investigations to gain knowledge and understanding of materials and their use within structures. You will also consider sustainability issues and how materials are specified, purchased and used in a sustainable way. In addition you will review and evaluate the use of different structural forms and how they impact upon design outcomes.

Opportunities to view a wide range of construction drawings will help you to become familiar with construction details.

How you will be assessed		
What you must show that you know	**Guidance**	**To gain higher marks**
Know about materials and their functions within structures	✳ Key materials are the materials that have a substantial content within the building and may include; steel, concrete, bricks, timber, glass and plastics ✳ Examples of the functions that materials may perform include; structural, thermal insulation, sound insulation, fire protection, light transfer, aesthetic appearance, water or moisture barrier, security, weather protection etc. ✳ An example may be a cavity wall that incorporates; bricks, blocks, wall ties, insulation, plasterboard and decorations to perform a number of the above functions	✳ Identify, clearly describe and justify the use of all the key materials forming the major structural elements and the external envelope of the construction project ✳ Identify and evaluate the function that the materials perform ✳ Examine a wide range of construction elements in detail and evaluate how different materials work together to perform different functions
Understand how to use materials in a sustainable way	✳ Remember sustainable materials may have an initial low carbon footprint or may help the long term carbon footprint of the project and reduce the need for extraction of fossil fuels ✳ Remember to look out for renewable materials such as softwoods that originate from managed forests ✳ Try to obtain the design teams views on sustainability issues surrounding the project and how they were addressed ✳ Use manufacturers website and published information to find out how their materials perform in sustainability terms	✳ Describe clearly, and justify the use of, a range of sustainable materials in use on the project ✳ Analyse, in sustainability terms, the benefits and drawbacks of all the key materials used on the project ✳ Consider the effects that the key materials may have upon the environment
Be able to evaluate and use different structural forms	✳ The structural form may include framed, cellular, cross wall or shell structures. Try to be more specific if possible for example a framed structure may be a portal frame, a space frame or a skeletal frame ✳ Advantages and disadvantages could include; cost, aesthetics, use of space, intermediate supporting elements, speed of construction, fire protection, flexibility of use, use of alternative claddings and finishes etc. ✳ Construction details may include eaves details, window head, jamb or sill details, substructure details. You will be expected to analyse a cross-section drawing of one of these details ✳ Remember you can use sketches to convey your understanding and to help illustrate your answers	✳ Identify, clearly describe and evaluate the structural form of the project ✳ Identify and clearly describe a range of suitable alternative structural forms that could have been used for the project including consideration of the advantages and disadvantages of each form ✳ Select, clearly describe and analyse a range of construction details

Unit 3 assessment guidance

In this unit you will be required to complete two separate assessment tasks. The first task requires you to analyse a client brief and produce appropriate designs for a building or structure that address the requirements of the brief. The second task requires you to demonstrate a knowledge and understanding of job roles in the construction design sector. Professional bodies such as the RIBA, RICS and the ICE all have useful websites that will help you to prepare for your presentation.

How you will be assessed		
What you must show that you know	**Guidance**	**To gain higher marks**
Understand job roles and occupational structures, and the importance of teamwork in construction design and related activities	* Remember that the focus here is on job roles within the design sector. This can include all work carried out by the various technicians and professionals prior to commencement on-site * Look into the 'pre-contract' jobs carried out by; architects, architectural technicians, surveyors, quantity surveyors, soil investigation technicians, structural engineers, civil engineers, electrical and mechanical engineers, planners, estimators, landscape architects, interior designers, etc. * Visit the websites of professional institutions and interview members of the various institutions. What do they offer and why do they exist? * Ask about their 'regulatory role', entry requirements, support given to members and disciplinary procedures	* Describe clearly and discuss all the key job roles including teamwork aspects and progression pathways within design of the built environment * Describe the interactions between supervisory, technical and professional roles * Explain and justify the role of the relevant professional institutions
Be able to create from a brief and evaluate a realistic design solution for a typical modern building or structure	* Carefully read and analyse the client brief before commencing your design work – make sure that you know what is required * Produce some 'room templates' to scale and you can then easily try different combinations of building layout * Produce some sketch ideas or 'proposals' before commencing your drawing board or CAD work * Remember to consider and comment upon the 'buildability' of your designs within your evaluation * Remember you need to produce, in addition to the above, floor plans, elevations and a cross section or a construction detail * A model may be used to evidence some of this design work and you may wish to provide an open model instead of a floor plan or a solid model instead of elevation drawings * Remember that if you use CAD 3D renderings and walkthroughs will provide further evidence of the effectiveness and aesthetic qualities of your design * Remember to evaluate your design against all aspects of the brief. Consider further improvements to your design and how you need to further develop your skills	* Describe clearly, illustrate and justify features that will meet all of the clients needs * Produce a design solution and portfolio of high quality design work that shows consistently precise attention to detail * Evaluate the final design in detail against all of the requirements of the brief

Unit 4 assessment guidance

Revision checklist	Completed
Can you identify and name the different types and components of foundations; and consider their appropriate use in different subsoil and ground conditions with both low and high bearing capacity	
Can you explain how foundations work by distributing loads over a wider area or transferring loads to a deeper high bearing capacity subsoil	
Do you know that setting out is the physical marking out of the building on the ground prior to work commencing	
Are you aware of the stages of excavation including: site survey, disconnection of existing underground services, demolition, site clearance, topsoil strip, deposit topsoil in temporary spoil heaps, excavate to reduce level, remove surplus excavated material from site, soil stabilisation (grouting or vibro-compaction), trench excavation, earthwork support, site fill and hardcore beds and compacting surfaces	
Are you aware of the differences between a brown field and a green field site in terms of excavations and site preparation	
Do you know that concrete is a mix of cement, fine aggregate and coarse aggregate; and are you aware of some typical mix specifications and the effect of different water : cement ratios	
Do you know about the need for steel reinforcement in some situations because concrete is strong in compression but weak in tension	
Do you know about simple formwork and the reasons for its use	
Do you know about different concrete finishes including: tamped, steel float, wood float and patterned. You will learn about slump testing and compression testing of concrete	
Can you identify and understand the use of: fork lift trucks, dumpers, mortar and concrete mixers, concrete pumps, piling rigs, pumps, hoists, tower cranes, excavators, backacters, breakers and compressors, loading shovels, angle grinders, masonry saws, electric drills, transformers, scaffolding and access equipment	
Are you aware of why construction plant is used i.e. to save time, work more efficiently and safely and work at height etc.	
Do you understand how the mechanisation of the construction industry has affected the types of buildings that can now be constructed	
Can you identify solid structures including cellular and cross-wall, framed structures including rectangular, triangulated and portal frames and shell or surface structures	
Do you know about substructures and superstructures, including the identification of major components and elements within traditional domestic construction	
Do you know about external walls, including detailing around openings in cavity walls and the function of the wall, structural, weather protection, sound reduction, thermal insulation, security and provision of natural light	
Do you know about external cladding including: tile hanging, timber cladding, profiled steel cladding, glazed cladding (patent glazing and curtain walling), brick cladding, concrete cladding and membrane or fabric	
Do you understand that steelwork is prefabricated off site and is erected using a crane, how the structural members are typically bolted together, the sequence of construction and how base plates have to be grouted once the columns have been finally positioned and plumbed	
Can you identify different types of floor, including solid, beam and block and suspended timber. You will also consider the functions of a floor including: provision of a level surface, sound reduction, fire protection, accommodation of services and environmental control	
Can you identify the main components of roof structures including flat roof construction, trussed rafter construction and roofing to framed structures; you will also be able to identify: trussed rafters, binders, wind bracing, common rafters, jack rafters, roof joists, wall plates, firings, ridges, hips, valleys, verges, eaves and gable ends	
Do you know about roof coverings, including built up felt, mastic asphalt, non-ferrous metals, tile and slate	

Revision checklist	Completed
Do you know how internal partitions are used to compartmentalise structures and perform to provide structural support, lateral restraint, fire protection, sound reduction and contribute to the provision and distribution of services	
Do you know about plastering, dry lining and decorations	
Are you aware that steel has to be fire protected to prevent structural failure in the event of a fire and how cladding (see above) is used for the building envelope	
Do you know that site practices that minimise the effect of a project upon the local community could include: community liaison, site security, agreed working hours, site access arrangements, car parking, timing of deliveries, safety talks, wheel cleaning facilities, damping down, acoustic hoardings, maintaining a clean and tidy site, effective plant maintenance, control of noise and membership of the Considerate Contractors Scheme	
Site practices that minimise the effect upon the natural environment could include: correct storage of materials, use of silt traps on temporary drains, local sourcing of materials, damping down, segregation of waste, recycling materials, correct storage of fuels and chemicals including use of bund walls and relocation of animal habitats	
Do you know how inappropriate site practices lead to depletion of fossil fuels and produce additional emissions that contribute to global warming	
Did you know that in-situ site based methods are used when buildings are constructed on site by construction operatives from materials and individual components	
Are you aware that prefabrication is a method of construction where the majority of the building structure is manufactured in a factory environment, off the construction site – with the rising cost of land and the drive to make houses affordable, prefabrication is steadily becoming the most economical method of production	
Are you aware of the advantages of pre-fabrication including: speed of construction, reduction in 'wet trades' reduces drying requirements, uses less skilled labour therefore cutting costs, improved standards of insulation, better and more effective quality control, use of sustainable materials, lowering the impact of construction activities on the local community eg shorter period on site and less site noise also prefabricated units can be more easily recycled at the end of their useful life and pre-fabricated units can be clad in a variety of different surface finishes	
Do you know that pre-fabrication requires the essential use of cranes and mechanical handling equipment because of the size and weight of the individual pre-fabricated components (typically bolted together once they have been lifted into position)	
Can you identify plans, sections, elevations and details	
Can you identify materials by reference to standard fill patterns or symbols including: brickwork, blockwork, concrete, damp proof course, subsoil, hardcore, metal, cement screed, insulation, stone, timber (sawn), hardwood (planed all round), softwood (planed all round), plywood, doors, windows and plaster or render	
Do you know about some of the common scales in use on construction drawings including: 1:5, 1:20, 1:50, 1:100, 1:200, 1:500 and 1:1250	
Can you identify time allocations and work sequences by looking at planning documents such as gantt charts	
Do you realise how some operations can overlap, some operations must follow others and how some tasks cannot commence until a period of drying time has occurred	
Do you understand the term 'critical path' and the concept of 'float' i.e. free time (float time) through routes other than the critical path	
Are you aware of how standard ICT can help with project management including a variety of CAD, word processing, payroll, costing and graphics packages	
You will know that programs such as Microsoft project can produce gantt charts and critical path analysis.	
Are you aware what is included in first and second fixing and how the terminology is used within construction planning for aspects of carpentry and joinery, plumbing, heating and electrical works.	
Do you understand that the performance specification states what results must be achieved eg thermal efficiency, load requirements etc; and the materials and workmanship specification states what materials and components should be used and the standard of workmanship that is required	
Do you understand that the bills of quantities are produced using a standard method of measurement e.g. SMM7 and that there are separate building and civil engineering standard methods	

Revision checklist	Completed
Do you know that bills of quantities are split into the following sections: preliminaries, preambles, measured works, PC and provisional sums and dayworks	
Are you aware that bills of quantities are used for pricing the work at tender stage and for monthly valuations during the construction stage and for the final account	

Unit 5 assessment guidance

In this unit you will use tools to produce a practical outcome. You will have the option to work in one of four different craft areas; brickwork, carpentry and joinery, painting and decorating or building services. In doing so, you will develop an understanding of relevant health and safety issues and the safe use and characteristics of materials. You will also contribute to a team presentation about job roles in construction. There is a wide range of manufacturers websites that will help you to find out about appropriate and alternative materials for your project.

How you will be assessed		
What you must show that you know	**Guidance**	**To gain higher marks**
Knowing about, use and be able to extend own implementation of health and safety practices in a construction craft environment	❋ Remember the difference between hazards and risk. For example materials on the floor are a hazard and there is a risk that you could trip over them ❋ Do not generalise; remember there are teachers, tutors, technicians, assessors and visitors who may be present in the workplace. Sometimes it may be the technician who is at risk when preparing materials for your use ❋ Find out what should be kept at the workplace in order to comply with the COSHH regulations ❋ Keep a note of all potential hazards and risks that you become aware of whilst carrying out practical activities	❋ Clearly describe all of the hazards and potential risks associated with the practical task including those associated with the materials used ❋ Identify all of the people at risk ❋ Autonomously and consistently demonstrate safe working procedures and use of PPE ❋ Observe, explain and justify the COSHH regulations ❋ Describe how your experience will help you to improve your knowledge and implement health and safety
Understand the working characteristics and safe use of materials	❋ Consider the properties of the materials you are using. What makes them suitable for your project? What are the advantages and disadvantages of the materials that you are using? ❋ Consider for example; hardwood vs softwood, facing bricks vs engineers, plastic vs copper pipe, emulsion paint vs eggshell, etc. ❋ Find out during work experience, or ask visiting speakers, about both safe working practices and methods of ensuring quality outcomes. Consider methods of protecting the work upon completion	❋ Clearly describe and justify the use of all materials required to complete your project ❋ Consider and discuss the advantages and disadvantages of alternative materials ❋ Clearly describe and evaluate a range of site procedures that promote safe and quality practical outcomes
Be able to use tools effectively to produce a practical outcome	❋ For your assessment you must take great care to complete work to the best of your ability ❋ Remember to record and report on all relevant checks and tolerances including where appropriate; main dimensions, square, level, plumb and face plane deviation ❋ Remember to comment as appropriate on; aesthetics, material selection, joint fit, dimensional tolerance, cleanliness of the work etc.	❋ Demonstrate a high level of skills to produce a practical outcome that shows consistently precise attention to detail ❋ Produce detailed and evaluative quality control records of the practical outcome
Understand the job roles, progression routes, occupational structures and importance of teamwork in the crafts and related activities	❋ Consider all the different craft roles within the 'create the built environment' sector ❋ Supervisory, technical and professional roles will include; site managers, buyers, planners, engineers, quantity surveyors, architects ❋ Consider the role of the main professional institutions such as the CIOB, RICS and RIBA. Can you find any others?	❋ Collaborate with others to clearly describe and discuss two different job roles, including teamwork aspects, within the craft sector ❋ Consider links and interactions with supervisory, technical and professional roles ❋ Describes and justifies the role of most of the relevant professional institutions

Unit 6 assessment guidance

In this unit you will learn how sustainability impacts upon the built environment and how the built environment contributes to societies and communities. You will also learn how the built environment can be improved to benefit both individuals and communities. In addition you will investigate and report on job roles in building maintenance and facilities management. Consider using a questionnaire to gain opinion of the impact of a development upon the local community.

How you will be assessed		
What you must show that you know	**Guidance**	**To gain higher marks**
Know how sustainability affects the environment	✳ Remember to consider, social and community issues, environmental influences, economic impacts and lifecycle issues ✳ Examples may include; how sustainable materials and processes are used, use of locally sourced materials to reduce emissions and pollution, sustainable site practice and sustainable maintenance ✳ The decisions made by the design team that affect the future maintenance of the building. Consider high quality, high initial cost, low maintenance cost solutions against low quality, low initial cost, high maintenance cost solutions ✳ Consider design life expectations of elements of the building. For example, some flat roofing systems may have a life expectancy of thirty years and others seven years	✳ Clearly describe and justify a wide range of relevant sustainable practices that are clearly linked to the maintenance of the built environment ✳ Evaluate the way in which decisions made by the original design team impact upon current maintenance issues
Be able to evaluate the contribution of the built environment to society and the communities	✳ Consider the role of both public and private housing ✳ Look at the ability of young people and first-time buyers to access the property market ✳ Compare the location and land prices with the type of property being constructed ✳ Consider how industrial and commercial property in the area contribute to employment, the economy and general prosperity ✳ Look into property trends and consider how demographic changes and interest rates influence property values	✳ Clearly describe and evaluate the local property market together with the factors that lead to the development of sustainable communities ✳ Evaluate a range of ways in which the built environment contributes to the creation of wealth
Understand how the built environment can be improved to benefit individuals and communities	✳ Brainstorm why properties and the built environment needs to be improved ✳ Consider the upgrading of buildings to current standards or regulations ✳ Think about how a change of use or the way people work or organise their lives. These may prompt the need to improve properties ✳ Consider sustainability, means of escape in fire, sound and thermal insulation, structural remedial work, upgrading the fabric of a building, redecoration etc. ✳ Remember to read through the unit 6 topics – produce a brainstorm of the factors that promote sustainable communities	✳ Clearly describe and evaluate a broad range of ways by which the built environment can be improved ✳ Justify the benefits of designing for future expansion ✳ Discuss a range of key factors influencing the development of sustainable communities
Understand the job roles, progression routes, occupational structures and the importance of teamwork relating to building maintenance and facilities management	✳ Investigate websites such as the RICS website and complete Internet searches on facilities management and property services. For example, search for the 'British Institute of Facilities Management' ✳ Consider the different roles that the crafts will have within property maintenance ✳ Consider writing to or contacting one of the professional institutions	✳ Clearly describe and discuss all of the key job roles, including teamwork aspects and progression paths, within building maintenance, property services and facilities management ✳ Describe interactions between craft, supervisory, technical and professional roles ✳ Explain and justify the role of the main relevant professional institutions

Unit 7 assessment guidance

In this unit you will gain a knowledge and understanding of how the built environment is maintained. You will also learn about the role of facilities management and support services and will analyse facilities management provision within an organisation. A copy of the facilities management structure of the organisation will help you with your analysis.

There are a number of websites that may be of assistance, for example look at the website of the 'British Institute of Facilities Management'.

How you will be assessed		
What you must show that you know	**Guidance**	**To gain higher marks**
Know about maintenance of the built environment	✳ Read the topics in this book especially the ones about planned maintenance and facilities management ✳ Your tutor may invite a speaker from the organisation you are studying. Prepare a list of questions in advance of the visit. If possible visit the organisation or buildings ✳ Ask about how the original specification for the building is affecting current maintenance ✳ Consider the sustainability issues impacting upon the maintenance provision	✳ Clearly describe all of the key processes involved in protecting, maintaining and managing a built structure ✳ Discuss and justify the underlying purposes and benefits of these processes
Understand how services are provided	✳ Comment on how the size of the organisation has an impact on the way that services can be delivered ✳ Consider the advantages and disadvantages of direct employment of maintenance staff against contracting with outside specialists ✳ Could some elements be covered under annual 'fixed cost' maintenance agreements? ✳ Remember also to consider, for example cleaning services, security services and catering etc. Brainstorm all of the services you can think of that may come under the banner of facilities management or managed services ✳ Ask what would happen to the structural fabric of the building if these services were not provided ✳ Brainstorm how the provision of such services provides economic and social benefits	✳ Clearly describe ways of organising and delivering a broad range of managed services ✳ Consider the impact of such services upon the lifespan of a built structure ✳ Discuss in detail the economic and social benefits provided by the appropriate use of managed services
Be able to analyse facilities management provision	✳ Consider how facilities management can feedback information on the performance of building materials ✳ Think about the role that facilities management can play in the client function and provide input to briefs and specifications for future developments ✳ Brainstorm the key features of the companies facilities management provision ✳ Ask if the company is willing to let you have a copy of their facilities management policy document ✳ You may have to evaluate; cleaning and housekeeping services, planned and routine maintenance, security, caretaking, management, reception, health and safety, lettings and general support services	✳ Clearly describe the key features of a company's facilities management provision ✳ Evaluate the benefits of each of the above key features and consider alternative approaches

GLOSSARY

Abbreviations   shortened versions of key terms, used so that all parties are clear on what is being drawn or explained

Absorption   when a substance enters the body through the skin

Acoustic   concerned with sound/noise; an acoustic hoarding absorbs or reflects back the sound so that it is not transmitted

Acrylic   a resin that is used in some water-based paints

Activities   the items on a chart; for example, excavate foundations

Adhesive   glue

Aesthetically pleasing   looking good!

Affordable housing   housing available to rent or buy at a lower rent

Aggregate   pieces of natural or crushed rock or stone, gravel or sand

APP   atactic-polypropylene

Arris   the edge of a brick formed by the meeting of two faces, e.g. header face and stretcher face

Auger   a large diameter drill capable of boring holes into subsoil

Bearing   surface supporting a load

Bearing capacity   the load the ground can carry (measured in Kn/m²)

Bearing stratum   a layer of soil or rock with greater bearing capacity that the soil above

Bed joint   the horizontal layer of mortar on which a masonry unit is laid

Bills of quantities   a set of descriptions of the work needed together with the measured quantities of everything needed to complete a project – they are produced using a Standard Method of Measurement (SMM)

Biomass   organic matter, e.g. trees harvested as a source of fuel; can also include recycled waste

Blinding   a compacted sand-bed

Blue collar worker   a member of the working class who performs manual labour and earns an hourly wage

Breeam   Building Research Establishment Environment Assessment Method

Broken colour   multi-coloured effects

Brownfield sites   sites that have previously been developed or built on. This may require the demolition of existing buildings and is likely to contain drainage, services and foundations that will require special attention during design and construction

BSI   British Standards Institute

Building   any structure with a roof that can provide shelter from the weather, for things or for people to carry on activities such as living, working or spending leisure time

Bund wall   a wall that surrounds a storage tank to contain the contents of a tank in the event of a leak

Carbon footprint   the total amount of CO_2 emissions produced by an individual, building or even industry

Cavity wall   two layers or 'skins' of wall held together by wall ties, usually made from brickwork (external skin) and blockwork (internal skin)

Cement   a grey powder-like substance that reacts with water and hardens to bind aggregates together

Chipboard   a board made by bonding wood chips with synthetic resin

CIOB   Chartered Institute of Building

Client   the person or organisation for which the building is designed and built and maintained

Combined loads — the dead, live and wind loads imposed on the structure

Compression — a pushing or squashing force that causes items to shorten

Condensation — water formed when warmer, damp air meets a cold surface

Conduit — a channel used to protect cables and wiring

Conservation — work carried out on any important or historic building or structure to keep it in its original state, often using special material or methods

Construction drawing — a drawing used to communicate technical information to different parties involved in the building process

Contract programme — the plan of works, usually a Gantt chart, showing when each part of the project will be completed

Conversion — the process of cutting trunks into usable planks of wood

Copping — a capping used to finish off and protect the top of a brick wall

Cross bearers — timber used to help stack materials correctly

Cross-lining — hanging lining paper horizontally on a wall

Curtain walling — a glazed cladding system used on some high rise structures

Dead loads — the fixed loads of the building itself

Defect — a fault that has occurred that needs correcting

Development — the construction of housing, factories, shops, roads and retail units

Dilapidated — run down and of no use

District heating system — a heating system that uses factories' waste heat and distributes it in pipes from house to house

Door ironmongery — any metal items that are associated or used with doors

DPM — damp-proof membrane, a barrier (e.g. polythene sheeting) that prevents damp or moisture entering the structure

Dry lining — a lining (normally plasterboard) fixed, with an air space, to the face of a masonry wall

Duct — a channel or pipe for a cable, heating or ventilation

Duration — how long each individual activity takes to complete

Dynamic — a dynamic load is a changing load, e.g. the workers moving about, carrying out maintenance

Efflorescence — the appearance of white salt crystals on the face of cement-based surfaces such as brick, block or render

Element — part of a project such as a floor, wall or roof, that performs a function within the building or structure

Embodied energy — the total energy consumed in the production of a building

Embossed — a pattern that is raised from the surface of the paper

Enforced — made to work, usually through the threat of some sort of penalty

Excavator — a digging machine that can swivel its excavator arm 180° or 360°; the most common is the JCB 3X

Exposed — opposite of sheltered, subject to the worst weather conditions

External envelope — the building elements (e.g. walls, roofs etc.) that enclose the internal space of a building

Fabricate — to put together, make from parts or create

Face plan deviation — a bump or hollow in the work, usually checked by holding a straight edge diagonally across the work and checking for gaps

Facing — the part of a brick that can be seen

Fall — a slope that allows water to flow from a higher to a lower level

Financial markets — where stocks and shares are traded between companies and individuals, commonly known as free trade

Finite	with a definite limit or end, not everlasting
First fix	all work done before plastering takes place
Flout	a tool with a flat rectangular face that can be used for applying plaster, mastic asphalt or a surface finish to concrete
Fossil fuels	non-renewable sources of energy extracted from the ground such as coal, oil and gas
Foundation	the base on which a building sits
Greenfield sites	sites that have never previously been developed or built on and form part of the natural environment
Greenhouse gases	gases that contribute to global warming, such as CO_2
Groundworks	heavy works that are undertaken below ground
GVA	Gross Value Added, an indication of how much each sector contributes to the UK economy
Hand tools	tools that are held rather than freestanding or major pieces of machinery
Header	a brick that passes through a brick wall from the inner to the outer face at 90° to the face of the wall
Hoarding	a solid security or safety fence around a building site. This is normally constructed of plywood and painted in the company's colours
Holistic	taking in the whole picture rather than looking at individual aspects
Hop-up	a small item of access equipment, usually handmade of wood, consisting of a single step and a working platform approximately 500 mm by 500 mm in size
Impervious	not allowing water to pass through
Infiltration	percolation of water into the ground
Ingestion	when a substance enters the body through the mouth
Inhalation	when a substance enters the body via breathing
Isometric projection	a method of showing a three-dimensional object in two dimensions. One corner is closest to the viewer with a horizontal lines drawn at 30 degrees to the horizontal
Lateral restraint	resisting a sideways force
Laying off	using the tips of the brush to ensure that the paint you have applied is even. Laying off also reduces brush marks
Legislation	laws passed by central government
Liability	responsibility for any problems that have arisen
Listed building	a building graded by English Heritage to preserve it for the future
Live loads	the moving loads of the people and objects within the building
Load	the weight of the building that is supported by the ground
LPG	liquid petroleum gas
Maintenance schedule	a program or plan of what will need maintaining, what needs to be done and when
Masonry	built of blocks, bricks or stone
Mechanisation	the use of mechanical plant instead of manual labour
Microporous	with small holes; in cladding, a microporous coating allows the timber to breathe
Modular size	the size of a brick including a bed joint and perpend joint: 225 mm long by 75 mm high
NHS	National Health Service
Nogging	a short horizontal timber cut to fit between studs in a framed partition

Ordnance survey	an organisation that has mapped the whole of the UK to a grid reference system and produces detailed maps of the UK
Orthographic projection	a drawing created using detail from one view. Different views are generated – plan view and elevation view – to allow the designer to see all the important information
Permeable	allowing water to pass directly through
Perp	short for perpendicular joint, the vertical joint between two adjoining bricks
Planning	the controlled development of buildings in the community
Plant	any type of mobile construction machinery
Plumb	vertical or upright
Porosity	the extent to which a surface will absorb moisture; a porous surface will absorb more moisture than a non-porous surface
Porous	with small holes that allow water to percolate through
Portable power tools	tools, mainly powered by electricity, which are small enough to carry
Product library	contains details on building products available for use on projects
Profile(s)	wooden 'stop ends' used as a temporary vertical abutment and to support the corner blocks once the line has been correctly set up to gauge
Purlin	a horizontal roofing member, parallel to the eaves or the ridge, that provides support to rafters or roof sheeting
Purpose-made rack	an item manufactured to allow material to be stored without getting damaged

Rake out	use a scraper or other tool to scrape along the middle of a crack to remove loose material before filling
Regeneration	the redevelopment or improvement of an existing site or area to bring it up to modern standards and enhance the quality of life of local residents
RIBA	Royal Institute of British Architects
RICS	Royal Institute of Chartered Surveyors
Rungs	the part of a ladder that your feet go on
Runoff	the water flowing off an impermeable surface
Sand blinding	a thin bed of sand, typically 25 mm thick, which protects the damp-proof membrane from the risk of puncture
Sanitation	when referring to paint, it means providing a surface or finish that is easy to keep clean
SBS	styrene-butadiene-styrene
Scaling	creating an exact copy of an area or item to a different, usually smaller, size
Screed	a mix of sharp sand cement (1:3) trowelled smooth in a bed 50–75 mm thick, sometimes reinforced with chickenwire to prevent cracking – it provides a smooth surface for the application of finishes
Seasoning	the removal of moisture from timber after conversion has taken place
Second fixing	all work done after plastering has taken place: e.g. installation of kitchen units, sinks, wash basins etc.
Services	electricity, gas, water and drainage to a property

Settlement	movement in the ground, usually caused by the building's load compressing the soil below, or volume changes in the soil caused by seasonal weather changes
Shade	a colour with black added
Sheltered	not exposed to the worst of the elements; usually protected from the wind and associated driving rain
Silt traps	a series of settlement chambers to intercept silt before it enters the main drainage system
Site set-up	the contractor's temporary services; for example, the cabin and fencing
Specification	when an architect creates a specification, they are saying which materials have to be used on the project; it will list all the project requirements as decided by the architect on behalf of the client
Spot priming	applying primer to small areas that have been stripped to the bare surface
Standard	an official way of making or keeping something all the same
Steel reinforcement	steel rods incorporated into the concrete to resist tensile and sheer forces
Stiles	the sides of a ladder or door
Stop and drain valve	a valve to turn the supply of water to a home on and off and to drain water from a system
Stress graded	timber that has been visually checked to ensure that it is free of defects such as knots, shakes, splits etc. that would reduce its structural performance
Structure	the frame or fabric of a building that holds everything up; the walls, floors and roof of a building are part of the structure
Stud	a vertical structural member in a framed partition

Superimposed load	the load applied to a structure: for example, the weight of furniture or items stored in the building, or the load imposed by snow on the roof
Sustainable	created and maintained in a way that lasts, without using up more and more resources, protecting resources for use by the communities of tomorrow
Symbols	figures or drawings used to represent a material or fitting that is to be used at that point of the building
Tang	the metal piece that goes into the handle of a scraper or knife
Technical information	relevant information and standards needed to successfully design a building
Tender	the process of bidding for providing a service to a specification
Tension	a pulling force that stretches items or increases their length
Thermal mass	a dense, heat-retaining material
Tint	a colour with white added
Topsoil	the top layer of soil, usually 150 mm to 300 mm thick, capable of sustaining vegetation
Tower crane	a crane sitting on a mast, comprising sections bolted together, which can lift material to great heights; these cranes tower over the project, and can climb up a structure as it is built
Tracked mini-excavator	small excavator that runs on tracks, so it is easy to manoeuvre on small sites
Tub paste	a ready-mixed wallpaper adhesive that is often used for heaver wallpapers and vinyls
U Value	the rate of heat lost through a wall in watts per m^2 per °C difference in temperature between the inside and outside air temperature ($W/m^2/°C$)

Ventilation   letting air in and out, to improve air quality and prevent damp and rot

Virtual testing   seeing how materials, components and structures will perform under different pressures and constraints by using a computer program

Walk through   a virtual simulation of how a person would view the property in 3-D if given a guided tour

Wood grain   the direction of growth and natural fibres in the wood

Woodwork   all of the elements of a room that are made of wood, e.g. skirting, doors

INDEX